Roughing it *Elegantly*

Roughing It Elegantly: A Practical guide to canoe camping: 1995
Midwest Book Achievement Award winner(Travel category):

Judge says: "Surprisingly thorough for all of the categories packed in. A very
handy resource for planning a canoe trip. This is a great little book. Very easy
to read and useful. Covers a lot of ground in a clear, concise manner."

****

"...From tents to strokes, weather forecasting to first aid, this book will aid the
beginning canoe traveler to take the first strokes onto the water."

From ***Canoe & Kayak***(October 1995)

****

If you've never gone canoe camping and want to, but hesitate at getting started,
Roughing It Elegantly is the book. ...I wish I had read this book before I
attempted a two-week trip through the Adirondacks. I would have avoided the
wet clothes, the fires that wouldn't ignite, and an inappropriate assortment of
ill-chosen food items.

Besides listing what personal gear you'll need for different weather conditions,
there's an entire section of healthful and delicious recipes for riparian cooking.
And if you don't know how to canoe, just follow the book's advice on selecting
the right canoe and paddle, loading and storing gear for ballast, avoiding
capsizing.

The last chapters offer a state by state synopsis of this country's regional canoeing
opportunities and list important recreational services, guides, outfitters, wildlife
departments, national and state park offices.

Small Press Magazine, Spring, 1995

****

What they said about the first edition of ***Roughing It Elegantly***...

"Excellent guide for novice canoe campers headed for the Quetico-Superior
wilderness.   Robert Beymer, ***Superior National Forest***

"Even beginners will feel at ease by following her well-explained, clear directions."   Woodstock ***Vermont Standard***

"Shows how anyone can safely and comfortably enjoy a wilderness experience."
Greg Leis, Executive Director, **Wilderness Inquiry**

"Outstanding guide to canoe camping...stylishly written...should appeal to all
outdoor types."   St. Cloud (MN) ***Daily Times***

"Pleasant, encouraging, environmentally-conscious,...a sensible, personal discussion of canoe camping."   ***Library Journal***

Roughing it *Elegantly*

A Practical Guide to Canoe Camping

by
Patricia J. Bell

**Illustrated by
Linda Oliver Isakson**

Eden Prairie, Minnesota

This book, as before, is dedicated to
To Don, Friend Spouse, husband and favorite canoe partner, whose idea this book was and who has ever been loving and supportive, and
To our Four — Lynne, Jean, David and Amanda — on whom we learned a great deal about canoe-camping.
            With love, from the would-be Elegant Camper

Copyright ©1994 Text Patricia J. Bell
Copyright ©1994 All illustrations including cover art Linda Oliver Isakson
Cover Design by Bruce Harrington
Indexing by Information Lost and Found

0 9 8 7 6 5 4 3 2
Printed in the United States of America

Second Edition

Publisher's Cataloging In Publication Data
            (Prepared by Quality Books, Inc.)
Bell, Patricia J.
    Roughing It Elegantly: a practical guide to canoe camping / by Patricia J. Bell; illustrated by Linda Oliver Isakson. —2nd ed. p. cm.
    Includes bibliographical references and index.
    LCCN: 93-74305
    ISBN 0-9618227-0-8

    1. Camping—United States   2. Camping—United States—Equipment and supplies   3. Canoes and canoeing—United States   I. Title

GV790.B45 1994   796.54'0973
                             QBI96-86

Contents

ACKNOWLEDGMENTS

Many people have contributed in many diverse ways to help in the current revision. I am indebted to all of them. Likewise, old friends from the first edition are not forgotten.

My brother-in-law, Dr. Robert F. Bell, a practicing dermatologist in Portland, Oregon, again contributed valuable comments on Health and Safety.

In our exploration of canoe camping in Florida's Ten Thousand Island region, Friend Spouse and I enjoyed the companionship and insights into primitive camping there with Smithsonian Associates Andrew Bertolino, Prue Perry, Paul Burkhart, Roy Larsen, Susanne Staats, and Lynn Haskell. Our outstanding leaders (from Wilderness Southeast, excellent outfitters) on the expedition were Cathy Sakas, a splendid, inspiring naturalist, and vivacious and skilled Jim Bitler. Canoeing in Vermont with Jim Walker (Battenkill Canoe, Ltd.) taught us much about river canoeing.

Thanks also go to Bob Gartner, for sharing his camping tips; to Joy Manlove for a teenager's viewpoint and suggestions; to our Connecticut friend Bill Everett for pointing out some important Algonquin Park publications.

I greatly appreciated all those who answered questions and sent material. In the U.S., identified individuals include Karri Morris, the Supervisor in the Reservation Office, Duluth Office of the Forest Service, who responded immediately, most courteously and fully to questions on Forest Service policies and recommendations; Shelly Smith at the Adirondack State Park Visitors' Center for her friendly help; Chuck Bartlett and others in the office) of the Ottawa National Forest in Michigan.

The Canadians were most helpful in providing information not only about their parks, but also about health and technique issues. In particular, there is Victor Miller, Park Visitor Services Officer (Quetico Provincial Park), who called in response to my letter and then sent a fat packet of material. He obviously also relayed my requests elsewhere. Thanks also go to Claire DeAngelis, Assistant Park Superintendent for Woodland Caribou Provincial Park for the marvelous, tantalizing packet of materials on Woodland Caribou Park, and to the office staff of Mike Walton, Chief of Visitor Activities, Pukaskwa National Park, for providing information on Pukaskwa and other Canadian National Parks, and to Murielle Bouchard regarding the Prairie and Northern Region of Canada's National Parks. Tourism Saskatchewan produces an excellent and thorough brochure (more like a magazine, really) that provides much helpful information. So many wonderful places to visit, and so little time to do it.

I am most grateful for the information from Janet A. Zeller, Disabled Padders Committee Chairman, American Canoe Association, Inc., for regarding paddling opportunities for disabled. It is heartening to know there *are* opportunities.

Because the generic names for many products are generally unfamiliar, though some of the trade names are at least fairly well known, we chose to use trade names of products over generic, not necessarily as an endorsement of that product, but because a name clarifies the type of product described. The following company and product names and trademarks are mentioned; I hope I have not overlooked any:

Advil, Avon, Bacitracin, Band-aid, Basic H, Benadryl, Betadyne, Bic, Bluet, Brillo, Camp Suds, Chapstick, Chlor-Trimeton, Coughlan's, Cricket, Cutter's Insect Repellent, Dacron, Di-gel, Dobie, Dr. Scholl, Fels-Naphtha, Globaline, Gore-Tex, Granite Gear, Halazone, Handiwipes, Hollofil, Jello, Joy, Kevlar, Lidocaine, Mirro, MSG Whisperlite, Murine, Muskol, Nalgene, Neosporin, Peak 1, Pepto-Bismol, Potable Aqua, PrameGel, Pramoxine, Purex, Ragg, Rappala, Scotch Brite, Sierra cup, Skin-So-Soft, Sleep-ez, Space Blanket, Sun Shower, Swiss Army knife, Teflon, Teldrin, Telfa, Therma-Rest, Tylenol, Velcro, Visine, Voyageur pack.

I also want to thank American Heritage, a division of Forbes, Inc., for permission to quote again the marvelous list from *The American Heritage Cookbook* and Hutchings' *California Magazine,* 1860, that begins Chapter 2.

I enjoyed having Eileen Quam and Theresa Wollner of Information Lost and Found as indexers, and Pat Ricci for the cataloging direction.

The talents of our daughter, Jean Bell Jarvis, whose illustrations graced the first edition, were not available this time. She is now Jean Jarvis, Doctor of Veterinary Medicine, and we are very proud of her.

The collaboration with the highly-talented Linda Oliver Isakson was an unexpected bonus. Her artistry illuminates the text and adds beauty to the cover, raising the book above the ordinary. I found her to be something of a kindred spirit on the outdoors, and thoroughly enjoyed working with her. What's more, thanks to her own professional expertise, I learned much from her.

And finally, as ever, special thanks go to Friend Spouse — my husband and favorite canoeing partner, — who encouraged me to write the book in the first place, supported me all the way during all the phases of creation and production, and in particular contributed heavily to all the material in Chapter 6.

...Patricia J. Bell
1994

ACKNOWLEDGMENTS, FIRST EDITION

I wish to thank specifically the following people—readers and critics for taking the time and interest to read the manuscript at different phases of completion.

Judy and Charley Hillger, Karen and Bob Seeger, all partners in Camp Upichuki, and Sandy Falkman for reading Chapter 2 at an early stage.

The Sawbill bunch—Frank and Mary Alice Hansen, Bill and Cindy Hansen—for reading the whole manuscript and for many helpful sugges- tions. Additional thanks go to Frank, as he is the one who lured us up to the Boundary Waters for the first time (as a family) when we had not yet been in Minnesota very long. It has proved toa be an addictive area.

Dr. George Freier, Professor Emeritus of Physics, University of Minnesota, for the section on lightning. First, he explained things to me, and then he corrected the manuscript.

Dr. Robert Pozos, [at that time] Director of the Hypothermia and Water Safety Lab, University of Minnesota—Duluth Medical School, who kindly read the section on hyopthermia, made corrections and offered useful and insightful questions to consider.

My brother-in-law, Dr. Robert F. Bell, Dermatology Department of the Portland (Oregon) Clinic, for valuable comments on the Health and Safety section.

In addition, I wish to thank J. L. Matthew-Rusnak, of the Customs & Excise Office, Fort Frances, Ontario, for reviewing the material on Canadian parks and for the suggestions and corrections offered.

Others who helped in various ways and are much appreciated are: Jini Coyle, Duluth Office of the Forest Service, who more than once responded immediately, most courteously and fully to questions regard- ing Forest Service policies and recommendations. Thanks also go to Tamara Meyer, park technician for Voyageurs National Park, and to Dave Elder for immediate and abundant information on Ontario's Quetico Provincial Park, and camping and fishing information.

Our son-in-law, Rich Hendricks, cheerfully shared his canoeing experience with me as well as his canoe.

Pharmacist Ben Allison provided helpful advice on the first aid and medications kit.

People who pointed a path for seeing this book into its original publication include Loris Bree (Marlor Press), Sybil Smith (Fins Publications) and Brad Thompson.

Sally Rhodes and Vera Koger from our years in Tennessee deserve thanks. Sally was daughter Lynne's Scout leader during Lynne's Brownie and Girl Scout days. I learned much from Sally when I accompanied the troop on camping trips, as I had never done any camping prior to that. Vera was my assistant leader when I later led our daughter Jean's troop. She was a seasoned and very adept camper and she taught me a great deal.

These two women in fact got our two older girls interested in outdoors life, and that in turn drew me into it. I learned a lot from our girls.

I also want to acknowledge the quotation at the beginning of Chapter 2, by permission, Copyright 1964 American Heritage Publishing Co., Inc. Reprinted by permission from *The American Heritage Cookbook* and Hutchings' *California Magazine,* 1860.

The book is greatly enhanced by the drawings done by our daughter, Jean Bell Jarvis, who also loves the North Country.

And finally, special thanks go to Friend Spouse, my husband and favorite canoeing partner, Don, who first raised the idea of my writing the book and who has encouraged me every step of the way.

...Patricia J. Bell
1987

ABOUT THE ILLUSTRATOR

The drawings and cover painting by Linda Oliver Isakson represent the merging of several forces in her life. A native of Ontario, Canada, she came with her ordained minister parents to the United States when she was in sixth grade, and has lived in Minnesota much of her life. As a child, she loved to ramble in the northern woods to discover trees and animals in diverse backgrounds. Entranced by the wild life, she recorded observations in drawings and paintings. Her delight in creatures emerges in the charming, lively drawings seen in this book.

Her natural talent developed with schooling; in high school she began studies in watercolor, oil and acrylic painting and sculpture. Later she was graduated cum laude in technical illustration and commercial design.

Her professional career has included creating commissioned fine art, graphic design and art direction for several large corporations. She has an extensive working background in design production and realization. Currently she is the founder and principal of Design Effects, a creative graphic design and set design firm based in Plymouth, Minnesota. Services provided include design consulting, concepting, copy writing, illustration, photography and production services utilizing Macintosh.

She shares her household with a pair of collies, Basia and Brieezer, and a pair of hedgehogs, Nefertiti and Tutankhamen, and their offspring, the only bristly personalities in the house.

Cornel Bunchberry

INTRODUCTION

WHY NOT ROUGH IT ELEGANTLY?

"To boldly go where no one has gone before..."
Mission statement of the starship *Enterprise*

It had been a day of hard work; fallen trees had blocked the trail on several of the portages. That can make life difficult if a tree is large and you are carrying a canoe, or if you have short legs and are carrying a good-sized pack. Now that was all that was behind us for today, and we had reached Trail Lake, our destination. Trail is a lovely little lake, with a shallow area down near the portage, and then it bends a bit, with the main body of the lake lying to the north. Our map said it had two campsites. The first campsite was up on a rocky rise and we landed to look it over. It wasn't quite to our immediate liking, so we went on up the lake to check out the other site. This one had a convenient landing area and a marvelous rock shelf where I could prepare meals without stooping, for a change. The tent site looked pleasant, and the latrine location was reasonable. Clearly, not only had the site been unused this season, it was seldom used. Furthermore, the site lay in the afternoon sun, a definite plus on this late May day. Friend Spouse (my husband Don) and I decided this would do very nicely.

We quickly unloaded the canoe, secured it and began the business of setting up a temporary home in the wilderness. Working together, we put the tent up in short order, and then set to our individual tasks in the usual routine of settling in. We had seen no other campers here in the Boundary Waters Canoe Area Wilderness (BWCA) since breaking camp that morning, and we wouldn't for another two days. We were in a contented mood as we shared some late afternoon refreshments. The lake was beautiful; down toward the portage, a large rock in the lake was currently home for a nesting gull who didn't seem unduly disturbed by our presence as we passed then or later when we went fishing. I prepared our evening meal; we ate, and as we often do, fished awhile after supper, enjoying those very special early evening hours. When it got dark, we retired to our tent and to the "snugginess" of our sleeping bags. Before we fell asleep, we could hear sounds of the forest — was that far-off call loons or was it perhaps wolves? We couldn't tell — it was appealing to think of it being wolves, with all the wildness that the notion evoked. Feeling very comfortable there on Trail Lake, we nestled in and slept soundly. In the morning we discovered a moose had crossed the camp in the night. And that delighted both of us.

Wilderness. You'll get an argument on what wilderness really is. If you argue that a wilderness is an area where no one has been before, the Boundary Waters area is not a wilderness, and by that definition, I suspect this world has few areas that have never felt human feet at some time or other. More than 300 years ago, French and Canadian fur trappers and explorers were tramping around this part of northern Minnesota and southern Canada. They were using portages and trails that the Indians had been using for untold generations before. Yet in this area of more than 3,400 square miles, where, for the most part, human movement from place to place is by foot or by canoe, it is possible to sense the natural forces in ways that are more elusive in ordinary everyday life. It is possible, with occasional jarring exceptions, to sense a world where man is not a major player. For many, the presence of trees — stately, or mere sprouts, or stumps gnarled and fire-scarred, the songs and calls of birds, the nonchalance of loons and ducks when you come up on them, the smells of the forest, the dignity of small animals that have not been corrupted by tourist handouts, the sounds of the winds — these can give a very satisfying taste of the wilderness.

True wilderness, such as described by that grand old man of the woods Calvin Rutstrum, is not readily available to most of us. Fortunately, there have been those such as Aldo Leopold and Sigurd Olson who believed in the importance of keeping portions of our country as wild as possible, not only to preserve unique areas, but because they believed that wilderness was very important to the restoration of mind and spirit. I know I learned very early that one of the reasons I especially valued our trips was that the wilderness restored my soul. We are deeply indebted to those stalwart individuals and groups who fought to establish the Boundary Waters Canoe Area Wilderness in northern Minnesota and Quetico Provincial Park in neighboring Ontario, areas dear to my heart. Other similarly wonderful areas have been preserved in at least a semi-wild state.

Compromises have been made. Most of us must be content with camping at semi-primitive sites that have been designated and equipped with steel fire grates and pit latrines. Even so, what we have can give a very rich and satisfying experience. In Quetico, the BWCA's sister park, the sites, while not officially designated as sites and lacking fire grates, tend to be "traditional" — they have been used for years, with piled-rock fire pits that have been constructed by campers. Quetico feels wild. The feeling is not diminished by the traces of earlier loggers that still remain. In the Ten Thousand Islands area of southwestern Florida, one can camp on islands, but still hear the roar of boat and plane engines.

My very first taste of the wilderness came with a very brief stopover on Lake Shagawa, near Ely, Minnesota, with my parents and sister. I was yet in my teens. To a child of southern prairies, it was a strange and wonderful place. Until then, pines and firs had been the forest of mountains. But here, there were no mountains. Just lakes and woods and bogs. It has been more than 20 years now since my husband, our children and I made our first tentative sally into the Boundary Waters area, and we fell in love with the region. Friend Spouse and I have returned, year after year, to camp there many, many times, and to enjoy its own special qualities.

We weren't always so comfortable in the wilderness. Nor was it always as easy as it is now. We had to learn how to paddle a canoe; we had to learn what was appropriate gear and how to cook over a steel-grated fire pit. We learned all that after we moved from Tennessee to Minnesota. At that time, our four children were fairly young. (Amanda, our youngest, was about ten when we made our first venture into the Boundary Waters country.) When our family first went canoe camping, we were dreadfully inept. It didn't occur to us to read up on how to do it, though then there weren't nearly so many books on the subject. It helped that our older girls, Lynne and Jean, had had some camping experience as Girl Scouts. We used make-shift equipment, which sometimes is almost as bad as the wrong equipment. Nevertheless, we learned. Did we learn!

Being a practical woman, I wanted to share what I had learned with others, particularly beginners and people from other parts of the country, to make their preparations for the trip and the trip itself easier and more pleasurable. Since I wanted to give them some ideas of what to expect, I decided to write this book. I wrote down as many of the things we do as I could think of for this book, which is a highly personal account. The title, *Roughing It Elegantly,* came almost immediately. Now roughing it elegantly appears to be a contradiction in terms. It doesn't mean wearing designer-labeled clothing, or carrying "fancy" gear, quite the contrary. Roughing it elegantly suggests camping with style, style that has to do with the manner of camping, and that comes from knowing about techniques, and choosing the best way. Think of elegance as mathematicians use the term, as the sense of refinement or propriety. Continued practice —

or experience — refines techniques. Elegant also carries the meaning of excellent, or characterized by dignified richness and grace of style. Canoe camping can be elegant by any of these definitions, even in the wildest of wildernesses.

I began to realize that canoeists and backpackers have several common concerns. Both experience an intimate contact with the immediate environment. Both must rely on their own strength for motive power, though the canoeist shifts alternately from arm power (paddling) to leg power (walking). Since they must carry their gear and food, they are concerned about the bulk and weight. Furthermore, it became apparent that while I was writing out of our experiences in the Boundary Waters of northern Minnesota, techniques and principles we had learned could be applied in other canoeing areas as well — Quetico and other Canadian Parks, Voyageurs National Park, the numerous Minnesota state parks with their fine canoeing, the Maine North Woods, New York's Adirondacks.

As I got deeper into the project, I began to read what others have written on the subject of canoe camping. What I found made trekking in the wilderness rather formidable, especially those books written in the 1970s and earlier. While canoeing and camping takes some physical effort, the newer equipment removes much of the difficulty that had been a major part of camping. This book should show that almost anybody could undertake wilderness camping. As a woman of, ahem, "mature years," I write from the perspective of a person who is not a professional guide, simply a person who enjoys the wilderness visits, even though the experiences may be infrequent, perhaps only once in a lifetime occurrences. Even persons with physical disabilities can enjoy the experience of canoe camping under several special programs.

While this is for those who are making their first venture into the Boundary Waters or into canoe camping, it may be helpful to people who already have some experience. I will suggest useful and effective ways to do things, from planning trip lengths, organizing the menus, to setting up camp. This book is for the family — and others like them — that we saw on one trip. The woman was sitting placidly in one of their three canoes, while her husband, more or less assisted by their four teen-aged daughters, transferred bags and sacks of things from the car to the canoes. She remarked to me that this was their first trip, and she really didn't have any idea of how to do things. She and I talked while Friend Spouse and I tossed our gear into our car trunk. They were planning to camp there on the lake. I was glad they intended to stay close in; they were not prepared for portaging out to other lakes. I suspected that the whole trip was Father's idea, and the family response was "Fine, whatever you say." I hoped all went well for them.

I hope they enjoyed their first Boundary Waters experience, because the BWCA, like neighbors Voyageurs National Park and

Quetico Provincial Park, is a special place, a vast wilderness with seemingly innumerable lakes and streams, remnants of the last glacial period. These parks run from the easternmost tip of Minnesota nearly half the length of Minnesota's northern border. Lying across the Canadian border, the boundary waters country evokes a sense of the old frontier, when the Indians, the explorers and the voyageurs who trapped for furs were the only people to go through the region. Traveling here in a canoe gives an intimate view not only of the here-and-now, with the physical eye, but of times long past, with the mind's eye. It is a trip for the imagination as well as for the mind and body. Because traces of human habitation and industry have been removed, one sees the country much as the old-timers saw it. In the here-and-now, you can see beaver lodges, some obviously old and long abandoned after their residents died. The imagination wonders what became of the lodges the voyageurs saw, as they trapped for furs in the 1600s and the 1700s; are those carefully constructed heaps of sticks now the bases for clumps of trees? Have the winter snows and spring floods picked away at the structures, leaving no trace of the former occupants?

While hauling gear and canoe across a portage, with mosquitoes whining around the ears, one can think of those tough little men sometimes toting upwards of some 200 pounds of pelts across the portage, then returning for the rest of the load and the canoe. It is no wonder that many of them were thoroughly spent by the time they reached their fifth decade, if mishaps or sickness hadn't already gotten them. Theirs was a life of tremendous hardship and effort, yet it had its own elegance. Of necessity, these men kept to essentials (and they had very clear notions of what was essential) and the most efficient way to get the work done.

Quetico provides a different mind trip. We have traveled along part of what once was the Dawson Trail, an early route intended to boost the development of Winnipeg. The Canadians have left remnants of the lumbering industry that was developed toward the end of the 19th century. Those moldering traces in the wilderness inspire a certain awe at the determination and effort needed to get the timber out.

Life was precarious then. It still is. One has only to look about the forest at downed trees, many of them broken or uprooted in storms. I still feel the chill I felt when we came to McIntyre, one of Quetico's lakes, and saw the broken tree trunks strewn about from some unnoted storm. A look at the shallowness of the root structure of a stricken tree, and the naked rock where the tree had been, will tell one that the soil, as such things are counted, is fairly young. Yet despite the rigors, life is abundant. The woods have an astonishing wealth of species of trees, shrubs, plants and fungi. The animal life is rich and diverse; and bird songs ring out. The North Woods give a marvelous opportunity for the close-up observation that the view from a canoe offers.

Most of the lakes are restricted to non-motorized boat travel, which also tends to cut down on the type of baggage visitors are apt to bring in. Entrance to the Wilderness is by permit only, and aims to keep down wear and tear on more popular areas and to ensure a reasonable degree of solitude for visitors. Likewise, access is limited to Quetico Provincial Park, with three of its entry points being through the BWCA.

As I said, the wilderness camper has only two ways to transport the gear — by paddling the canoe and by carrying gear and canoe across the portages from one lake or stream to another. It's amazing how that one fact of lugging stuff causes a marked rearrangement in what one considers necessary to have along. Only the diehard backpacker has reason to be even fussier about the weight of baggage. Reputedly, a really determined backpacker is so concerned with reducing the weight to be carried that he will strip tea bags of their tags. Since more time is spent paddling than portaging, the canoeist doesn't need to be quite so persnickety.

The ancient Romans had a word — *impedimenta* — for all the equipment and gear. The root of the word is *pes,* or foot, and the prefix *im-* (as in *impede*) carries a strong suggestion of a person tripping over a collection of stuff. Impedimenta could well describe the gear and its handling by the inelegant camper.

Friend Spouse and I have wilderness-camped for many years, with all, some or none of our four children, and we are convinced it can be done with style and grace. Over the years we corrected our gear and improved our techniques so that now we can paddle efficiently, go on and off portages with a minimum of fuss, set up a comfortable camp, and eat well. We can enjoy the wonders and pleasures of the wilderness, and minimize its discomforts because we have learned to do what has to be done as efficiently as possible.

We have come to realize that elegant camping intensifies the richness of the wilderness experience. A concept arose: the Elegant Camper is one who uses appropriate equipment in appropriate manner, respects the environment by being as unintrusive as possible, and considers the campers who will follow. Further, the Elegant Camper has a sense of his or her skill and physical limitations. Friend Spouse and I are not professional guides, just simply people who love the wilderness and respect it for its wonders and for its power. We have been concerned when we have seen groups of youngsters under the direction of persons who were clearly less than fully adept. While for the most part wilderness camping is an activity safely enjoyed by large numbers of people, it is not without its dangers. The risks are diminished by knowledge and careful practices. Furthermore, the concept underlying the techniques — simplicity, efficiency, appropriateness and thoughtful planning — are immediately applicable to any sort of camping trip, be it wilderness, backpacking or group.

However, when all is said and done, camping is still strongly affected by personal tastes and values. One can read all or little of what the experts have to say, can acquire equipment and have at the wilderness. In time, a personal style based on personal choices and values will develop. Elegance is not restricted to any one equipment list or set of menus.

Technique is an important part of elegance. The ways I describe are not the only ways to do things, but they work; we've tested them. Many of the things we do are quite simple and may seem glaringly obvious. I thought about whether I should include them. Then I remembered the legendary little Girl Scouts who were out on their first campout. Their leader told them that their cooking pots would get quite black over the campfire, and they should be sure to soap the pots well to make them easy to clean. The girls eagerly set to and thoroughly soaped them — inside and out. Things are not obvious if you haven't seen them.

Two of life's basic necessities — food and shelter — are of even greater importance in the wilderness. If the expedition organizer flubs badly on either of the two, he or she should bear in mind there might be a strong temptation for the rest of the group, to leave said organizer behind — out there! So we will look at the matter of pacing the trip, weather expectations, selecting equipment and clothing, at health and safety, at planning menus and cooking, at the satisfactory cooking fire, and — to get at the really elegant part — how to put it all together for a pleasant, minimum impact sojourn in the wilderness.

So, in this book, we will look at important aspects of wilderness vacations. I will tell you what we have found of use so you can test and see for yourself what you can use to rough it elegantly.

Bon voyage, mes voyageurs!

Polygala Gaywings

1

ARE WE READY TO GO?

"The best-laid plans of mice and men gang aft aglae."
— Robert Burns

One of the most obvious questions before the onset of trip planning is Who is going? This has immediate bearing on the amount of gear, the menu planning, the length and the pace of the trip, as well as the sort of daily activities that may be involved. Other questions quickly follow. How many will be in the group? Where will we go? What is the purpose, or philosophy, of the trip? What is the general age of the group? Does the party include young children? What are the physical capabilities of the members of the group? The abilities of the weakest of the party markedly affect the pace and the nature of the activities.

We will plan for the expected elements of the trip — this means selecting the gear we will need, the clothing, the food, basic but mundane items such as toilet paper, toothpaste, soap, bug repellent, sunscreen, and rain gear.

Further, we will plan for the unexpected things that could occur. We can plan until we are blue in the face, and still there may be unforeseen occurrences. The wilderness is not a controlled environment, for sure. We can study forecasts and trends, but the weather will be what it will be. The bugs may or may not be abundant. The water levels may or may not be what was expected.

The trip planner will consider what sorts of things can go amiss and what steps to take to minimize the effects. Despite the greatest care, injuries *will* happen; people *will* get sick. And some people will be careless and lose gear.

PHILOSOPHY OF THE TRIP

When you begin planning your trip, you need to decide the "philosophy" of the trip. What are you expecting of it? Are you going for the adventure or just to relax and get away from it all? Are you going out a short distance and then stay put for the duration, or are you proposing to make a circuit — "traveling"? (It helps if all in the party agree on the trip philosophy, too.) The philosophy you choose has considerable impact on what you take with you. If you are going to stay at a particular destination, with a minimum number of portages to deal with, then you can afford to take extra gear, food and "playtoys." If, however, you expect to be traveling, then you should take a careful look at what can be left behind. On one of our longer and more strenuous trips, we carried about ten pounds of extra food alone more than was necessary.

We have found that it takes us about two days to get into the full swing of camping. Muscles need to be reminded or taught about the efforts of canoeing and portaging. The internal clock needs some adjusting to a different pace. The digestive system needs to adjust to a rather different diet, and particularly if trips are more than a couple of days long. For this reason, if the trip being planned is a "traveling" rather than a fishing trip, we usually try to arrange for the third day to be less strenuous than the first two and keep the distance low on the first two days. You'll find that by easing off on the first couple of days, you'll have more strength on the days following.

We have also found that it is sensible to build a rest day into the schedule, even though you may not use it. This provides a time "cushion" to allow for resting a bit if the previous days have turned out to be more strenuous than expected, or if it rains, or some other reason appears. More often than not we have come in from our trip a day ahead of schedule simply because we didn't use the rest day. You may choose to stay in camp on a rainy day. Traveling in the rain is not particularly fun. It is virtually impossible to stay dry, even with rain gear, as your skin continues to do its thing of excreting moisture that has no opportunity to evaporate. This leads to feeling chilly, which in turn takes more energy. In addition, the gear gets damp and heavy. I am talking about a day where the rain has begun early, before traveling starts, rather than when showers come up later in the day. Things get a lot dirtier, too, with rain.

DESTINATIONS

If you take the time to find out as much as you can about your proposed destination, and to think out what you are going to do and what you will need, and how you will cope with situations that might arise, you greatly improve your chances of a successful trip. While this book is primarily about the BWCA and Quetico Provincial Park, many of the techniques I will talk about apply in other wilderness regions as well.

An exciting part is planning where you will go. Park officials describe the BWCA as having over 1 million acres; they describe Quetico as covering 1,800 square miles. The BWCA is somewhat smaller at nearly 1,600 square miles. (The Appendix provides a conversion table for equivalent distances. See Appendix — Distances and Areas.) This region offers prime canoeing, but there are other places for great canoe camping. The Quetico/Minnesota Boundary Waters are part of a stretch of canoe country, remnants of the glacial ages that run clear to the Atlantic. This belt has certain similarities — granitic and gneiss floor, great forests (or their remnants), streams and lakes. The same natural forces that created the Boundary Waters region also were at work in northern Wisconsin, on the Upper Peninsula of Michigan, in New York state, in New England, the eastern part of Saskatchewan, and the central and southern reaches of Manitoba, Ontario and Quebec.

For a vastly different canoeing environment, consider the coastal waters off southwestern Florida. There, the canoeist works with navigational charts and pays close attention to the times of the daily tides. The point is, be sure you get the appropriate maps and charts for your intended area and do some homework before you set out on your first trip. Even then, as Sessue Hayakawa said, "The map is not the territory." (See the Appendix — Canoeing in Canada and Canoeing in the United States for additional information.)

WHERE SHALL WE START?

First, decide where you intend to enter your canoeing area. You then need to get maps of that area or areas where you plan to visit. There are several producers of maps, and all will have a large, overall map that shows the sectional maps available. (See Appendix — Map Sources. Also see Canoeing in the U.S. and Canoeing in Canada.)

What maps show changes according to the demand of their general users. In our early years, we camped following the copyrighted 1952 versions of the Fisher maps. They simply showed roads, the shapes of the lakes and streams, locations of islands, portages and their lengths, all laid out on a grid with a 6-mile base. (They cost $.50 then.) Later we got a McKenzie map of the same area, dated 1982. It was gridded at one mile intervals, much more helpful in determining distances and planning trips. In addition to the basic information provided in the earlier Fisher maps, the McKenzie showed topographic features such as swamps and hills; contour lines showed shape and elevation of land features and lake depths as well. A trip planner does well to note such details as a series of contour lines very close together near a route. The message is the terrain is steep. The character of the terrain is particularly interesting to anyone with physical problems.

The current Fisher maps (the F series, periodically reviewed for accuracy and updated by the Forest Service) have added topographic features plus information of interest to hikers — hiking entrance points and trails and campsites accessible by trail. Both the McKenzie and the newer Fisher maps are clear evidence of the growing interest in travel in the Boundary Waters area. Both are quite dependable on campsite locations. However, it should be noted that the McKenzie maps for Quetico do not show campsites for the simple reason that the Canadian park does not have *designated* campsites.

Traditionally, in the BWCA, portages are measured in rods (a rod equals 16½ feet). Somehow, a portage of 320 rods doesn't sound quite so bad as one a mile long. A short portage of 150 meters is about 10 rods, or 55 yards. (Short portages like that are rather a nuisance. It takes as much effort to unload and reload the canoe, no matter the distance, and the tendency is to not bother with efficient pack loading for a short haul.) A Quetico portage typically is only about 73 rods, or 401½ yards, or about four-tenths of a mile long. In the southern part of the Boundary Waters region, where we have traveled often, portages are longer, which caused us at first to think more lightly of the Quetico portages. While on the whole, the lengths are shorter, they are by no means necessarily easier. Maps of Ontario's Algonquin and Killarney parks likewise use meters.

Good maps are essential; they should also be current. We have found that things change over the years. Sometimes campsites are closed to heal from extended use. Saying that beavers alter water features is an understatement. I know of several instances where the portage trail had to be changed because a beaver dam caused flooding of the old trail. A strategically placed dam can remove the need for making a portage at points upstream. I'm not sure that knowing that a particular portage is quite steep is necessarily the best thing for a novice canoe camper to know. It can be scary, even daunting. On the other hand, being able to read a map and determine that there are some difficulties ahead is useful in planning realistic and reasonable day's distances.

A canoeist who travels in the wilderness such as this never views waterfalls the same way as a non-canoeist. Knowing a waterfall drops 32 feet between the levels of two bodies of water implies that there is a *minimum* of 32 feet between the levels of the bodies the waterfall connects. The reality of that fact is that the portage trail, or any portage trail, for that matter, will climb, and it will drop. In reality, on longer portages, there will generally be at least two such climbs and drops as other drainage patterns seek the stream. The point of interest to the canoeist, then, is not necessarily how long the portage is, but how steep, and what kind of footing it has.

The Laurentian Divide runs from the south in the BWCA through southern Quetico. On the south side of the Laurentian, water flows eventually to Lake Superior and ultimately to the Atlantic Ocean. The old voyageurs called it a Height of Land, which would imply that at least some of the portages cross some of the higher stretches in the area.

In traveling the lakes of Voyageurs National Park and Canada's wilderness parks, maps are vitally important. The importance of current maps is underscored by a remark in the Friends of the Algonquin's "Canoe Routes of Algonquin Provincial Park." It states that the angle of degrees between true north and magnetic north is as of 1985, and that the declination of the compass needle is increasing annually 8' in the park area. This sort of change over time can make quite a difference.

There is a book (in two volumes), quite comprehensive, that describes all sorts of BWCA canoe trips from various entry points and discusses the trips in terms of distance, difficulty, and characteristics (how many rivers, lakes, portages, etc.). It is Robert Beymer's *Boundary Waters Canoe Area: Volume 1: The Western Area* and *Volume 2: The Eastern Area* (see Appendix — Useful and Interesting Reading for books on this area and others). If you don't have any particular entry point in mind, Beymer's books are invaluable with descriptions of many possible routes, and are quite readable. He lists the intensity of use of the various entry points, very useful in planning for a high-quality wilderness experience. His *Paddler's Guide to Quetico Provincial Park* is likewise enormously helpful in planning trips through that park, and to my mind, is even more interesting. Each of his books includes a general map of the zone, which is great for an overview. *A Paddler's Guide* has a more intimate tone, as he talks of the history of the area. The Canadians have left traces of the activity of the previous century, while the Forest Service has tended to remove traces of human habitation in BWCA. We have taken several trips in Quetico with his book in hand and found the trips greatly enhanced by his observations of "historical" relics. In both the BWCA and in Quetico, we have enjoyed reading his descriptions of routes we had taken. We have traveled a number of the trips and find his recommendations of time and distance reasonable, particularly if the party prefers to "travel."

Another useful, though less comprehensive, book is *A Paddler's Guide To the Boundary Waters Canoe Area* by Michael E. Duncanson. It too lays out a number of trips that are interesting. The time and distance he recommends are reasonable.

HOW MUCH TRIP CAN WE DO?

You need to consider the "shape" of your trip. Will your trip be a loop trip, or will you start at one point and end at another? We personally are biased toward loop trips or "yo-yo" (out and back the same route) routes as opposed to being either dropped off at a starting point, or picked up at the end, as with a river trip. Shuttling means you are dependent on someone else being where you need them to be, and you must arrange accordingly. However, in many regions, arranging for a shuttle is really the only practical way to go. I like Beymer's suggestion to have someone drop you off at the beginning of the trip, with your vehicle at the end. Then you are free to come in at your own speed and time.

Whether your route follows rivers or lakes makes some difference, too. If the route is primarily river, check to see whether you will be going up or down stream. Many of the little rivers of the BWCA are rather slow and sluggish. Their primary challenge may come with the shallowness that can be seasonal, or with obstructions such as logs or boulders. (A swampy area in wet weather may offer no difficulty, but during low water — mud, actually — your work may be cut out for you.) Some of Quetico's rivers, though some (notably the Maligne) are the drains for large lakes and drop a considerable distance over their length. The force of the current of such rivers can provide a substantial challenge for the canoeist.

Let's look at some instances. Friend Spouse and I are adults well past middle-age in fairly good physical condition. I believe we are competent paddlers. Because we like certain creature comforts, it is a given that we have to make a second carry on almost every portage. Let's compare two trips of roughly the same distance (that is about seven miles, actual distance, a day's travel), the same number of portages, and nearly identical total portage length. The first, Sawbill Lake to Phoebe Lake, we have covered in just over 5 hours. It has one portage of 285 rods — almost nine-tenths of a mile — that is long, but otherwise easy traveling. The second trip, the Louse River loop from Trail Lake to Mesaba Lake, has the same number of portages (seven), and virtually identical total portage length (497 rods actual distance). Yet that route took us a tough 6 ½ hours travel. Beymer describes this route as "challenging." It is not an overstatement.

In actual practice, the 1 ½ miles of portage become 4 ½ miles, since we generally double-portage. The same 5 ½ miles of canoeing is generally the easier part. Actually, I like making a few portages on a trip. Portaging makes an opportunity to use a different set of muscles, and it is a relief to get out and stretch. Since each portage is different, the change of scene offers interest, except to the canoe carrier, who sees little but the ground ahead. To ignore or minimize these walks through the woods is to miss out on another side of the lakes and river country. Likewise, after a good workout for the legs on portage, it is quite pleasant to sit back down in the canoe and use the arms again. Change is indeed restful, and we don't usually dally very long at the end of a carry. But, as I say, we find traveling 6 to 7 hours quite enough. If, however, the route is mostly by water and the wind either a tail wind or very light, we can stand to travel longer. The greatest distance we have done on a single day was some 20 miles, with one portage. It was a day late in the trip, when we were at peak strength, and that made a difference.

TRAVELING

A traveling day may go something like this. We wake fairly early, about 5 in high summer usually. If our plumbing doesn't tell us it's time to get up, the birds do. (Apparently the gulls tag one gull with the job of reveille. The wake-up call at 4 A.M. in high summer rouses the others, and then *all* the birds are up for the day.) We dress and stuff the sleeping bags. Friend Spouse packs the sleeping bags and other stuff in the housing pack and takes down the tent while I prepare breakfast and clean up afterwards. The use of camp stoves shortens preparation and clean-up times, but it still takes upwards of two hours from the time we get up until we move out. It seems to be much the same, whether there are two or six of us. At any rate, we are usually out on the water by 8 a.m. or earlier. A big reason for starting early is that as a rule, the lakes are calm early in the day, and it is a shame to waste easy paddling. You are also more likely to see animals early in the day.

An ordinary traveling day would find us at our chosen destination — at least its lake — by somewhere around 2 or 3 P.M. On our second long trip in Quetico, we found ourselves traveling longer days and were consequently thoroughly bushed at day's end. We traveled longer because camping places tend to be further apart, though there wasn't the competition for them. Selection of a campsite adds a little more time. Then we would set up camp, with pitching the tent the first item of business. If rain threatens, the second item of business is to put up the tarp. While I tend to rolling out the bedrolls, Friend Spouse tends to site details. We have a snack, rest, fish, or whatever, until supper time. Quite often, the wind comes up during the middle of the day, and it might blow rather hard until about 7 P.M. If it is windy, we will wait to fish until after supper, when the wind drops.

Others may be more inclined toward a later time for getting up and so have a later hour for moving out. And since in high summer (late June and July) it doesn't get dark until well after 9 P.M., some like to get in as much traveling as possible. There's nothing wrong with that, either. A leisurely pace, though, is part of the pleasure. However, particularly in high summer, those who make earlier stops usually have a better choice of campsites. Personally, I don't like to have to rush to prepare the evening meal, and I don't like to have to clean up in the dark. The same goes for setting up camp.

Which brings us back to planning the trip. Look at the map to see where your proposed day's distance should put you, and make sure that the distance includes campsites. It is also well to have a back-up plan in mind in case you have chosen a popular lake and find, on arrival, that all the sites are occupied. Several times, we have gotten the next-to-last campsite on a lake at 2 P.M. Theoretically, this shouldn't happen, and probably seldom does, as the permit system controls the number of parties into a zone and is supposed to spread them out so that all the campsites are never in use at once. However it is prudent to consider whether the next lake with campsites is a reasonable distance. What I am saying is, don't plan your day's destination to match your energy limits.

TRAVELING WITH CHILDREN

If you are a novice to all this, and particularly if you will have youngsters in the party, you should keep a couple of principles firmly in mind as you plan your first wilderness forays. There are degrees of wilderness, according to one's taste and capabilities. Determine what you really want and can deal with. For better prospects of a peaceful, happy trip, involve the kids in the planning.

First of all, keep it short. Start with brief trips (under 5 days). Second, keep it simple. Don't try to learn to do everything the first time out. If camping is new to you, don't try for elaborate cooking. Set up a base camp and use it for day trips in the surrounding area. The campgrounds in the National Forests are great places for developing your skills. You have the wonderful surroundings of forests and their denizens, a bit of the feel of wildness, but still have some of the amenities that simplify things for beginners. National Forest campgrounds generally will have designated campsites, with tent pads, fire pits and picnic tables. Close by will be the facilities (enclosed latrines). In some instances, firewood is available (for a small price). We started with camping in the Superior National Forest and paddling on the lakes at hand. It is not a bad way to go, particularly with children.

Alternatively, in Minnesota and Ontario (and undoubtedly in other areas around other National Forests and parks), there are resorts scattered around the fringes of the wilderness. These can be excellent spots to introduce younger children to wilderness (with a little more comfort).

As I said, 6 or 7 hours is quite long enough for a day's traveling; this was true when our children were along and holds equally true now that we are older. How much actual distance this is depends on how many portages, how long or difficult they are, and whether said portages require more than one trip. The amount of time also depends on how strong and vigorous the weakest, or slowest, member of the party is. One veteran canoeist who advises campers says that he thinks that 2 miles an hour (this is water distance, not with portaging) is a reasonable pace to base a day's distance on. That's fine, for some, especially if it is mostly water travel. I think that's quite a distance for novice campers or young campers. In some regions, wind direction and intensity can make a big difference in the distance traveled, and in coastal areas, the tide is a major factor in planning the starting and ending times of a day's trip.

How do you keep the kids happy?

If the kids are big enough to introduce them to trail travel, as on portages, you may need some tricks to keep them interested and in pleasant spirits. Portage time is a prime opportunity to encourage the youngsters to become good observers. Again, keep it simple. If there are several carries on the day's travel, focus on a single sort of item a day. One day's observation may center on plants and flowers. How many different flowers did they see? (Don't worry if you can't name them.) Note that some plants and shrubs may be abundant on one portage and perhaps missing altogether from the very next one. What is it that makes this portage different? Is the trail sunnier than the last one? Is it rockier? Kids also should know that all collecting should be done with the eyes and ears alone.

It's fun for young children to learn to recognize the well-known denizens; the tiny red squirrel, the chipmunk (whose name comes from the Algonquin word for squirrel) with his *lederhosen* look, the loons, the stately great blue heron, the ubiquitous gulls, the beaver and the moose all are easy starts.

Another day's attention might be directed to listening. (This calls for quiet on the trail in order to hear.) For instance, the different species of woodpeckers have different pitches to their drumming (some drill like jackhammers; others roll like snare drums). The blue jays' positive attitude as they scream "Do it! Do it! Do it!" greatly amuses me. The white-throated sparrow, *the* voice of the woods, has two-note whistle, followed by a bouncy triple-note. (I know; some people say the bird says "Peabody," but I don't believe it.) In some areas, the bird has a slightly different dialect, in which the two-note whistle rises, rather than falls.

In some more remote areas, we have heard the woods "talk." As we travel along the portage, we seem to hear people talking, though we can't quite understand what they are saying. When this has happened, we were in reality all alone in that area. One advantage from portaging quietly is the greater likelihood of seeing creatures out and about on their daily business. More than once we have been delighted with catching sight of a spruce grouse very close to the trail. This is a rather trusting sort of bird, which has gotten it the nickname of "fool hen."

Listening is fun in camp, too. All the things observed or heard during the day are subjects for sharing in conversation over dinner or lunch. Several kinds of frogs, for instance, live in the North Woods, and they all have their own calls. One island camp on Quetico's Sturgeon Lake faced the swamp near the portage, and the resident inhabitants sounded like a carpenter's crew, hammering away.

If your background is up to it, you and the kids could make a bit of a game called "Making A Living." This considers the question of how people survived in the wilderness in times gone by. You could look for plants that provided food and raw materials for the Indians who used to live in the region.

Another ploy passed on to me by a mother of young children is story telling. You can make several variations on this. One is to tell a story in installments, from portage to portage, in the manner of the old movie serials. Depending on the age of the kids, story invention can be passed around. One person starts a story on the first portage. Another picks it up at the next one and develops it further. And so it goes throughout the day's travel.

In the evening, after dinner, try the technique introduced to us by the Wilderness Southeast people. Make a daily list of things seen during the day, or phenomena noticed. One of the group could read the previous day's list as an opportunity to add items neglected or omitted. It is a wonderful way to learn to focus. You *see* things and you tend to remember more.

For me, Boundary Waters trips have always also been mind trips as well. One of the biggest mind trips is to try to imagine what it must have been like for people passing through the area in times past. A variation might be what a trip through the area might be like in 20 years or 100 years.

ATTITUDE IS IMPORTANT

Another consideration in your trip planning and even more important on the actual trip is the attitudes brought along. It is well to remember that you will be roughing it; you will not have the usual comforts of home (and shouldn't expect to); there will be hard work involved, and the weather may not cooperate. A cheerful acceptance of what the wilderness presents helps very much. A willingness to do what has to be done also makes things go easier. We all know that a grouch in a group can make matters unpleasant for the rest. Adopt a basic philosophy to the effect that this will be a *wonderful* trip; if, however, perchance things go wrong, we are equipped to cope. If you planned to deal with these variables occurring, you have improved your chances for rising above or going around unexpected difficulties that present themselves. And then the chances are that it really will be a fine trip.

PERMITS AND REGULATIONS

One other important point in your planning: you will need to get a permit to camp in the BWCA (in Quetico and other parks as well). As the number of visitors to the region has grown, so has the load on the available campsites and the vulnerable terrain. In consequence, the managements for both areas have instituted a system of issuing permits, the idea of which is to limit the number of visitors to any given zone at any one time, and to distribute them a little better. There is currently a $7 reservation fee if you book ahead, which is a good idea, because then you are assured of a share of the space. If you wait until the day you want to go into an area during the peak season, in say July or August, you face the possibility of no permit available on that day — or possibly the days on either side of it. Holidays (Memorial Day, Labor Day, and Independence Day) bring heavy visitation; weekends likewise are heavy, but early to mid-week days are better. Permits are available through the Forest Service and the canoe outfitters or resorts in the area. See Appendix — Canoeing in the United States for useful addresses.

Reservations are generally necessary for the more popular Canadian parks also. See Appendix — Canoeing in Canada for details. (Reservations or permits of some sort may be necessary in other parts of the country for similar activities. See the Appendix.) Group size in the BWCA has been limited to 10 at a campsite; in Quetico, the number was 9. However, efforts are being directed to reducing the party size and number in both parks. In 1993, discussion pointed toward eventually limiting party size to 6.

IRIS

2

HOW DO WE CHOOSE THE RIGHT STUFF?

*An 1860 list of the "necessaries of life" for an eight
day's trip in the mountains of California:*

8	lbs. potatoes
1	bottle whisky
1	bottle pepper sauce
1	bottle whisky
1	box tea
9	lbs. onions
2	bottles whisky
1	ham
11	lbs. crackers
1	bottle whisky
½	doz. sardines
2	bottles brandy, (4th proof)
6	lbs. sugar
1	bottle brandy, (4th proof)
7	lbs. cheese
2	bottles brandy, (4th proof)
1	bottle pepper
5	gallons whisky
4	bottles whisky (old Bourbon)
1	small key whisky
1	bottle of cocktails, (designed for a "starter.")

— From Hutchings' *California Magazine,* 1860

After planning the trip, the second order of business is getting the
camp gear together. Camping can be a memorable experience with
a lot of bad memories if mistakes have been made in getting the
equipment together. As with so many of life's endeavors, camping
goes much better when you use the "right" things. Certainly it is easier
to camp elegantly with carefully selected gear. Let me emphasize one

point: elegance in camping requires quality, durable material, quality workmanship and sensible design. It does not need to be the most expensive. Whatever the item, it should be capable of easy packing (and of being packed) or it becomes a pesky nuisance. It is much more pleasant on a portage trail when one is not loaded up with a slew of stray items, or tormented by uncomfortable lumps poking one's back. Some of the portages are long, or difficult, or both, and the extra aggravation is definitely not needed.

Greater efficiency on a trip is a worthwhile goal. It is smart to determine what will be needed for a successful trip and for the most likely contingencies, especially problems that could arise. Then organize your gear and all so that the least amount of effort is needed to deal with it all.

Further, you don't need to acquire everything at once. If you are planning to rent equipment, it is a good idea to learn what you can rent, and where, well in advance of the proposed trip. Our friends the Hansens, the canoe outfitters at Sawbill Lake, like many canoe outfitters, have a complete equipment rental service; they will completely outfit any group with gear and food if the group has let them know what they want. This is what canoe outfitters do very well. This is also a very good way to learn what and how much you will need if you haven't read helpful books such as this. Other general rental companies will have some camping equipment, but you do need to look carefully into what they have, and everything you need may not be available.

For people coming in from some other part of the country, it is very helpful to talk with outfitters. Every area has certain quirks and idiosyncracies, and the local people generally have found particular items better suited than others. One minor example: hats. In the North Woods, a hat (for summer time) should be capable of shedding water. Such a hat is not so comfortable in southern areas, where more interest lies in keeping off the sun, yet letting the air cool the head.

One other angle on the matter of rental. For more than 18 years, we rented canoes. We could have paid for a canoe with what we spent on rentals, but we did not have to deal with the problem of storing the craft, much less the decision-making for buying one. Home space is thus a criterion on this buy/rent question, and certainly applies to other gear. Further, we were not ready to decide on the kind and type of canoe to buy.

Borrowing equipment is also a possibility. Just make sure that you return it in the best possible condition, and above all, clean. Just don't do what a few over-zealous souls have done; don't wash the tent — or other coated materials — in the washing machine. You will ruin the water-resistant coating if you do.

Now to the specifics. I have broken the list into several categories — travel, living, sleeping, cooking, personal gear, clothing, and fishing. See Appendix — Master Check Lists for the areas discussed. If you don't plan to fish, just skip that. However, fishing in those northern lakes and cooking the fresh catch are very much a part of the richness of the wilderness, and fresh fish definitely makes a meal elegant.

TRAVEL

Let's start by looking at packs. All the gear is, or should be, carried in packs of some sort. (I'll say more about loading them later.) It is worth noting that in most outdoor excursion-type activities such as backpacking, hiking, mountain-climbing or canoeing, each has special requirements, and consequently, while some of the equipment is interchangeable, there are good reasons for the particular items to have been developed. There is no such thing as a truly all-purpose pack. What works for a backpacker will have some shortcomings for the canoeist, and vice versa. Finally, pack manufacturers *are* recognizing that women of assorted sizes are actually wilderness-tripping!

On some of our early canoe trips, with the four children, we tried using duffel bags (purchased for the kids' trips to Scout camps) for carrying things such as sleeping bags, etc. It was a mistake. We used them a few times and found them very difficult for the kids to carry. These were the old-style bags, about 3 feet long, with a handle strap and one across one end of the bag. Even with only a sleeping bag and some personal gear, it was about three-fourths as long as a kid, much too long to carry over a shoulder, and much too long to carry by the handle. A good-sized adult could manage one over the shoulder — I have seen men carrying a duffel bag slung atop a backpack, which seemed to work pretty well for them, but I wouldn't want to carry one that way. It is not easy for smaller people to handle. Duffel bags (*Duffel*, like Duluth, is a place name) are not designed for easy carrying over a portage of any length (longer than say 5 rods — that is, about 80 feet or a little more than a tenth of a mile), and they also can be awkward beasts to stuff into a canoe.

However, like so many other pieces of equipment, technology has brought changes. The present-day duffel is stubbier than its elders: our old ones were some 36" long. The bigger ones today can range in size; one company's largest is 28" x 14" x 14 overall, or some 5488 cubic inches. The newer ones also may feature compression straps that stabilize the contents, or they may have end pockets. (One of the problems with the old-style duffel was its floppiness unless it was totally stuffed.) While a duffel bag would be a royal pain in the lake country of the Boundary Waters, it serves very well where the travel is all river or coastal water, with no portages. The key point to remember here is *appropriate*. Are you selecting the right type of equipment for your trip?

The classic Duluth pack, the traditional canoe pack in this region, is essentially a canvas envelope with leather shoulder straps with no cluttering outside pockets to catch on canoe sides or thwarts. It was developed for canoe travel and still is difficult to beat for hauling gear. A Duluth pack sits well in a canoe; it is reasonably easy to haul in and out. Three centuries of use have produced some improvements in the materials used in making the pack, but the simplicity of the basic design developed by the long-ago fur traders has not been surpassed. Improvements have come in the form of sturdier, lighter-weight materials, padded shoulder straps, and special features such as flat internal pockets for maps, etc. Its straps are adjustable for adapting to different sizes of people to carry it. (Friend Spouse and I have refined our technique to the point where we know who will carry which packs throughout the trip and set the straps on all packs accordingly.) It also has the virtue of being fairly inexpensive, especially when compared with an internal frame pack. A #2 Duluth pack has been our pack of choice for food. It can hold upwards of thirty to thirty-five pounds, or about a week's worth of camp meals. We chose the smaller #2 over a #3 because of the sizes of the people who would be carrying it.

In the past, traditional packs and pack frames were often used in conjunction with a tumpline. A tumpline is a leather strap that passes across the forehead from either side of the pack. It is appropriate with very large or very heavy Duluth-type packs, especially on long portages. Like the pack frame, it enables the weight of the load to be distributed better. When Eric Sevareid, the famous reporter, was a teen-ager, he and his friend Walter Porter made a canoe journey from Minneapolis to Hudson Bay. One thing he mentions was how he came to hate that tumpline. In recent years, I have begun to see occasional mention of tumplines in some of the specialty catalogues.

If you are making do with whatever you have on hand, avoid any piece of luggage that requires carrying by a hand strap. Anyone who has toted a suitcase in an airport has a notion of the weariness ahead. Pick the piece with a shoulder strap over the one with only a hand grip.

Our pack collection currently consists of two traditional-type packs, two internal frame packs, a small backpack, and until recently a pair of all-purpose packs (known in our house language as the "Little Bastards"). After renting packs a time or so, we bought the two Little Bastards and a pair of #2 Duluth packs. (This was more than 20 years ago.) The choice was partly determined by price, partly by the carrying capabilities within our family.

We didn't know much about packs when we bought the "Little Bastards," since retired. (Yes, we name our packs; each has a certain personality, and a name provides immediate reference.) These, as we learned, were badly designed and wretchedly uncomfortable pieces of equipment. Ostensibly small back packs, they were impossible to adjust to fit with any degree of comfort anyone over 5' 6" and virtually so for anyone else. Friend Spouse refused to carry them. The front pocket had a zippered closure; the two side pockets were covered by flaps that buckled. (Those pockets were a real pain in hauling the pack out of the canoe.) However, I liked their external pockets, and for years one of them was my pack of choice for housekeeping gear.

Later, when only Friend Spouse and I made up the party, we purchased the "Big Green Honker," a #3 size Voyageur. The Voyageur, made of heavy-duty Cordura nylon and with padded straps, is an updated version of the classic Duluth. We use it for our sleeping bags, air mattresses, other sleeping paraphernalia, and spare clothes. That sort of stuff is bulky but not particularly heavy, so it is quite feasible for me to carry this larger pack.

Backpacks are often designed for use on either an external or internal frame. Frames make it possible to put a prodigious amount of material into one working unit. We have seen people in the BWCA with external pack frames, though such is not my pack of choice. However, a loaded external-frame pack is awkward to get in and out of a canoe. The belts can hang on the canoe gunwales, causing increasing aggravation as the number of portages increases.

The newer canoe packs with internal frames are easier to handle. These packs feature a system consisting of shoulder straps, chest strap and hip belt that make it possible to adjust the load more comfortably to the bearer. A major feature of this new breed of packs for canoeing is the system of compression straps along the sides. These adjustable straps make it possible to "fine-tune" a load so that it is very firm and secure. With the proper adjustments, it is possible to carry a substantial load (even more than the usual weight) with a

smaller degree of discomfort. These same straps can cause some annoyance in loading and unloading, as they tend to catch on the side of the canoe. A primary — and important — difference between canoe packs and backpacker's packs is that a backpack will have several compartments accessible at any time; a canoe pack, with a single opening, has greater protection from rain or from water sloshing into the canoe.

Big Blue and Miz Blue, our newest packs, represent this latest technology. Big Blue is an internal frame pack like those just described. Of our various styles of packs, it is the most comfortable to carry, and generally holds the heaviest load. (Friend Spouse carries it.) Miz Blue, the woman's version of Big Blue, is somewhat wider, and not so deep, and can be adjusted much better to my female frame. It is by far the easiest pack to portage I have ever used. (See Appendix — Equipment Sources for further discussion.)

In choosing or loading a pack, consider carefully its center of gravity, or where its heaviest part will be. The center of gravity of any load you carry on your back should be well above your hip joints. Otherwise you will be thrown constantly off-balance because the load is distributed badly and you will tire much faster from the inefficiency of poor load distribution.

We replaced "Little Blue," a small backpack which we used for camera gear, water bottle, lunch, rain gear and other small stuff for day-tripping after some 10 years use. Sometimes I used to "double-pack" it with the Big Green Honker (our shelter pack), carrying Little Blue in front, or Friend Spouse perched it atop Big Blue. (Carrying two packs — one front, one back — is double-packing.) The current Little Blue is designed for attaching to a canoe seat or to one of the big packs, or it can be carried as a shoulder bag. A day pack is a great piece of equipment for a younger child (say 8 or 9 years old) to handle on a trip. It is a reasonable load for a youngster and solves the problem of handling some of the overflow items that are going along. As the youngster gets bigger, he or she can handle a small pack that contains the sleeping bag and whatever extra clothes are being carried; in short, the child carries his own gear. Just try to keep the weight of the pack to a quarter or less of the child's weight.

Fanny packs are useful for day tripping, but they are uncomfortable when worn while carrying a pack on portage. For a woman answering Nature's call while on the trail, they are a real nuisance.

Maine canoeists traditionally used pack baskets. While I have never seen them used in Minnesota, they are beginning to show up in Minnesota stores (see Appendix — Equipment Sources). The late noted outdoorsman Calvin Rutstrum said he would remove the harness from his 12-inch basket and then put it into a tradtional pack. The same result is achieved with a sturdy cardboard box with much less cost and weight. Pack baskets start somewhere around $60, and I frankly don't see them offering any advantage over a proper canoe pack.

It should be noted that packs are not inexpensive items. A very basic #2 Duluth will cost upwards from $50. The internal frame packs can run from $140 to $200. If you are just beginning, consider renting the equipment, or borrowing it from friends. Learn about the differences before spending big money. If you are buying, get the best quality you can (and that doesn't necessarily mean the fanciest piece of equipment); pay for good material, good design, and good construction.

It is worth noting the carrying capacity of our various packs. (I will talk about packing everything later.) A Duluth pack carrying a week's worth of food weighs about thirty-five pounds; the Voyageur is larger; Big Blue can easily hold 60 pounds or more, and the day pack with our rain garb and Don's camera stuff carries about 15 pounds.

CANOES

Let us assume that you have not purchased a canoe or paddles for your trip. A canoe is an appropriate item for renting until you have enough experience with canoeing to decide that you enjoy it well enough to buy equipment and that you have been·able to form some notion of what works best for you. Buying a canoe is no simple matter and really is best considered after you have some outings behind you. After a few expeditions, you will have a better idea of what kinds of trips you like to take — extended tours through the wilderness; simply going up to a lake and settling there for the duration; day-tripping, whatever. Then there is the matter of what kind of water will you be dealing with — flat water, rapids, rivers, or big lakes.

As with gear for other outdoor activities, certain canoes are better suited to particular conditions than others. Rent a few times, so that you get the feel of handling a canoe. If possible, try different brands and types of "expedition" or "touring" canoe, as opposed to a racing or a river canoe. Talk to knowledgeable people at stores that specialize in outdoors equipment or other people who canoe with some frequency. You should be able to try out several canoes before you buy one.

Great interest in design configurations has arisen with increased activity in several aspects of canoeing. Different types of situations call for different types of canoes. The canoe that is great on the large open lakes won't work as well for river travel or white water. After many years of renting whenever we went to the BWCA, we finally bought a canoe that was designed for touring, or lake paddling with a loaded canoe. Cat's-paw, our 18-foot touring canoe, is wonderful for our Boundary Waters trips; loaded, it goes easily across open water, even headed into the wind. Unloaded and on winding rivers, it is an absolute and unwieldy dog. Its length keeps it from being highly responsive, again especially in a wind, or on a narrower river. But loaded, it handles beautifully in rough water. On the other hand, a canoe designed for river travel or white water will not perform as well as a touring canoe. After paddling in Vermont rivers in agile, stubby little canoes, we bought canoes that are wonderfully maneuverable for canoeing on southeastern Minnesota rivers, but they give Friend Spouse hernias just thinking about portaging them.

What should the canoe be made of? Wood, or plastic, or fiberglass, or aluminum, or some other exotic material or combination? The technology of materials used in canoes has undergone remarkable development in recent years, with a dazzling array of possibilities open to you. It is possible to buy a wooden canoe (even a birch bark one), a classic wood and canvas, aluminum, fiberglass, Kevlar or other special synthetic material. During this past decade, the technology of canoe making has developed dramatically. The push has been toward an ever lighter canoe (to the great joy of the canoeist who has to portage the craft). The old wood and canvas canoes tended to get even heavier — upwards of 90 pounds in some instances — toward the end of a trip, as the wood absorbed water. The aluminum canoes that were the result of the transition from war-time manufacture of aircraft fuel tanks were an improvement, as they were lighter than a wood-and-canvas model, weighing in the neighborhood of 75 pounds (this is where we came in as canoeists). They were very durable and required little maintenance, which made them attractive to many paddlers.

A great many outfitters used aluminum canoes almost exclusively until recent years. Their canoes need to be very durable with the use they get, as it is a deep rock in the Boundary Waters that does not have aluminum scrapings on it. Aluminum canoes, commonly 17-foot ones, are reasonably light — weighing some 63 (lightweight) to 75 pounds (standard), a manageable load for a strong adult or two smaller people of approximately the same height. But more and more, we are also seeing touches of color from fiberglass canoes. The Kevlar canoes are in the range of 45 pounds. Increasingly, outfitters are providing smaller and lighter one-person canoes for solitary tripping as well as Kevlar canoes.

Experts or veteran paddlers will favor one material or another. For instance (and all this is speaking generally), aluminum canoes are lighter than wood or wood and canvas, but they are noisy in the water. Wood is beautiful, but requires a great deal of careful upkeep. Fiberglass is sturdy but can be quite heavy. Kevlar, a relative of Teflon, is extraordinarily strong, very light-weight and very expensive. Market pressures however, have led to combinations of materials that meet the popular criteria of light weight and strength. The budget and the back become major considerations here. The lighter canoes have definitely opened up wilderness canoeing for women — for anybody less than tremendously strong.

It all boils down to what is appropriate for *your* particular time, place, use and budget. And even then, a certain amount of personal prejudice enters in. When you rent a canoe, the problem is solved for the moment, and you also have an opportunity to develop your own prejudice based on experience.

PADDLES

Selecting your own paddle is an important choice. Like the canoes, the paddles have also been affected by technological develop-ments. You will find variations of material, shape and size.

The component material range is not so great. Generally, paddles are made either of wood or of plastic and aluminum. Canoeists have continued to seek out lighter equipment here, too, with good reason. Consider: you may be paddling something like 30 strokes a minute or more. You may be actually paddling 5 hours in the day. That's *seventy-two hundred times* a day you lift that paddle. If you are using a 22-ounce paddle (a fairly typical weight), you will have moved some 9,900 pounds — over *four and a half* tons — in the course of that day — and that's just paddling. The wooden paddle is a thing of beauty, particularly if it is a new one, and some are incredibly light. Ojibwa paddle-makers at Grand Portage make beautiful spruce paddles that weigh less than a pound.

As with the canoes, you can find paddles that are made of composite (synthetic) materials, or that are made of combinations (wood with foam core, for instance). Weights here range from as little as 11 ounces (a racer's favorite).

Outfitters have long used plastic-bladed paddles because they are inexpensive, very durable, and require no real maintenance. They weigh a bit more than wooden paddles, ranging from about 23 to 28 ounces. What I have liked about them is their very smooth shaft. Any roughness on the shaft can lead to blisters on the hands. Wooden paddles need to be maintained carefully to keep that smoothness of shaft and handle.

The cost is a factor: the plastic-bladed paddles are *much* less expensive. You can get one for less than $30. The wooden or synthetic (not to be confused with plastic) ones run between $45 and $200. (And then there are the high-tech racers' paddles.) Again, it makes sense to rent until you are reasonably sure you want to continue making trips.

Canoes of some sort are found in many places in the world. Just as the styles, materials and designs vary according to the materials available and the nature of the water ways, so the shapes and types of means to propel them differ, too. Generally, in the BWCA, the traditional paddle shape is a broad blade. In Quetico, the Canadians often use a paddle much like the traditional Ojibwa paddle, with its long narrow blade. Out east, you may be more apt to find the so-called beaver tail, which is rather narrower than the Minnesota style. We are most accustomed to the broad-bladed paddle. Some experts point out that a narrower blade is easier for people with less upper body strength.

Canoe racers often use a bent-shafted paddle. We have seen those used several times on our trips, and they are showing up with greater frequency in the stores. While they may be more efficient in the water, their shape makes them a bit unwieldy on a portage. For the average wilderness-trotting canoeist, I still think that the shapes developed by the Indians are still as valid today as they were 300 and who knows how many more years ago.

The other crucial point is the length of the paddle. It is very important — and I cannot overemphasize this point — to ensure that the paddle is not too large for the paddler. Depending on the brand of paddle, the lengths come in 1- or 2- inch increments. The most common lengths are between 50 and 56 inches, though longer and shorter are available in some styles.

If the paddle is too long, the paddler can not make an efficient stroke and expends more energy than is necessary for good movement in the water. Particularly if youngsters are going to be paddling, and it is a first-time experience for them, great care should be taken to outfit them with properly-sized paddles. There is absolutely nothing to be gained by carelessly setting them up for an unpleasant time and thus possibly ruining the wilderness experience for them for good and ever.

What is a good length? Certainly not as long as from floor to your nose (many veteran canoe paddlers think the old Boy Scout advice for that length was very bad). Better is from floor to chin and even shorter. Actually, when you start shopping, you will find that there is any number of ways to determine the "proper" length. The dealers who sell canoe paddles have ideas, and I suspect they are also very helpful. One way is to check is to grasp the paddle with both arms extended directly forward. If the paddle is about right, one hand will be just back of the hand grip and the other just above the blade. If for some reason the right length is not available, I think it is better to go a little short than too long. You can paddle faster with a shorter paddle. True, you won't get the depth of stroke, and consequently the power, with a short paddle, but you won't suffer the fatigue of overextending the reach. Old-timers like Calvin Rutstrum and Theodore Cheney advised a longer paddle for the stern paddler. The fatigue factor is important, too; it can lead to accidents. It is always a good idea to take along an extra paddle, in case you lose or break one.

LIFE JACKETS

Canoe travelers should also automatically include life jackets, or personal flotation devices (PFDS), in the canoe. Do *not* go out into the wilderness without life jackets. Get the proper size to fit well, too. Do *not, repeat, do not,* rely on flotation cushions. It is helpful to get jackets of different colors or with some other distinction to make it easier to identify one's own (as in keeping track of stuff on a portage). Since Don and I have identical ones, I marked mine with a yarn tie on a buckle. Wear the jacket while on the water, especially if your swimming skills are minor. Even if you are a strong swimmer, wear it. The lake waters are cold, a hazard to keep in mind at all times. In fact, Minnesota law requires that a United States Coast Guard-approved PFD *for each person* be "at hand" at all times. As Bill Hansen at Sawbill Canoe Outfitters pointed out, no one drowns with a PFD on. Canadian water safety law requires, in addition, that all canoes be equipped with a bailing can which is an excellent idea wherever you paddle.

A helpful item in the canoe is a clear plastic map envelope; there are several one the market. Friend Spouse likes to have it with the map of the day on a pack in front of him as we paddle so that he can refer to it for locating a portage or campsite.

LIVING

SHELTER — THE TENT

"Living" includes the matter of shelter and outside "housekeeping" for your home in the wilderness. We did not buy tents until after we had rented tents several times. By then we had gotten some notions about our needs. The ones we acquired at that time were well suited to park and campground camping (we were trying lots of camping), but proved too heavy and bulky for wilderness trips. We have since made two replacements.

Tents certainly are not what they used to be — hallelujah! The wilderness tents available when we started going out in the early '70s had to be supported by ropes strung to trees, and it was a good trick to find trees obligingly placed. Further, they were canvas, heavy stuff, and even heavier when wet. I no longer remember where I once read a description of the business of waxing a tent with melted paraffin to make it water-resistant. Part of the lore of those earlier times was the warning not to touch the wall of the tent (or allow anything else to) during a rain because it would permit water to wick through. A ground cloth was an absolute necessity, as the tents then did not have floors built in.

Technology provided an elegant improvement with the self-supporting tent. Good quality tents (and the field is quite competitive) are free-standing, made of light-weight rip-stop nylon. The material used today cuts the weight considerably: a 4-person tent weighs under 10 pounds. One splendid improvement is the water-resistant floor (picturesquely described as a bathtub floor) that is now found in all good tents. (A ground cloth placed under the tent protects the floor from the little nicks and pricks that come with use. It also offers some insulation against the ground drawing off body warmth.)

Most have mosquito netting over all openings that can be zipped shut from the inside as well as the outside. Being able to control the ventilation adds considerably to the comfort of the tent. We enjoyed our first tent with a screen door, even though we had to open the screen to close the main door when rain came up or it got too chilly. The designer of our newest tent dealt with that problem: the main door, or weather door, can be closed from the inside, without having to open the screen. We were also delighted to note that more and more tents are designed with "front" and "back" doors — splendid for ventilation, and even nicer that occupants don't need to crawl over the other to go in or out.

Nowadays tents generally have a rain fly, or second "roof," great insurance against a tent leaking during a rain. One of our earlier tents did not have one. We were camping in early October, and on the second evening, Friend Spouse remarked that the glorious sunset was an excellent sign that we would get rained on that night. So we rigged a fly by using our plastic tarp to cover the tent. Sure enough, rain fell in the night. It sounded like we were sleeping in a popcorn popper, but we were warm and dry.

Over the years, we have found that we get rained on at least once during any trip of at least 3 days. We have learned to expect it and to plan accordingly. If the weather is rainy, keep things that are inside the tent (if it does not have a full fly) from touching the wall, as that encourages water to wick through.

In camping supply stores, you'll find tents described as three- and four-season tents. Unless you are quite positive you intend to winter-camp (after October in Minnesota, the canoeing is *much* harder), a three-season tent will do very nicely. The popular dome tent, for instance, often is a four-season tent, as its shape is well-suited to shedding a snow load.

One feature now standard on good-quality tents is the tent pole sections are threaded with shock cords, which makes setting up the tent much quicker and easier.

Another point to consider is size. The market offers a rich selection of sizes and shapes — domes, mummy styles (for solo backpackers), ellipses, and even more exotic shapes besides the classic A-frame tent. Several years ago, we bought a four-person A-frame tent, even though later only the two of us used it. We got the larger size because our eldest daughter Lynne occasionally went with us. We enjoyed the extra space, especially on rainy days, and the larger size added only about 2 pounds over the smaller size. We have since replaced it with a two-person dome tent which is a couple of pounds lighter than our old one, yet has similar floor area.

Some veteran canoe-goers prefer to use as small a tent (thus lighter) as possible, essentially what a backpacker would choose. The lighter weight usually comes from a sacrifice of space. Canoeists look at tents a little differently from backpackers; they generally prefer a roomier tent, as they are more apt to be wind-bound than the hikers, and a larger, taller tent is a more pleasant place to hole up for the day. When our four children were young and going with us, it was more comfortable to use two smaller tents rather than have everybody in one large tent. Our present tent weighs about 9 pounds, not a bad weight for canoe travel.

One useful trick is to string a high-line inside the tent from one end to the other and use it to hang clothes on overnight. (Such lines are on the market now. You can also buy a mesh "hammock" or loft for this purpose, an inexpensive item. I enjoy having a place to put small stuff.) This gives your clothes a chance to dry and air out a bit. We did this, as usual, once time when we camped in Montana's Gallatin National Forest and that night the temperature dropped to 28°F. The next morning, we could just reach up, collect our underwear and put it in the sleeping bag to warm up a bit before putting it on.

THE RAIN FLY

A tarp, or rain fly, is a good thing to have, especially if you plan to stay put in the same site for several days. We don't often use this, but nevertheless we always carry it "just in case." It is useful as a secondary shelter, and is certainly valuable to have if the weather turns rainy. When the two of us hit rainy days, we can retreat to the tent to read or sleep. But if the group is larger and if children are along, this is clearly not a satisfactory solution. If it rains on a traveling day, a tarp makes the setting up of camp a good bit more pleasant, and it offers a bit of shelter to get the fire started and to prepare a meal. You can get a plastic tarp, or one of woven polyethylene. A good size is approximately 9' by 12'. Good quality ones will have grommets not only at the corners, but at mid-points on the sides as well. Lines from these mid-points give additional precision in controlling the tarp. In addition to a ridgepole rope, you need ropes at the corners: A good length to erect it is 20 to 25'. There's more about rigging tarps in Chapter 6.

SHELTER EXTRAS

Tents are a part of shelter, but not the whole story.

Put a small whiskbroom in the tent bag for cleaning out the duff, or leaf debris, and the like that gets tracked in. You can find small whisk broom/dustpan sets in outdoor equipment stores. I like the trick an acquaintance uses. He includes a small oriental rug to use as a door mat.

If you think you'll do a lot of camping, you may want to invest in a vestibule to the tent. This is a sort of extension that can provide some ten square feet or so of additional space. We have never gotten one; since most of our canoe trips involve moving every or nearly every day, we didn't want the extra weight.

HOUSEKEEPING DETAILS

At either end of the season (May or as early as September), we take a Space Blanket. An absolute must for early or late season camping, we routinely use it throughout the season. This is an aluminized sheet of plastic, very light, and effective to have under the sleeping bag and mattress pad when the weather is cooler. It prevents loss of body heat to the cooler ground. We put the Space Blanket under our bedrolls so that the aluminized coating can reflect our body heat back to warm us. (Actually, in warm weather, you'll want to face the shiny side down, to keep from reflecting your body heat back to you.) Don't put it over you; the body moisture given off during the night condenses on the underside of it and then gets the sleeping bag wet.

Rope is essential. I say rope: I mean cordage, preferably nylon or polypropylene, and it is possible to find it in quiet colors (other than bright yellow). It is inexpensive, durable and lightweight. (Polypropylene has several virtues for the canoeist: it is not stretchy; it is very slow to rot, and it floats.) You can find ⅛- inch (3 mm.) braided nylon cord, which is just fine for most camp use. (I think this is what some call parachute cord.) You can also get a 300–pound test nylon cordage that is lightweight. The one-quarter inch (6.5 mm.) nylon braid, up to 30-pound test, is quite adequate for raising a tarp for secondary shelter. If you are starting from absolute scratch, you can buy a hank or two of lightweight, heavy-test line. Otherwise, scrounge around and use what you have on hand.

An assortment is appropriate. You need a very sturdy one of at least 20' for the ridgepole of the tarp. You need one long rope for a ridgepole to lay the tarp over, and then you need four shorter and lighter cords to tie to trees to stretch the roof out. Part of the trick is to find the trees growing conveniently for erecting the "room." Our rope collection, actually gathered rather haphazardly over the years, has four or five pieces in the 15–18 feet range, and while often the length may have been excessive, there have also been times longer pieces would have been useful. So I'd say have at least four stout lines (they can be left attached to the tarp, or not) at least 20' long.

Expert campers and outfitters agree the most effective way of preventing bears (we're talking about the basic, common black bears — *Euarctos americanus* — which may be cinnamon or brown as well as black) from carrying off the food pack is "flying" — hanging — the food pack. (In the Everglades, you fly the garbage to keep the raccoons from it.) I'll talk more about ways to fly it in Chapter 6. Two 50-feet sections of ⅜-inch polypropylene (#7.5) rope will do for this.

An assortment of additional shorter, light lines is useful. These can be fairly light, so long as they are good and strong. One standard use is a clothesline for hanging the towels; since tree distances vary, it is useful for that line to be 6 or 8 feet long. We generally tie on a 10- or 12-foot line to the canoe as a painter, for pulling it up and tying it for brief stops. (Put this piece in a place where you can get it quickly and easily or tie it onto the canoe when you launch the boat. Use a small bungee cord to keep the hank out of the way.)

A small assortment of bungee cords is useful, too. Small ones (6 inches or so) can be used to fasten fishing rods together, or bind up surplus painter, and so on. Of course, there are other times when you'll need a piece of string for whatever reason, so take some string as well. In our day pack, I have my "bag of tricks" — a quart-size zip-lock bag with the compass, several bungee cords, extra shoe laces, a spare quick-release fastener, several adhesive bandages, a couple of pre-moistened towelettes, a whistle, and other odds and ends that might be needed.

Put in six to ten clothes pins, too. They are useful for hanging towels and to hang other stuff to dry. On one of our Quetico trips, rain came up in the night and blew into the tent before we realized it was raining. Morning brought an end to the rain, but also it brought a very strong wind. Clothespins anchored the sleeping bags to the line to dry. Plastic bags — assorted sizes, from garbage-can size down — are always useful. Have several.

A small folding saw is very handy. We acquired a Sven saw (then about $12) that is a joy. It folds into itself with an overall length of 22 inches. There are other types of good camp saws that have come on the market since we got ours. Quetico people recommend carrying a small saw rather than a hatchet.

The writers of the older books on canoeing (1970 and earlier) included an ax in their lists of equipment, rather than a hatchet. I have been on a few portages where an ax, or better still, a chain saw, would have been useful. But now, with more people going into the wilderness, the Forest Service people advise leaving the hatchet at home and taking a saw instead. I am told (and it sounds reasonable to me) that an ax or a hatchet is the Number One source of injury and damage. Generally, there is an abundance of small wood — sticks of assorted sizes — within fairly close range of a site. We used to carry a hatchet for splitting larger pieces of deadfalls into smaller firewood, though in recent years we have tended to cook more with a camp stove. Friend Spouse says that if you can't break a piece of wood over your knee, it's bigger than you need anyway.

At one time, a collapsible camp shovel was considered an important piece of equipment. Now, it is officially discouraged by the Forest Service. For one reason, too many people were following the now-discredited practice of digging a trench around the tent to carry away rain water. Such trenches scarred up the place something awful. We routinely carried a shovel, but eventually concluded it was more trouble than it was worth. Its main use is cleaning out the fire pit, and a backpacker's trowel will do that just fine.

Forest Service regulations stipulate that fish innards must be buried well back away from lake edges and camp sites. Again, other places, other techniques. Primitive camping in the coastal islands of Florida requires digging for personal sanitation. The backpacker's trick of carrying an ordinary garden trowel is a good one and generally, a trowel would suffice. (Inevitably, light-weight backpacker's trowels have appeared on the market.) Keep in mind that in Quetico, as in some other places, there are no permanent latrines. A trowel or small shovel is very much in order there.

Comfortable sitting spots, particularly with a back rest, at camp sites are rare. Few of the BWCA and no Quetico camp sites have picnic tables. One or maybe two string hammocks are pleasant, if your site has well-situated trees. Several types of camp seats have appeared on the market. This again is a point where one considers extra weight versus additional comfort. We greatly enjoy having a couple of the sling-type camp seats. After a day of paddling and portaging, the back rests are wonderful. From my experience, I would suggest that a camper with hip or leg problems take some sort of portable camp stool. The logs that have been placed around fire pits may not be a very good height for a person with joint problems.

You may need supplemental illumination. In northern Minnesota (and other sites in corresponding latitude) in May, daylight comes about 5 A.M. and dark by 9 P.M. In July, daylight comes about 4:30 A.M. and full darkness settles about 10:00 P.M. States with hunting and fishing regulated according to daylight hours will issue tables of sun-up and sun-down hours for the appropriate seasons. In mid-August, it is dark by 9:30, so we need only a flashlight for urgent nocturnal trips. Take at least one flashlight for every two people, or one per tent. It need not be large; there are some very powerful small lights on the market, some hand-held, some mounted on a headband (somebody really had a good idea here). Take fresh batteries; having a spare bulb is not a bad idea, too. We usually leave the camp all ready for the night when we go out to fish and then go straight to bed when we come in.

Many campers travel long into the day, and evening finds them cooking and clearing up in the dark. They need more lighting gear. Many people have a candle lantern for use in the tent; I don't like the idea of a flame in the tent. We have never carried a gas lantern, though we have in years past seen parties with them. The main reason is that our pattern of activities doesn't call for one, but other very cogent reasons are that a gas lantern is bulky, and more to the point, the globes and mantles are very fragile and subject to breaking. If breakage occurs, you are then carrying dead, useless weight, and that doesn't appeal to me at all! Other highly portable camp lanterns have appeared on the market since the first edition of this book.

By all means, include a small roll of plumber's duct tape. It is marvelous stuff for toughness and versatility. It will patch, for the moment, a hole in a canoe or a cooking pot, a rip in pants, or deal with whatever unexpected calamity of whatever dimension that might appear.

A fun optional item is a Sun Shower. Friend Spouse was given a portable solar-heated shower for a birthday present, which we of course tried out on our next trip. It is great for those trips when you stay put, as it takes several hours for the water to get to the desired 90 degrees. We were traveling, so only about two hours of heating time were available. But the water was well warmed for dish washing, and it was nice to have heated water for rinsing.

Again, what it all comes down to is deciding what creature comforts are really important to you, and whether what it takes to have those comforts is worth the extra effort.

SLEEPING

Sleeping bags can be quite an investment. The first point to consider before buying is the temperature range when you will most likely be camping. There is a rather formidable array of bags, with a choice of stuffing that determines how much cold can be kept out, a range of weights, and even a choice of shapes. Again price is a final consideration.

You should look carefully at your expected pattern of camping: What time of year do you generally go? How many days in a year do you camp? How many years do you expect that you may go camping? For choice of stuffing, down is probably the warmest. A down sleeping bag is very light in weight, scrunches down to very little space, and is expensive. One big problem with it is that is vulnerable to moisture. Wet, it loses much of its insulating qualities, and is "really bad news when it's wet." I know from experience about sleeping in a wet bag; I recall one wretched rainy night when the tent leaked onto my sleeping bag (my first one, and it wasn't down), and I had to sleep in a rather constricted position the rest of the night. Not nice at all! There are several synthetics that work quite satisfactorily, such as Hollofil, and they are less expensive than down. I feel it is pointless to get the very finest down bag if you are going to do the bulk of your camping in the hot months.

The first camping items we acquired were sleeping bags for the kids on their Scouting camp-outs and we added bags for ourselves. They were good quality, for the time, and relatively inexpensive.

Those first bags were comparatively heavy and quite bulky. After the kids left home and Friend Spouse and I began to do more serious camping, we bought new bags that could be mated. This pair had nylon shells filled with 3¾ pounds of Dacron Hollofil II. In August, they could be too warm. Pricewise, they were more expensive than our earlier bags, but still not so expensive as down. They occupied about the same space in the pack as did the earlier, unmatched pair. Then a couple of years ago, after the zippers began to give consistent difficulty, we decided to replace the bags rather than repair them. (It cost something like $40 a bag to get a zipper replaced, and we had used those bags for some 10 years.) As we have gotten older, we have looked to lighten our loads, so we decided on down replacements.

We had purchased compression sacks (another handy little equipment item!) for each of the Hollofil bags, but discovered that we could put *both* the down bags into one compression sack. (We knew down was less bulky, but that was a revelation!) We could also leave the bags mated and just stuff them in. This cut the time and effort to pack bedding. We do love our down bags for their ease in packing.

Some people like the mummy bags. They don't take much sleeping space and are very cozy, since they don't have much area to be warmed. A newer variation of the mummy is the semi-mummy, which has a little more feet and leg room, and can be mated to another, much like the rectangular bags. (Our down bags are this type, and they don't constrict the feet as I had thought they might). Others — couples, that is — may prefer the practice Friend Spouse and I long used. When we first replaced our old bags, we got matching ones that could be zipped together. This takes more sleeping floor space, but is undeniably much cozier than each snuggled in his or her own bag. Wilderness camping is a very physical business. Paddling the canoe, portaging, setting up or taking down camp, tending to meals — all take a lot of effort, and a comfortable night's sleep makes a big difference on a canoe trip.

Some sturdy souls claim to be quite comfortable with their sleeping bags directly on the ground. However, Friend Spouse and I are not of that school. Sticks and stones *will* dent our bones, so we prefer to use some type of mattress. Several choices are available. Backpackers and some canoeists choose a foam pad. Several types are available, with a moderate range of cost and bulk in packing. For a number of years, we used high-quality air mattresses which were very comfortable. However, Friend Spouse hated the evening ritual of inflating them, particularly if we were on the move. They were heavy, a small trial in completely deflating them for packing, and on occasion, they tended to flatten during the night.

They also skidded apart. The sleeper sometimes woke to find that he has slid off the mattress before morning, an unpleasant discovery. Several years ago, we acquired a newer type of mattress (the Therma-Rest) that combines the lightness of foam with a self-inflating quality, and we like this product very much. Inflated, it is only about an inch thick, and I frankly didn't expect much of it. I have been pleasantly surprised. A couple of light straps keep them from drifting apart in the night. Other similar products are now on the market.

A mattress or sleeping pad serves as some insulation between you and the cold ground, an advantage. Unless you make your bed on a spot that has been baking all day in the sun, the ground temperature will be considerably lower than your body temperature. The heat from your body flows to the cooler ground, and if the temperature difference is great enough, you may feel cold long before morning. An insulated ground cloth such as a Space Blanket or a foam pad will make a big difference.

You can also get a small inflatable pillow, or simply pack your spare clothes in a pillow-shaped bundle. A sweatshirt or sweater (whatever you are carrying) also works well. If you decide to look around, the stores catering to the backpacker are probably the most productive.

So there you have it on shelter and bed. The main thing is to consider very carefully just what you require for comfort; compare those points with the market offerings; then consider how much you are willing to spend when you are ready to buy. See what you already have that will serve. The things I have suggested are simple, but they will keep camping from being austere. You don't need to outfit for a royal safari, but at the same time, you don't need to be uncomfortable. Keep in mind that you *don't* have to buy everything at first. Rent the more expensive things; that way you can find out at minimum cost what sorts of features matter.

When, and if, you do buy, select carefully, because the tendency is to adapt to what you have and not change items unless you lose or damage them. Shop for good design, good quality material and good workmanship for the most lasting satisfaction with the items. I know I would have continued using many items we had without question until I started writing this book and found there are other things and other ways of doing.

COOKING GEAR

When we first began to do much camping, our cook gear consisted of the mess kits the kids had acquired for their individual trips to camp. That didn't work well for a family of six. So early on, we got the classic nested aluminum camp kettle sets. Such kits usually have the basic necessities for cooking in relatively compact form. The pots or kettles with wire bails were earlier known as "billies." (Remember the line from "Waltzing Matilda" about the jolly swagman who waited camped under a koolibah tree and waited while his billy — kettle for his tea — boiled?) I like ours and have used them for many, many years.

However, what you want for a camping trip depends on your basic philosophy on eating. One school of thought could be called the Minimalist. This group goes for the simplest meals with the simplest or least cooking. Adherents choose meals that can be prepared by adding boiling water or by boiling a bag in water, with only one or maybe two pots for the entire meal. There is absolutely nothing wrong with this style if it appeals to you. After a long, hard day of traveling, simplicity is a positive virtue.

We have tended to look at the evening meal as an activity and a pleasant time, and I like to do a certain amount of cooking. Don and I find that a diet of the freeze-dried meals tends to become monotonous very quickly. Also, we like to fish, partly because fish adds an element of interest to meals. Camping, with the portaging and all the rest, provides enough difficulty that to be able to look forward to the meals is a real joy. So our particular style ranges from one point to the other, depending on the conditions of the trip.

KITCHEN STUFF

What you get with a cook kit depends on its size. Our old set, made by Mirro and acquired when the six of us went camping, has cooking pots in 2-quart, 4-quart and 8-quart sizes (the 8-quart holds the whole collection), two fry pans (one of which is the lid for the 8-quart pot), a coffee pot, six plates and cups, and two fry pan handles. This is great; I have frequently used all but the 8-quart pot in preparing a meal. (I usually carry one or two plates and cups extra.) A set for four will have an 8-quart and a 4-quart kettle, the 10-cup coffee pot, two pot lifters (or fry pan handles — same thing), one fry pan, and cups and plates for four. I have in recent years added another small non-stick fry pan with a folding handle, and we were given a beautiful little wok.

It is possible to get nested sets in stainless steel. They cost more and generally have smaller pots. Their advantage over the aluminum primarily lies in their being sturdier. It is much more difficult to melt out the bottom of a stainless pot than an aluminum one.

One point to remember about using light-weight cooking pans. They do not distribute heat well; unless you are very watchful during the cooking process and stir frequently, you'll get hot spots immediately over the heat source and the food will burn easily.

Think about what equipment will be needed when planning menus. Don't forget that some things require a mixing container before cooking (though you can use a good heavy-duty plastic bag for that). I rarely use the 8-quart pot for cooking; it serves as the container for the rest of the kit, though I use the lid as a fry pan. A plastic bag could serve as the collection container — it depends on what you are using. The bag keeps it all together and that's handy; it is also fairly clean. Generally, our first night meal will have one prepared item carried in a plastic container. This then serves as a bonus mixing dish.

Some Minimalists recommend taking 4- and 2-quart pots (no coffee pot!), with plastic bowls rather than plates, and insulated mugs rather than the usual plastic or aluminum ones. The mugs are appealing, especially in the cooler seasons; drinks come to the surrounding air temperature rapidly in the plastic cups. They *are* bulky. (There always seems to be a tradeoff.) Likewise, Minimalists consider a spoon sufficient, maybe a fork for fish, and a knife superfluous. Nevertheless, I like to take the old chow kits (knife, fork and spoon which fasten together for storage); we use all three pieces, depending on what's to eat. You might like a "spork," a combination spoon and fork.

For cooking, I include a pancake turner and add a long-handled wooden spoon if the group will be more than two. My spoon was originally a little too long to fit in the housekeeping pack, so I shortened it in the pencil sharpener. You can get or make a "kitchen organizer," which is a fabric carrier with pockets for various implements.

A good fish fillet knife (such as Rappala makes) will take care of the usual food preparation needs, such as slicing salami, cutting cheese, and of course, filleting all those fish you will catch. As we have gotten older, we have tried to reduce our load, with varying degrees of success.

CAMP STOVES

The emphasis on no-impact camping has led to a marked trend away from using camp fires for cooking. I had thought including a small camp stove in our housekeeping pack was a rather indulgent practice since I used it primarily for making coffee. Some days, if we were traveling and wanted to get off as quickly as possible, the camp stove made a hot breakfast possible with a much shorter clean-up time (not to mention preparation time, with the building of a fire and soaping the pots). Or, if I had planned a cold breakfast, at least we had hot coffee.

However, we became converts to the camp stove mode during a trip to Quetico one summer when open fires were banned. Southern Ontario was suffering from drought conditions that year, and Park personnel called to tell us that open fires were forbidden. (When we arrived at the Park, we even had to produce our stove before we were allowed to enter.) The resulting experience marked a major change in our procedures.

More and more canoe campers as well as backpackers are using the camp stoves for the cooking they do. Camp stoves occupy another area of changing technology, with a wide variety developed for specific conditions and circumstances. What we are talking about is variations on small stoves that have been developed for backpackers.

Generally speaking, a stove is designed to be reliable, compact, lightweight, safe, stable, and suitable for use with a relatively small pot. I would say that stability under larger pots is of some importance. Backpackers seek the ultra-light model; winter campers want one that will light at very cold temperatures. All want dependability and ease of operation. Fuel choices vary, according to needs of the activity. Simplicity of lighting and operation are also highly desirable. Be careful in your selection to get one that is not too light or delicate.

If the party has several people in it, and the decision is to shy away from building campfires, the meal preparation process is speeded up with two stoves. I would not recommend taking a 2-burner stove, though; it is just too cumbersome for easy handling. Some stoves, such as the Coleman Peak 1, have fuel reservoirs built-in. Another type, such as the Bluet, uses a fuel canister that is discarded when the fuel is all gone. The burner unit taps into the canister, and starting a new canister can be a rather tricky business. A third type, such as the

MSG Whisperlite, uses a refillable fuel bottle, attached by a hose connection to the burner.

The stove we have long carried is a 1-burner Coleman stove, with its own aluminum carrying container which could double as cooking equipment. (I like the idea of a rigid container for the stove; the stove is better protected against the rough treatment the pack gets. While we now use stuff sacks for our stoves, I don't feel very comfortable doing it.) We had bought the stove years earlier with the notion of using it on weekend motor cycle trips, though the trips never happened. We have since acquired a Bluet and an MSG Whisperlite, typical of the lighter — and more expensive — models available.

Coleman states their Peak 1 stove carries enough fuel for a typical 3-day, 2-night trip. I am not quite sure what is considered a typical 3-day trip, but the statement does suggest a useful capacity. One veteran camper who uses a stove almost exclusively says that 2 quarts are sufficient for minimalist cooking for three people for a week. Please note the word "minimalist." It should be kept in mind that there are a great many variables — how big your party is, how much cooking you and your party will do, what kind of cooking, whether it will be for only one or for two meals a day. You can fill your stove and carry additional fuel in a metal fuel bottle for one trip and see how much you bring home.

As with other major items, the best bet is to think about what you want to do on a camping trip before buying a camp stove. Backpackers are not season-bound for their activity as canoeists are. Since they can plan to travel year-round, they are interested in a stove that is easy to light and reliable at much lower temperatures than the canoeist experiences. The Whisperlite, in fact, is designed for reliable operation in very cold weather, but as a consequence of this feature, lighting it involves warming its fuel line, making its use somewhat more complicated. The Bluet or Coleman is much faster and easier to light.

Several of the outdoor magazines such as *Canoe* or *Backpacker* regularly run articles reviewing outdoor equipment. One month, it may be canoes; another, stoves; yet again, rain wear. These are very helpful in identifying features and disadvantages. A shopping trip (either in a store or through a good catalog published by a company that concentrates on outdoor gear) will let the price of the item decide for or against its purchase.

One accessory that frequently proves itself invaluable is a windscreen for the stove. My favorite is a little 5-panel folding aluminum screen that is tall enough to shield the Bluet stove and part of a pot sitting on it. Its folded size is about 10" x 3.75" and the weight is about a half-pound, well worth every ounce, too.

FUEL OPTIONS

Nowadays, fuel options range from white gas to kerosene to butane. A container for additional fuel, assuming a longer trip or heavier use, should be of metal, preferably designed for fuel, and used for no other purpose. Butane comes in a cartridge and is more expensive. The empty cartridges should not be abandoned, either. The Coleman Company, not surprisingly, sells white gas that is best known as camp stove fuel. It is generally available in 1-gallon containers, and this makes greater flexibility possible. *(Never* use automotive fuel for these stoves!)

We compared our three stoves with their fuel for a particular trip. The Whisperlite is a tiny unit; apart from its fuel cartridge, the Bluet is, too. Our old Coleman 1-burner seemed much heavier. But by the time the fuel and fuel container is figured in, the tiny stoves are about equal. The Coleman is heavier.

If you are taking extra white gas for fuel, don't forget the little filter funnel for filling the stove. While the fuel is especially formulated for portable stoves, it does have impurities which can — and will — gum up the works, especially after sitting for a period of time. (For this reason, you should drain your stoves before storing them.) Filtering the fuel while filling prevents the need for dealing with that problem. Water also can condense in the tank.

We take both matches and a couple of disposable butane lighters, such as a Bic or Cricket, preferably the lighters that have adjustable flames. We put one lighter in the housekeeping pack (along with matches in a waterproof container), and at least one of us carries another. It is not a bad idea to have matches (in a water-tight container) in several other places. Use good wooden kitchen matches, and not the paper "gopher" (you know, strike one, go fer another) matches. Strict safety-minded persons prefer to see that at least one lighter and a few water-proofed matches are carried on the person.

OTHER KITCHEN STUFF

Take at least two sturdy pot holders or oven mitts. There is no need to risk burns of any degree.

On a trip, I store my pot scrubber inside the cook kit. I like Purex's Dobie; its sponge wrapped in nylon mesh makes it very good for dish washing, as the sponge holds enough soap to be useful and the mesh is effective for scrubbing. Scotch Brite is a good item, too, particularly for final cleanup. I don't recommend steel wool pads for canoe trips; they get very messy, even though they are wonderful for keeping pot exteriors clean. (In a pinch, a steel wool pad can be used to help start a wood fire.)

Some people use aluminum foil freely in their everyday world. I don't; a roll of foil may last six years or longer. (I am rather repelled by the enormous amount of energy expended in refining the aluminum, with it then being so readily wasted.) Eventually the roll gets down to a reasonable size suitable for the camp kit. I have long since quit carrying it in its own packaging; the box is unnecessarily bulky without being particularly useful. After I ripped my hand on the cutting edge a time or two, I decided not to include it. I really don't like to use foil on camping trips, but there are times when it is useful, mainly to cover the pan in which I am cooking bread, and with care, that piece can be used twice. One objection to foil on a trip is that it does not burn completely, and it is disgusting to find foil remains in a fire pit. The Elegant Camper packs out *all* used foil to dispose of at home, preferably at an aluminum recycling point, and this includes the foil packets freeze-dried meals come in, too.

You could if you like add disposable towels such as Handiwipes. There are times when pre-moistened towelettes would be nice as well. I think in fact they will be a part of our standard equipment. You can maintain a somewhat higher standard of personal hygiene; they are not bulky; they can be easily burned in the fire pit, and they take up less space than a towel. Some people include paper towels. We have carried the tag end of a roll for years, and on one trip, said towels came into service when the toilet paper supply gave out prematurely.

In addition to our basic traveling cooking gear, we have a supply of useful items to draw on. The assortment includes plastic bottles and tubes (these can be opened from the bottom for filling and then closed with a special clip), some plastic boxes, and heavy-duty plastic bags. The small plastic bottles medicine samples come in are excellent for spices. It is worthwhile to invest in several of these items, but make sure they are meant for outdoor life. I cannot overemphasize the importance of good, secure lids and tops. The food pack and housekeeping pack undergo pretty rough handling during a trip and contents security is no small matter. I would have on hand at least the following:

  3 or 4 plastic bottles, in quart, pint and half-pint sizes
  1 tube (for packaging peanut butter or jelly)
  1 or 2 small plastic jars with good screw-on lids, my preference
      for peanut butter)
  Heavy duty plastic bags

WATER

It is important to drink plenty of water every day. I will talk about treating water in Chapter 3, Health and Safety. You can use a collapsible water jug (such as the so-called Jerry jug) that will hold about 2 gallons (8 liters). This is a manageable size, as water weighs about 8 pounds per gallon. (I detest the jugs, though; they are really difficult to fill.)

Carry a bottle of water or a canteen for personal drinking water throughout the day. (One quart per person is recommended.) Nalgene is a plastic often used in manufacturing camping equipment designed for holding food and water. Theoretically, it transmits no taste of its own. Also you could carry a collapsible cup, such as a Sierra cup, in your shirt pocket. Don't forget to treat your water before use.

Canoeists traveling coast lines and among Florida's keys *must* take their fresh water supply with them. Heavy plastic 5-gallon containers are a manageable size. I stress *heavy* plastic. Raccoons, ever avid for fresh water, with their sharp teeth, will easily get into lighter-weight jugs. Five gallons per person per day is the recommended amount.

This makes up the basic gear for the whole business of food and eating. As you see, it is possible to be elegantly equipped, even with old gear, so long as it suits the purpose.

SPECIAL EQUIPMENT FOR SPECIAL CONDITIONS

When we canoe-camped in Florida's Ten Thousand Islands region, I was impressed with one piece of equipment our guides had. Instead of using the soft packs that are customary and practical in the North, they had food and food preparation equipment stored in stout wooden boxes that were banded with metal, much like the old steamer trunks. The aim (and a highly successful one) was to keep out plundering raccoons. The truly ingenious idea with the boxes was the use of strapping in each inside corner of the box and the lid, where a short section of aluminum tubing could be inserted. *Voilá,* the lid then became a table top at a reasonable working height.

PERSONAL AND SHARED GEAR

You already have your own list of the personal care items you can't do without — things such as a comb or brush, toothbrush and toothpaste. (Don't start in on a large tube just for this trip; a small one or well-started one will do just fine. However, I should tell you the really environmentally-conscious camper uses a mixture of soda and salt and spits away from the lake, and not into it or the immediate camp site area.) Sunglasses are a must to reduce the effects of glare from the water. You can avoid dropping them in the lake or sitting on them or whatever mishap by wearing them on an eye-glass chain or an eye-glass holder for active people. But let's look at some other considerations.

Soap is a very basic need. I tried the motel-size bars of soap (it seemed the thrifty thing to do) — once. They are okay for personal use, but are just not up to the rigors of dish washing. Since their capability is limited, I prefer an all-purpose soap. Use a biodegradable product — one that breaks down and is absorbed without harm by the soil or water. Even then, be careful where you wash or dispose of your soapy water; the labels don't tell you how long it takes for the stuff to degrade. At the same time, avoid getting soap or whatever in the lake. Dishwater and the like should be dumped 100 feet back from the water and away from the camp site to reduce attraction for flies and little critters.

For years I relied on Fels-Naphtha. Half a bar fit nicely into the standard humble plastic soap box and accommodated personal hand-washing, pot-soaping, and dish washing for a week. Basic H is another product popular with environmentally-conscious people. Camp Suds, a "soap" concentrate developed for outdoor use, too is a good product. A small bottle lasts a week for our ordinary use. I question the biodegradability of commercial liquid household dishwashing detergent. One well-known detergent, Joy, lathers well in brackish water.

Other basic items that are shared and may be packed together are toilet paper, towels, sunscreen (essential for everybody, and absolutely vital for anyone who doesn't have much of a tan — sunburn can be miserable), and insect repellent. Towels should be sturdy, not the heaviest quality, but not the flimsiest, either. The objection to the heaviest type is that it takes too long to dry out between uses. If you're traveling, the towels are packed away damp and it isn't too long before they start to stink. The flimsiest sort just doesn't do a decent job of drying, especially if dishes for several people have to be dried. Towels on the market made specifically for camping are worth getting, if you absolutely don't have anything around the house that will do and expect to camp quite a bit. They absorb well, yet dry rapidly.

A self-zipping plastic bag keeps the toilet paper dry, yet available. I make a practice of carrying in a shirt pocket a day's supply of toilet paper (in a sandwich-size plastic bag). A woman appreciates the convenience. It's a lot handier than having to dig in the pack, especially if it's a traveling day. One roll of two-ply paper lasts the two of us about a week. An all-female group will need more toilet paper than an all-male group.

Put the sunscreen and bug repellent where they are easy to get to. I generally put them in the day pack or in a shirt pocket. I will discuss sunscreen and insect repellent in more detail in Chapter 3.

You should also have a repair kit of common or shared personal items, such as tweezers, good nail clippers, which are also handy in the fishing tackle box, a couple of needles and thread (double duty: pick out a splinter or sew on a button), safety pins of assorted sizes, a small mirror (this could also be used as a piece of safety equipment) and an emery board or nail file. (It may sound silly to say trim your fingernails *and* toenails before you go, but it is really pretty good advice. Fingernails may snag in the course of a day's activities, and long toenails can make the feet complain after a long portage.) Our small whetstone fits into the kit — a metal Band-aid box — with these items. You should also have a first aid kit, and each person in the party should know where it is. (See a list of important items in the Appendix — Master Checklists.)

THE PERSONAL STUFF

At least one of the party should have a pocket knife. The classic favorite is the Swiss Army knife, which comes in numerous versions. These have all sorts of useful implements and are a delight to the gadget-happy individual. Friend Spouse used to wear a small hunting knife on his belt, but found it to be something of a nuisance, with the sheath catching on the pack as he would load up; he uses his Swiss Army knife instead. Carry a small whetstone or some other kind of sharpening stone or ceramic honing stick; dull knives are more dangerous than sharp ones.

ODDS AND ENDS

Include a small pad of paper or notebook and a pen or pencil in a sturdy plastic bag; the day pack is a good place for this. This is handy for notes to yourself, but if a real emergency were to arise, you are able to send a note describing the location and situation with a camper who is heading back.

And why not take a mini-tape recorder to record the impressions and events of each day? Expand on your notes when you get home and you'll find you can recall much more later when you think about the trip.

Friend Spouse goes back and forth from year to year on whether to take his rechargeable shaver or to let his beard grow. Many men have no objection to the minor discomfort and scruffiness of a new beard, and not having to fool with shaving may be one of the pleasures of the trip. I repeat: each person will determine, in time, what is important and what is not.

One of the party ought to take the overall responsibility of keeping track of gear and supplies on a trip. The importance of this was demonstrated when we took a lunch break at a campsite that was at least one or two days away from an entry point. At the latrine, a previous group had inadvertently left their supply of toilet paper behind. (And then there was the hapless individual who dropped the entire roll in.)

Some sort of lip protection such as a lip gloss or Chapstick can be very comforting.

In recent years, I have come to appreciate the value of a walking stick on canoe trips. In first instance, I turned an ankle while on a trip in Quetico. The damage was not severe, but I found walking on portages much easier when I used a paddle as a support. It was particularly useful on keeping balanced going across rocky areas. The following year, deterioration in my hip joints required some assistance with walking. The hiking stick I had acquired proved to be very helpful. Orthopedists will tell you that use of a stick takes nearly half the load off a joint. A stick also helps maintain balance on difficult trails.

THE "TOYS"

Some people might like to carry a good handbook on flowers or birds with them to become better acquainted with woods life. My experience is that you will hear more birds than you are likely to see, and for that reason, a bird book would be so much extra weight. More useful would be recordings of songs to aid in identification, and there is a tiny cassette player with "cards" containing bird calls. (See Appendix — Equipment Sources for where to find things.) But for spring and summer, the flower book is nice. I watch for the pink moccasin flowers (and I know several places where and when I can expect to find them), and I watch for other little flowers that grow in the woods. Familiarity is part of the pleasure of going each year about the same time over areas where we have traveled before.

Other special interest handbooks could be taken: July and August often provide an abundance of mushrooms. Just don't be surprised if you find you don't really have time to look things up. In fact, this very busy-ness of a wilderness trip is one of the things that makes it particularly relaxing. Most of the activities, whether paddling, portaging, cooking or fishing, require that you give them full attention, but it is not a stressful sort of attention. You find that you are very much in the "right here, right now," with the usual daily patterns and concerns pushed well back, and this is quite refreshing to mind and spirit.

If you want to take books to read; choose paperbacks rather than hard covers (they are lighter to carry), and try for everybody to take something the others haven't read.

Moccasin Flower

CLOTHING

Let's now turn our attention to clothing. The key here is suitable clothing, and for suitable, read *sturdy*. You may want to use what you have on hand (still not a bad reason for choosing particular items). However, if you happen to have woolen shirts and pants for cool weather camping, so much the better, as there has been general agreement among experts that wool is far superior for cool weather. This is another area of changes because of technology. Some of the newer fibers are displacing wool with qualities of warmth, lightweight, and abilities to repel or wick away moisture. You pay for these qualities.

In researching for the first edition of this book, I found that some veteran canoe campers prefer pants made of poplin, twill, or corduroy to jeans, noting that denim is very slow to dry after getting wet, and is consequently colder. So I bought a pair of cargo pants of 65 percent polyester and 35 percent cotton. (Cargo pants, with all their pockets, are wonderful. I have each pocket assigned particular tasks.) We have gotten rained on, and indeed, these pants dried faster than my partner's jeans. I was pleased with the purchase.

The beauty of poplin or twill is that the fabric is tightly woven, with a smooth surface that is resistant to snagging debris; softer surfaced or loose-knit fabrics are not. Let's face it. You will be picking up smoke and dirt on your clothes; you do not need bits of leaves or twigs sticking to them to track into the tent and work their way into your sleeping bag! Long pants with elasticized ankles close an easy meal stop for ticks. If your pants have cuffs, you may want to turn them down so that they don't contribute to the trash collection.

PANTS

Some canoeists wear shorts in the woods. Personally, the thought of having large areas of my skin exposed as a buffet for the bugs does not appeal to me, and I am not particularly eager to invite sunburn. Besides, you can expect that some of the time will be cool. If the proposed trip is going to last more than 5 or 6 days, you could take both long pants and shorts. Or you could choose "Marie Antoinette" pants, where the legs zip on. That way, you can have your cake of warmth and protection, or eat it, too, and give those legs some sun. But my choice would be to take a second pair of pants. I wouldn't even do that for a trip under 7 days.

Friend Spouse loves a pair of suspenders, rather than a belt, for camping trips.

SHIRTS

As for shirts, the old principle of layering works well here. Start with a T-shirt and work outward; you need a long-sleeved shirt for protection against insects and sun. (For summer, a chambray shirt is wonderful.) The standard practice is to put on a tank top or T-shirt under the shirt. You may well be grateful to have included a long-sleeved shirt: I have known times in late July when one felt really good under the shirt. In the early morning and late in the day, the outer shirt feels cozy. As the day warms up, it can be removed. But on those portages, the long sleeves provide more protection against those bugs that are out for blood. For cooler seasons, a canvas, chamois or wool shirt is excellent. Chapter 4 gives a more precise definition of "cooler."

Then in addition, again depending on the time of year and location, some sort of light jacket, such as a nylon shell, zippered-front sweatshirt or wool or chamois shirt, is valuable. In the BWCA or other northern areas, the jacket may be lighter in high summer, but you should take something, even in August.

If you are shopping for camping clothes, look for a firm surface that is less apt to collect trash. Give a high priority to clothing with pockets; shirt pockets with button-down flats are even better. Not having pockets to put stuff in is a nuisance. Cargo pants or shorts are well-supplied with them.

IS COLOR IMPORTANT?

Color seems to have some minor importance that marks a real difference between the canoeist and the hunter or the backpacker. Customarily, the hunter wears at least some items of a vigorous and fluorescent color — bright orange is highly visible and recommended. There is good reason for this. No hunter, dear to his life's companion, wants to be deer to some other excited hunter. Likewise, many backpackers, particularly solitary ones, prefer to use at least some bright color on their persons. High visibility is a safety factor.

The Elegant Canoeist, on the other hand, wants to be as unobtrusive as possible when going into the wilderness. As a result, you'll find that the stores specializing in outdoors equipment feature tents, tarps, and the like in quiet blues, greens, grays, and tans. Clothing is likewise quietly colored in medium and darker tones. These don't show dirt quite so badly, either. Gray is marvelous for this.

Some research indicates blue attracts mosquitoes (black flies, too). This makes some sense when you consider that many insects' vision operates into the ultraviolet range of the spectrum. Blue is a border to that edge of the spectrum, and is perhaps to insects' sight rather like dogs hearing high sounds that are beyond human detection. We have noticed mosquitoes and black flies seem to gather more on darker blue than on light blue. With the number of them present, and all the females more or less competing for blood to nourish their unlaid eggs, color choice for mosquito deterrence seems rather irrelevant. My observation is they choose individuals over color. Some people, to their discomfort, evidently are more appealing to mosquitoes.

You may feel uncomfortable with the idea of not changing clothes more often while you are out. Console yourself with the idea that the natural aroma is much less attractive to mosquitoes, thought I'm convinced that a really hungry mosquito will bite *anybody*. If the two shirts are beginning to take on backbones of their own, they can be swished out, one at a time, dried in the sun and put back on. After all, who expects the standards imposed by a hot water heater, a washer and drier to hold in the wilderness?

In the old days, we took a complete change of clothes along on a week's trip. (This was in addition to the basic items already on the list.) Now we have reduced that to a change of underwear and socks. We eventually learned that the fewer in the party, the more each had to carry, so the list of non-essentials grew, and that included extra clothes. If you have planned enough layers to deal with the likely weather changes, you should be fine.

SLEEPWEAR

Sleepwear was, for me, long a problem. I have finally settled on a loose shirt such as a T-shirt, and a pair of pants — panties if the season is high summer, a lightweight pair of warm-ups if the weather is cooler. Silk long johns are just fine. In the higher latitudes as well as the higher altitudes, don't count on the nights being warm. In cooler seasons, a pair of socks — take a third pair — for sleeping keep the feet warm, and consequently the whole body feels warmer. Some recommend a hooded sweatshirt as good sleepwear. This would be particularly appealing in cooler seasons, providing for much warmer sleeping since the head is a major drain of body heat. It is amusing to read earlier books on camping and what the old-timers said about their practice of sleeping nude or near-nude. Now, consider the current tendency to mixed-group or family campers.

Night clothes, extra socks and underwear can be stowed in a nylon stuff sack which could then be used as a pillow. Or you can use what's at hand, such as a plastic bag such as shoe stores use.

It is very much to the point to get out of your daytime clothes when you go to bed. Residual dampness in your clothes will lead to chilliness in the sleeping bag. I first heard of this years ago from Sally Rhodes (Lynne's Scout leader and a veteran camper), and found it difficult, in

Tennessee, to believe. I know better now. What's more, clothes are more pleasant if they have had a chance to air out a bit.

You need a hat of some sort. Different regions produce favorite types of head wear. You will expect the hat to be useful; you do not want one that will be a nuisance. As apparel, it serves three functions: it shades the eyes from sun glare off the water; it reduces the target area for the ever-present bugs, and it may be called on to keep the raindrops from falling on your head. A hat also can serve as a tool, particularly in fanning a reluctant fire into life or bailing water from a canoe. What kind of hat is really a matter of personal taste, so long as it can meet its obligations as just outlined. I would not recommend a straw hat for the North Woods, for instance. Friend Spouse has used a billed baseball cap, though now we have acquired Gore-Tex "crusher" hats. These are great: they can be rolled up; they shed rain, and with the brim turned down, the water is directed over your collar instead of into it. They can be quite warm in high summer.

Gore-Tex is amazing material. It was originally developed for use in repairing cardio-vascular and soft tissue patches, as Gore-Tex grafts let in air but not bacteria. This gate-keeper quality makes it highly suitable for keeping water out while letting air pass.

This then is the basic summer collection. For cooler weather, you can add additional layers — long johns (silk, wool, or polypropylene), a wool or chamois shirt, a hooded sweatshirt. Sweatshirts with handwarmer pockets are great! The fabric chosen is also important. Cotton is cool, but absorbent and slow-drying; silk and wool are warmer. Acrylic is warm and dries quite rapidly when wet. Polypropylene is effective in wicking away moisture from the body.

FOOTWEAR

The other crucial items of your clothing are footwear. Some people wear hiking boots for canoeing. In cool weather, a low-cut leather boot would be warm. Some wear light boots for traveling and change to smooth-soled shoes in camp. L.L. Bean offers canoe boots that are well-regarded. This is not say you should pop out and buy a pair. Rather, it suggests a sort of standard to compare with what you have on hand. You should avoid heavily-treaded shoes or boots, as they can inflict considerable damage on a rather fragile environment. Further, boots with heavy lugs pick up an *awful* amount of dirt in damp conditions, and they track it into the canoe or the tent. The sneaker is an excellent choice. The soft rubber, tracked soles give sure footing for portages that may range from dirt path to beaver dam to rock-pile to out-and-out bog or any point in between, but the soles are not so damaging to the soil environment as heavier-cleated shoes. A fabric upper means that the shoe is light and will dry rapidly if gotten wet. I keep a pair of aerobics shoes that are no longer good enough for class, but still are comfortable enough for walking portages. Like the rest of camping clothing, shoes are never fit for public appearances, especially if they had to portage through a really boggy area.

Friend Spouse and I have long argued the advisability of wearing high-topped shoes for canoeing. He contends they give greater protection to the ankles. If I had been wearing high-tops, perhaps I would have been less likely to have turned my ankle on a Quetico trip. That may be so. However, I think that, as with so many of the items used on a canoe trip, one must weigh the cost of the item along with the number of times it is likely to be used, and whether that rates a high priority on the purchase list. What you do depends on what you have, how much you are willing to spend and how much you are willing to carry. But for high summer, the best bet is a lighter shoe. In cool and wet weather, a rubberized boot has some attraction. Certainly, in any event, if portaging is likely, sandals are totally inappropriate.

Some canoeists like to wear wool socks, such as Ragg socks, under the theory that wool dries faster than cotton and thick socks cushion the foot. (A friend of ours who canoes in the southeastern U.S. wears Ragg socks with his boat sandals.) The idea is appealing in May or September, but hands and feet are areas the body uses to dissipate excess heat, and that's much harder to do with heavy socks. Technology has produced something better than cotton athletic socks. Silk or polypropylene sock liners are very comfortable, and they dry very rapidly. In combination with Gore-Tex booties, they not only keep your feet dry but also warm during either end of the season.

If you go camping quite early or quite late, as in May or September, gloves and a stocking cap can be very welcome. Fingerless fishing gloves work pretty well for canoeing and fishing. They keep the hands warm and thus functioning, but also make it possible to do whatever tasks that call for finer finger control.

RAIN GEAR

Finally, what if it rains? The traditional rain gear has been the poncho, and we have a collection of ponchos that we have used over the years, but frankly, we have found them unsatisfactory in a variety of ways. We each wore out an inexpensive two-piece rain suit of waterproofed (coated) nylon which was originally chosen for motorcycle riding on rainy days. The suit had a pair of pants with elastic-gathered ankles and drawstring waist and a hooded, zippered jacket. They folded down to a fairly compact size (the folded pants could go in the jacket pocket), and the jacket worked very nicely for wind protection for a cool evening's fishing. Their replacements are PVC-coated nylon, with coated leggings, rather than pants. (On one July trip, the weather turned damp and chilly. I put on the leggings over my long pants, and the retained warmth soothed my aching hip joints.) Though the jacket is vented, you can still work up a major sweat inside the rain suit on a portage.

Since you are carrying the rain suit anyway, put it on if it starts to rain! You risk chilling, even in high summer, as your body attempts to keep warm with wet clothing on. Let your rain garb protect you when it rains, and particularly if the wind comes up.

There are more expensive rain suits available. Good, light gear is made of Gore-Tex. On the other hand, check the clothing sources for people who have to work outdoors, rain or shine. You should be able to find practical wear at lower cost.

An unpleasant consequence of rainy days is wet shoes, socks and feet. One sensible suggestion is to change to dry shoes when you get to camp, and then on the next day, put the wet ones back on for traveling. It is rather amazing how the shoes will dry from the heat of your feet. Likewise, with the socks — if you have a strong suspicion that the next day will again be wet, save your clean dry socks for camp. You'll appreciate them.

SAVE IT FOR CAMPING

Over the years, I have accumulated clothing that I reserve for wilderness camping. The pile includes a pair of twill cargo pants, a sturdy belt, a T-shirt, a chambray work shirt (daughter Jean embroidered it), a T-shirt and warm-up pants for sleeping (though lately I've shifted to silk long johns instead), underwear that is adequate but not the sort one would necessarily want to be found in "in case there is an accident," and three pairs of socks (one pair is for warm feet at night). For a trip, I will add at least a warm-up jacket, a hooded sweat-jacket and a long-sleeved T-shirt. Friend Spouse's collection is similar. You just as well keep camp things — towels, clothes, socks — to themselves, because after a wilderness sojourn they'll never be fit for polite society. So use them just for camping and don't worry about how they'll look. It is elegant to have everything already together should a notion for a spur-of-the-moment trip occur.

People planning to travel in other wilderness areas will find it helpful to talk with local outfitters. Every area has certain quirks and idiosyncracies, and the local people will have found particular items or techniques better suited than others.

THE TRIP HOME

While you're packing, remember to pack a kit with clean clothes for the trip home. We make a special point of having a change of clothes in the car, which we change into just before we start the long drive home. One time, the six of us simply piled into the car, dressed as we were when we came off the last portage, and drove the 5-hour trip home. The aroma in the closed car was almost unbearable! Since then, we change, put all the dirty clothes into the trunk of the car, and wash at least hands and face at the first opportunity. We're still grungy, but not so redolent and disreputable-looking if we stop somewhere along the way to eat.

Sometimes, depending on where you enter the wilderness, it may be possible to take a shower at the outfitter's or a resort. That's very pleasant, and clean clothes feel wonderful. When you are packing for the trip, make a list of what all you put in the car pack — shampoo, clean underwear, clothes, shoes, a spare jacket, etc. We have found that all the planning tends to focus on the canoe trip and not the return. If you wear a jacket out on the trip, have one for the return, and preferably not the same one.

FISHING

Many people, for various reasons, do not choose to fish while they are on canoe trips. However, this is about the only time of the year that we go fishing, and for me, it is a very special part of the trip. I particularly enjoy going several lakes into the wilderness, selecting a campsite and staying put for several days with the specific purpose of "terrorizing the walleyes." This is not to say that I do not like "traveling," or moving through the country each day; I love to do that. But to select a campsite and settle in for a few days with an eye to fishing is to have a number of extra pleasures of a very special kind.

When we go to fish, we often go out in the morning, after we have had our breakfast and cleared up — good housekeeping practice. Really dedicated fishermen would have been out before breakfast, and we have done that, too. But to go fishing in the morning is leisurely, and it feels good to get in the canoe, maybe taking a bit of lunch along, maybe not, and go out on the lake and paddle around to find a likely spot. If the fish are biting there, great. We cast awhile. When we tire of that, or decide it is not productive, we troll around for another spot. There is no pressure, no urgency, just the pleasure in the day and in the sport. After all, what we are after is merely enough fish for the next meal. There is no point in catching much beyond that, as we have no way of dealing with the surplus. If it is windy, we just head back to camp. We do that anyway around noon, because the fish don't seem to be any more interested at that time of day than we are. Around noon, it seems like the whole forest sort of stops to take a little rest, and we do likewise.

Then around four o'clock, we may decide to take a whack at catching our supper, and we go out again for about an hour. I like the business of watching to see how windy it is. The wind very often comes up during the day and then drops a bit late in the afternoon. If it hasn't dropped much by then, we wait until after supper. By the time we have eaten, cleared up the dishes and settled the camp, it is about seven o'clock, the wind has finally dropped, and it is time to go out.

I really think that this is one of the very best times of canoe trips. I love going out on the water and watching some of the shifts that occur between day and night. The song of the white-throated sparrow which we heard throughout the day, and is to me the quintessential sound of the northern forests, begins to give way to the cries of the loons and then to the night calls of the thrush who sings us to sleep.

We frequently see beavers going about collecting food; we see them swimming in their territories, and we hear their loud warning slaps as they announce our presence. We have seen otters and fretted about our fish catch. We have seen a cow moose and her calf emerge from the lake onto another island. Occasionally we see a mother mergan- ser, or sawbill duck, with her little flock as they poke around the shoreline for food. We have been within 10 feet of loons, elegant in their black and white markings, as they sit on picket in their particular areas, and it seems every little lake up there has at least one pair of resident loons. Some evenings, the sunsets are truly spectacular. One needs to be a bit suspicious of Mother Nature and her bounty, though. When the sunsets are spectacular, make sure the camp is well tucked in for the night, because the chances are good for rain before morning. We sit quietly in our canoe, and paddle softly as we troll around our chosen fishing spots, or sit and cast toward the promising areas. With the dropping of the wind, the lake becomes mirror-like; the evening is rich in color and rewarding to the spirit.

It's even better if the fish are biting. One year, we were in the BWCA about the time the May flies were molting. It was quite lively out on the water: all these flies were dropping on the water, and something was clearly after them. It wasn't long before we learned that it was suckers, or dogfish, that were the source of all the activity, but we had come for walleyes.

FISHING GEAR

I won't presume to tell *anyone* how to fish, or what to fish with. Some good books on fishing in the BWCA are listed in the Appendix — Useful and Interesting Reading. I will simply tell you what we do, which is about as simple, therefore elegant, as could be. Friend Spouse inherited quite a bit of fishing tackle from his father, including a rather large tackle box. Clearly, we didn't need all of that for our trips. So we bought a small tackle box, one that fits neatly into a pack, and carefully sorted out what we might need. We have given each other good rods and reels — relying on the advice of experts on the type of equipment for the kind of fishing we do, and I cannot overemphasize the importance of recognizing the *kind* of fishing. Being something of the fidgety sorts, we like to troll, and we like to cast. Poking around in camping and sporting goods stores and talking to people is most informative. There are good rods that have been designed for activities of this sort. One, described as "very elegant," is packed in a 12-inch unbreakable case.

If you propose to troll, take a reel of replacement line, because trolling kinks the line up something dreadful. If the line has not been replaced for a season or two, it may have to be done in camp, and that is a nuisance. The line removed should be either packed out or burned;

it should *not* be left in the water or just lying around out in the woods or around the campsite. It is hazardous to the resident wildlife, as they can get fatally entangled in it.

Friend Spouse glued Velcro strips on the inside of the canoe with which we can simply strap the rods in and therefore not have to carry them as "trash" on portage. This works wonderfully well. The trick is finding a glue that will make a lasting bond with synthetic materials.

If you plan to do a fair amount of fishing, you can reasonably carry more gear. If the trip, however, is for traveling on a daily basis, then we pare down to bare essentials and as small a box as will accommodate the basic gear. Space is a greater constraint then.

Many avid fishermen prefer to go after walleyes with live bait. In Canadian and Minnesota parks, there may be restrictions on the type of live bait, specifically *no* minnows or other little fish. We almost never use live bait, except maybe a leech or two that we collect ourselves. Instead we have collected Rappalas of various types, as we have found them far more effective than any other type of artificial lure. We use both sinking and floating types, and generally the floaters are more successful. Friend Spouse often sets up what is called a Lindy rig, with a small lead weight on the line about 3 feet from the lure. This pulls the floater down to a desired depth. We have found that we are less apt to get into the trouble of hanging up on the rocks than when we use a sinking lure. We have both dark- and light-colored Rappalas. I have pushed for having at least two of each type, so if we find that one particular type is the hot one for the moment, the other person can switch to the successful variety. Many accomplished fishermen use lures with single rather than treble hooks.

Wherever possible, Friend Spouse has removed hooks, leaving only the one treble hook at the rear of the lure. This improves a fish's chance for survival (with catch and release), as extracting all the hooks if the lure is swallowed just about dooms the fish. There is a growing tendency toward the use of barbless hooks for catch and release.

Just as you expect to get rained on at least once, count on losing at least one good lure a trip. On one memorable trip to Quetico, we gave up four to the Spirits Of The Water in a single evening!

In the tackle box you should have a pair of needle-nosed pliers, a stringer for all those fish you plan to catch, an assortment of sinker weights, spare line, some extra hooks, and maybe a couple of bobbers for really lazy fishing. A good nail clipper is very handy for nipping line ends when a new snell or hook is attached. We carry the clippers in the tackle box and let them do double duty for personal gear, but it wouldn't hurt to have clippers in both tackle and personal gear.

We generally carry a small dip net, but we are trying to improve the landing techniques to where it is not crucial to landing a fish. One thing I have learned is not to grab the line between the rod and the fish in this landing process and to let the spring action of the rod handle the shock of the struggling fish. A flopping fish caught on a lure with two sets of treble hooks can really do a job of getting all entangled in the net. (Another good reason for removing one set of hooks.) It is more elegant to do a cleaner job of landing the fish in the canoe without the hassle of a net, anyway. One with a short handle is a lot easier to portage than a long-handled one, especially when it is tucked away in the food pack.

That then is basically it for fishing: good rods, reliable reels with good line, a modest-sized tackle box thoughtfully outfitted, and maybe a net.

We have found that evenings are generally our most productive times. *If* the evening has been quite productive, we face a problem that we haven't completely solved. What do you do if you have several fish? Friend Spouse hates to come in and clean a fish that will be breakfast, and with good reason. It's dark; the mosquitoes are out in force, and the fish is fresher if cleaned in the morning. Leaving the fish on a stringer is not good; most will die before morning, and they are prime targets for turtles and mink, and we have more than once lost all our catch that way. We have tried a mesh fish basket, but it was too small for practical use, and a larger one would have been awkward to pack. So we wind up with him cleaning the fish, putting it in a closed pot which is then set in another pot with some water in it, and the whole thing hung from a near-by limb. The water layer cools in the night air and keeps the fish cool.

Walleye for breakfast — that sounds good!

Canada Mayflower

3

HEALTH AND SAFETY

*Providence protects children and idiots. I know
because I have tested it.*

—Mark Twain

In planning a trip, we always have to consider the possibility of injuries or illness while in the wilderness and to be prepared to deal with them. This is a matter of elegance, though it is equally a matter of elegance to do one's best to prevent or avoid mishaps.

Most accidents can be prevented by using appropriate equipment and clothing, by paying attention to what one is doing, by exercising patience, by not getting in a hurry, and by paying attention to one's limits of strength and energy. It is also to the point to pay careful attention to the conditions of weather and your immediate environment.

I want to emphasize *using appropriate equipment,* all three words. Fatal accidents are infrequent in the BWCA, but they do occur. One a few years back involved a party of two men whose canoe had swamped while they were paddling on a large and windy lake. Only one survived, and it was 24 hours before the other was found. They had refused life jackets from the outfitter from whom they rented the canoe. The U.S. Coast Guard requires one personal flotation device (PFD) per person in every boat. In this instance, there was a token nod to the regulation: the victim had a threadbare boat cushion (evidently all he had). When canoeing, *especially* on cold waters or on a windy day, a boat cushion is simply not appropriate equipment. Disaster in a canoe can occur with appalling swiftness. If you are struggling to keep a canoe headed into the wind, you don't have time to stop to put on a life vest. If you are sitting on your cushion, rest assured that when your canoe swamps or overturns, it will not be sticking comfortably to your rump (which would be a poor place, since it would force your head underwater). No indeed. It will go bobbing off on its own merry way. So wear your PFD whenever you are in the canoe and above all, put it on *before* you start out on a windy lake.

It is not within the scope of this book to teach first aid. When you think about it, the very term *first aid* implies that additional treatment may be necessary, and presumably will be given by a professional. However, at least one person in the party should have had training in traditional first aid care. Ideally, at least one in the party should also be trained in cardio-pulmonary resuscitation (CPR). If a member of the party is stricken with a heart attack, or struck by lightning, CPR might be enough to get the victim going again. Reading in a book about how to do it just before going out is simply not adequate (and is, therefore, inelegant preparation). The cold hard truth of the matter is that unless breathing restarts before 12 minutes have passed, the chances of resuscitation are very slim.

Let's consider for a moment the realities of wilderness camping. While a permit may be necessary to start a trip, there may no particular procedure for announcing the completion of your trip. (If you are renting from an outfitter, he could be more concerned — for the property.) The Forest Service recommends leaving a trip itinerary with someone, and it should include the name of the group leader, the entry and exit points and dates, the license number of the vehicle parked at the landing, the color (where known) and number of canoes, and the number and names of people in the group. The Canadians do likewise. (Minnesota law requires that *all* water craft on Minnesota waters, including canoes, be registered, and at this time (1993) includes canoes from other states, even if those states do not require registration. That registration number could be useful in identifying a canoe.)

However, the sorts of mishaps most likely to happen are the four Bs — bruises, bites, blisters and burns — and one C — cuts. Splinters and sprains are less common but possible. Other untoward, more serious events to consider include getting snagged with a fish hook, the consequences of a canoe upsetting, overheating, and being caught in a lightning storm.

To repeat: as a rule, injuries are avoidable. From our experience, I believe fatigue and haste are leading contributors to camping mishaps. Another cause of mishaps (and some of the most potentially dangerous) is an exaggerated sense of one's capabilities (or conversely, an insufficient awareness of one's limitations). However, we should not overlook a fourth that can be lethal: some might call it stupidity; some might call it carelessness; some simply ignorance. In the long run, it is inadequate assessment of the situation that could be fatal.

That said, let's talk about the little things that are more likely to happen. A checklist of items to include for health and safety is included in the Appendix — Master Checklists.

DEALING WITH THE COMMON MISHAPS

Let's take the four Bs — bruises, bugs, blisters and burns — first. Bruises are the simplest to deal with — you can't do anything except to admire the changing coloration from day to day. (I was puzzled about the appearance of bruises on my upper arms and my wrists until I realized I was getting them while hoisting on my packs. Shins get their share of bruises, too.) If a bruise is really sore, or a fall threatens to raise a lump, you apply a wet pack to the spot for a while. If the pack is cool enough (the lake water is cold; the evaporation rate is high), it will help. The cold application will reduce swelling.

BUGS

In Minnesota, insect repellent is absolutely essential. Probably that is true in most parts of the United States. About 170 species of mosquito flourish in the United States; not many of these go for human blood. Minnesota has some twelve species of mosquitoes of assorted sizes, deer flies, black flies, common house flies, and more recently, ticks. These are the usual offenders in the Boundary Waters parks; other regions (geographically and anatomically) suffer with chiggers as well. Mosquitoes commonly get the bad name; their "Humming Chorus" at bedtime is annoying, as is their way of swarming about one's head on portages. It's hard, when the critters are swarming about you, ravenous for your blood, to remember that mosquitoes are a vital protein source for little ducks and play a more important role in wildflower pollination than may be commonly realized. However, the deer flies and the black flies get my vote for the worst producers of sheer misery. Not only are their bites sometimes painful at the time of infliction, the effects linger and often get worse. The gnat-lke black fly is quite common in June, and sometimes in May. The deer fly is larger than the black fly, with a rather distinctive wedge shape. The familiar (all *too* familiar) house fly takes its turn in August.

For years, Cutter's Insect Repellent was unbeatable for discouraging mosquitoes and other biting insects. (It doesn't do much about those that simply walk over your face.) Now there are some new challengers, and very effective ones, too, particularly those containing N, N-diethyl-meta-toluamide, known as DEET. The thing to look for on the label when you are buying bug repellent is the concentration of the active ingredients, and DEET in particular. Cutter's has commonly used a concentration of 33 percentDEET with 17 percent other active ingredients. Now Cutter's also offers their Cutter's 100 (Cutter's Maximum Protection), with 95 percent DEET and 5 percent other unspecified isomers (compounds that are chemically related). Muskol lists 100 percent DEET on its label. Other brands appear from time to time on the market; check the labels and compare prices. Another welcome newcomer to the market is a black fly repellent.

The trick in getting the most out of your bug repellent lies in how you use it. We have been told that DEET works by the interaction with body heat, not by clothing. That is, spraying it on your clothes only won't help. To get the most good out of it, apply it to your skin. Don't forget to dab some on shoulders and arms before you put your shirt on, and dab the ankles before putting on the socks. Those suckers can drill! I never cease to wonder at how so small an insect can have a drill tube that can go through clothing and skin to reach blood. Treat the stuff like $70 an ounce French perfume rather than like hand lotion, particularly with the higher concentrations, and touch it up periodically if the perspiration is flowing. We have found that in high summer, one 1-ounce bottle of Cutter's will last the two of us a week. Half a 2-ounce bottle of Muskol has seen us through two weeks, though admittedly, on one trip the bugs were not so bad. However, on another trip, we used almost an entire bottle. So don't go with only a partial bottle. It is a good idea to start a trip with at least a full bottle. One other point worth remembering is that research indicates mosquitoes are drawn to sweet odors, so avoid perfumed items.

Some of the current research indicates that DEET seems to have some effectiveness as a tick repellent. With the current concerns about ticks and Lyme disease, this is hopeful news. Again, in the effort to avoid ticks, it makes sense to close the cafeteria — cover the skin.

However, some people are quite sensitive to high-powered chemicals. They can find some products on the market made of various plant-derived substances that are also effective as bug repellents. One common substance is oil of citronella. Many people swear and avow that Avon's Skin-So-Soft bath oil is effective. Its effect may come from the oil of citronella used in its formulation.

One point to keep in mind is that there is probably nothing short of a glass block that will keep the bugs off. As the manual for the continuous-clean oven puts it, it does to an "acceptably clean" level. Insect repellent reduces the annoyance to an "acceptable" level, but not to a complete absence. It is too much to expect the chemicals to keep all the bugs away for hours.

Avoid aerosol containers. They are bulky and on an effective ounce per ounce basis, more expensive. I prefer to carry small bottles of sunscreen and repellent. It's easier to deal with several small ones than one large container.

Clothing can be treated to make the entire garment bug proof. Several of the camping supply catalogs list such garments. You can do it yourself, but the process is a bit tedious. Rub the repellent on your palms, then rub the garment. Repeat this until you have used about 2 ounces (over the whole jacket). It will be effective for several days unless washed off. Do keep in mind that DEET is quite detrimental to coated nylon and some other plastics. In fact, Muskol's labeling cautions against over-application, and goes on to warn that the stuff will "damage synthetic fabrics, some plastics, furniture finishes, paint and linoleum.")

You should be alert for ticks on your person. Wood ticks are fairly common, especially in early season. Deer ticks (called bear ticks in Wisconsin) at present are not yet a severe problem in northern Minnesota, thought the Park Service issues cautions regarding deer ticks and the possibility of contracting Lyme disease. Ticks are slow-moving critters, and happily for us, they are unable to rush to prime blood sources. Dr. Michael Osterholm, Minnesota state epidemiologist, says between 18 and 30 hours may elapse before a tick gets around to biting. You should know the procedure for removing attached ticks.

You can be avoid much of the potential problem with ticks simply by making it hard for them to get to skin, and to check daily for them. Ticks can be a dreadful problem for deer and moose. In Minnesota, the poor moose suffer terribly from so-called winter ticks. In 1989 the moose population dropped to nearly half its numbers, with ticks the basic problem. As with humans, scratching may provide temporary relief, but in reality only exacerbates the problem. Big bald spots on a moose in winter caused by frenzied scraping can be fatal. Oklahomans have seen similar problems with ticks infesting deer in such numbers as to drive the animals frantic with irritation.

I recommend keeping bug repellent and sunscreen in a self-zipping plastic bag (freezer-weight); you can't keep the stuff from slopping down the sides of the bottle, and it is not good for a lot of products.

MISERY RELIEVERS

Several commercial products, packaged for carrying convenience, take different approaches to topical (skin surface) relief. Although itching and pain are closely related, the most effective products to relieve itching are topical anesthetics (which decrease sensation), rather than analgesics (which relieve pain). If the object is pain relief, the topical anesthetics can do the trick in removing the immediate discomfort. Safe topical anesthetics include products containing Lidocaine or Pramoxine (PrameGel). A dermatologist advises against Benzocaine-containing products, as Benzocaine is a potent sensitizer. Topical antihistamines (Benadryl or Pyribenzamine cream) have a mild anesthetic effect. Analgesics such as aspirin, ibuprofen (e.g., Advil), or acetaminophen (e.g., Tylenol) will also provide pain relief and are much more effective when taken internally. A paste of aspirin and water applied to bites also provides relief. Aspirin and acetaminophen also work to reduce fever or inflammation and can be helpful for a severe sunburn.

Counter-irritants used in topical analgesics work by a substitution of feeling. That is, the sensation they cause is more pleasant or less annoying than the pain or itch of the irritant being treated. You can expect that if the product has a strong smell, such as that of menthol, camphor or ammonia, you are dealing with a counter-irritant. These are familiar and safe counter-irritants and can be helpful for itching as well as pain.

Any of these preparations should be kept out of eyes.

A small tube of a cortisone ointment (typically containing 0.5 percent hydrocortisone) is helpful. Remember to be very sparing with any steroid. A steroid should never be used with a cut or the like, as it will mask any sort of bacterial infection. It too should be kept out of the eyes.

Itchy bug bites may respond well to a soda paste application. (We have carried a packet of baking soda for years.) Mosquito bites usually fade without any treatment. Deer flies and black flies (gnat-like little devils) can be another matter. On some people, these bites result in itchy or painful swellings that take a day or two to unleash their misery. Stings by wasps or bees are not to be ignored; be watchful for signs of violent allergic reaction. People who have known allergies should pack emergency antidotes. One of our worst mishaps occurred in a National Forest Campground before we had started our trip into the wilderness. We were setting up camp; the kids were gathering firewood. Suddenly our son, badly stung by wasps, ran yelling back to camp. Immediate application of baking soda paste to the stings soon brought relief.

One old remedy for bug bites or wasp and bee stings, no longer particularly recommended, is meat tenderizer, which is based on an extract of a papaya enzyme. Some people may develop an allergic reaction to the papain.

If any in your party is easily or severely bothered by bug bites, you might consider including an antihistamine. I have found that bites that had continued to itch severely over several days quiet down with a round of antihistamines. A dermatologist with considerable experience with allergies strongly advises carrying an antihistamine. It would be helpful if a severe allergic reaction should occur. Chlor-Trimeton (in 8-milligram doses), which is available over the counter without a prescription, is a suggested possibility. Teldrin is a similar product. A pharmacist advises me that 8-milligram doses are usually in a sustained-action preparation. The 4-milligram doses that are also available are faster acting. Another antihistamine that is helpful is diphenhydramine, which is a major ingredient in such sleep preparations as Sleep-ez. Likewise, if you come from outside the Upper Midwest, it is possible you may come across dusts or molds or pollens that could set off an unexpected allergic reaction. It is not that the Midwest has unusual or fierce allergens, it is that they are different. For that matter, anyone visiting another region could have a problem with local irritants. I became aware of the problem on a trip to Palenque, Mexico. Throughout my life, I have never been bothered by hay fever or the like. But as we came into that jungle area, I developed a horrendous case of weepy eyes and drippy nose that left me when we moved on out of the area a couple of days later. It was this experience that caused me to include antihistamines in our routine traveling kit.

To reduce the number of bug bites, use insect repellent and "close the cafeteria" — wear long sleeves and pants. Rainy days can be very trying as the mosquitoes eagerly seek warmth, shelter and blood.

BLISTERS

Blisters are most likely to develop in two areas. If you are paddling for unusually long periods of time (especially with a paddle handle that may be a bit oversize), or are wearing rings (I usually leave *all* jewelry at home), you may get blisters on your hands. Rough spots on paddle handles can also contribute to blister formation.

You may develop blisters on your feet if you are wearing unaccustomed shoes or ill-fitting socks. Equipment doesn't have to be beautiful, but it should be appropriate. Clothing — and that does include shoes — should be comfortable, and socks should not have holes in them. Some veteran campers advise wearing two pairs of socks; the second sock reduces friction between foot and shoe. Moleskin (Dr. Scholl's is a well-known brand) is a popular means of guarding against blisters.

What if you do get a blister? An assortment of small bandages is useful. The idea is to wash the afflicted area (reasonably clean — Betadyne or soap and water) and put a clean buffer, such as a Band-aid, between the blister and the rest of the world. Telfa pads, or some other non-stick materials, are good to include. A Red Cross First Aid instructor pointed out that a fabric bandage, rather than plastic, with adhesive is kinder to the skin and generally holds better, too.

BURNS

Burns are potentially the most serious of the four Bs. With a burn, the first step is to cool it, and this is true whether received from too much sun or by a hot pot. That lake out there is full of cool water, and a towel or some such piece of cloth, dipped in cool water and applied to the burn is not only comforting but helpful. Leave it there for more than 2 or 3 minutes, too. (One rule of thumb is cool the burn for twice the length of time of getting the burn.) The application of a cool wet cloth for 20 minutes or so can ease much of the discomfort from a severe sunburn. A dampened tea bag (if you are carrying any) is likewise an effective remedy. Don't use one that has just been steeped in boiling water: let it cool first. Baking soda applied as a dampened poultice also eases burn pain. Or you can carry a tube of an antiseptic or antibiotic cream (Neosporin is a good one). However, soap and water are as effective as the antiseptics sold over the counter and are a good bit cheaper. Include in your kit several Band-aids of assorted sizes and some Telfa pads, just in case.

You can avoid burns by using sturdy pot holders or mitts when moving cooking pots.

USE A SUNSCREEN

Avoid sunburn by protecting the skin with clothing or a chemical sunscreen. Products containing Padimate O, Oxybenzone, Ethylhexyl p-Methoxycinnamate, singly or in combination provide good protection. (PABA — para amino benzoic acid — has caused problems for some people and is almost never used in sunscreens any more.) Sunscreens currently on the market are labeled in a rating system for SPF, or skin-protecting factor, of at least 15. (A number of 15 means that protection allows remaining in the sun fifteen times the time expected to produce a burn.) The higher the number, the greater the blockage of skin-damaging rays. Choose according to your skin type and the amount of protection you want. If several will be sharing the sunscreen, select the highest rating needed or the protection level appropriate for the most vulnerable of the group. Get one that is also labeled "water-resistant," as perspiration can otherwise slyly reduce the protection; "water-resistant" will wash or rub off slower.

As well as the usual ultraviolet B, or UVB, blocker, some new products also contain a blocker against longer light wave length (ultraviolet A, or UVA), which is useful for people with allergies to sunlight and for those taking certain drugs that produce an allergic reaction when combined with sunlight.

Several medications increase the skin's sensitivity and make it much more vulnerable to burning as well as increasing susceptibility to heat-related illness. Some of the more commonly used ones are tetracycline (primarily used for acne), sulfonamides, and certain medications used to regulate blood pressure. If you are regularly taking medications of any sort, checking with your doctor or pharmacist before you go out could save you grief or misery.

It is well to read the label (nowadays, it is well to read — and heed — the label, no matter what!) if you do not usually use sunscreen. Whether you want to be well protected from the sun, or whether you are quite eager to get a tan is your personal choice. What I am saying is simply consider the possibility of a burn and make your plans accordingly. Don't forget that you can acquire a much worse burn on the water than on land, as the water surface reflects and "bounces" around the burning rays. Likewise, don't forget that while an overcast sky may filter out the bright light, it does not filter out all the rays that tan or burn. If you haven't been going bare-legged before you start your trip, be aware that the skin on your legs and feet is just as susceptible to burning as your face, if not more so. And anyone who has burned the backs of the knees can tell you about excruciating pain. A sunburn can be most unpleasant. It doesn't need to happen.

SKIN BREAKS

Cuts, for that matter, any wound that enters the skin, can be more troublesome. The accepted procedure with any cut is to let it bleed briefly to clean the wound and then stop the blood flow. With small cuts, usually an adhesive bandage snugly applied will do the trick. The aim is to apply enough pressure to close the wound and to stop the bleeding. Some antiseptic should be included in your first aid kit. Betadyne is an iodine compound that is excellent for cleaning wounds. It comes in ointment or liquid form and can be used much like a soap for cleansing a wound. (Medical people use often Betadyne instead of alcohol for routine skin cleaning.) Pre-moistened towelettes, particularly those sealed in their own little foil packets, are good to include for cleaning the area around a wound, though soap and clean water also do an adequate job.

If the cut is a bad one, with brisk or "pumping" bleeding (which implies arterial damage), it is very important to control the bleeding immediately. The best way to do this is by immediate application of pressure. Once clotting has begun and the blood loss stopped, you can clean up the wound and apply a clean bandage. If the cut is on the arm or the leg (which is most likely, from using a hatchet ineptly or hurriedly), elevating the afflicted area while you are applying pressure will call gravity to your assistance. It is harder for the heart to pump blood to a part of the body that is higher than the heart.

With a bad cut, it is easy to use up a fair supply of clean gauze or the like in stopping the bleeding. One a camping trip, the supply of available material is not as large as it is at home. For this reason, I usually include a couple of sanitary pads. They are compact; some come individually wrapped to stay clean, and should continue to be so if tucked into a self-zipped plastic bag. (If you have access to a sealer for boil-in-the-bag packaging, this is a good time to use it.) Include a roll of adhesive tape and a small box of gauze for a clean dressing on a cut or blister.

Poison ivy flourishes in the BWCA, though for many years we never saw any. We have seen a lot of it in Quetico. If (and that's always a big if) you know you have come into contact with it, you can avert some damage by prompt, thorough and repeated (two or three times) washing with any good detergent or soap; used promptly, this will deal with the oils that cause the problem. You can expect this treatment to take care of the problem unless you are already quite sensitive. If that is the case, you no doubt carry your own preferred treatment materials.

THE EXTRAS

I usually include some simple medication such as a small bottle of aspirin or aspirin substitute such as acetaminophen or ibuprofen and some antacid tablets such as Di-gel or Pepto-Bismol. We routinely carried Di-Gel for several years, but after a foreign trip, where we had occasion to deal with the threat of diarrhea, I make a point of including Pepto-Bismol. Research has shown that bismuth compounds (Pepto-Bismol is one) are the most effective in dealing with diarrhea. These should be packaged in water-tight containers (a small bottle with a good lid will do).

I don't usually expect to use either aspirin or antacid on a trip, but there have been times when a long day of sun glare provoked a headache or a rigorous day of canoeing taxed unaccustomed muscles to the point where sleep was elusive. Likewise, if one of the party has managed to get a very severe sunburn, one or two aspirin or aspirin substitute tablets can be taken to combat the inflammation. If you are including baking soda in your kit, that can serve to deal with the occasional case of upset stomach. Baking soda is good stuff. It's useful for applying to burns or bug bites, to soothe the disturbed tummy, and in solution, to boil loose burnt-on bits of food. (Even elegant cooks sometimes have sticking problems.)

Include a small bottle of Murine, Visine or other eye drop products to deal with specks that might get into the eye. Contact lens wearers are already aware of what they do in their daily care routines. They should know that routine cleanliness is more difficult in the woods.

Warning! People tend to get a bit casual about using these powerful chemicals for protecting their hides. Veteran Wilderness Southeast guides urge extreme caution about putting sunscreen and insect repellent above the eyes. They can easily (in hot weather) mix with sweat and run down into the eyes, with excruciatingly painful and dangerous results. It is easy to forget the power many of our "personal" chemicals — insect repellent, sunscreen, deodorant, etc. — have to create effects other than what they were meant to combat.

Constipation may occur for any one or a combination of several factors. The change in diet may do it. Doctors speak of a condition called "bashful kidney," where the individual (often a male) has difficulty urinating if someone is around. The lack of walls and doors around the wilderness latrine can likewise be quite inhibiting. The tension that results from an unfamiliar or exciting activity likewise can cause the whole system to tighten up. Those concerned by the problem may choose to include a mild laxative in the health and safety kit. The problem should be averted, though, by including fruits and whole grain cereals in the menus. Oatmeal, granola, dried apricots and peaches all come to mind as meeting the specifications. The level of physical activity, especially on a "traveling" trip will also contribute to the feeling of well-being.

FISH HOOK REMOVAL

Fishing with artificial lures means plenty of opportunities to get snagged with a hook, whether while detaching the lure from somebody's clothes or disengaging it from a flopping fish. (Friend Spouse has begun taking one set of treble hooks off our lures.) If a hook gets embedded in flesh, the first thing to do is to remove the plug or lure from the hook with the needle-nosed pliers. Then clean the area around the hook carefully with some Betadyne or soap and water. If the injury is quite shallow, you can cut the shank of the hook and push it on through.

If the hook is deeper in the flesh, this is a thoroughly unappealing technique. The better procedure is to get it back out the way it came in. To do this, tie a long, heavy piece of string on the round part of the hook (this is the "bend" or shaft of the hook). Put pressure on the shaft and push down on the shank of the hook, to free the barb from the flesh. Now, jerk the string sharply. The hook should come out the original wound without further damage.

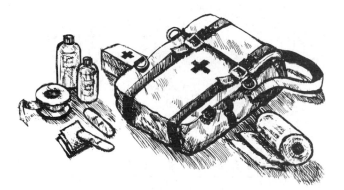

PRECAUTION IS PREVENTION

Really, though, the Elegant Camper will reduce the chances of injuries occurring. Appropriate clothing and equipment — and using equipment proper to the task — do quite a bit to insure safety. Poorly maintained equipment — here, that often means using dull knives or hatchets — can lead to cuts and bad bruises.

To my mind, the injury most threatening to a canoeist is a broken leg or arm, with a sprain not far behind. If there are three in the party, a broken arm is not so great a problem; there are still two to portage the gear and paddle the canoe, and the victim is mobile. Aside from making the victim with a serious leg injury as comfortable as possible, there is not much to do except wait for another party to come through. If you have already made camp, fine. Just stay put. If not, get settled as soon as you can and sit tight. In high summer, the wait would likely be fairly short, maybe as little as a couple of hours, particularly on some of the more popular routes. Toward either end of the season, or in the more remote areas, the wait might extend to a couple of days. The Red Cross recommends packing a rigid splint for joint injuries, and several types are available. It should be quite clear by now that good planning includes informing someone of your plans, so that if an undue delay occurs, someone would be aware of your absence, and perhaps have started to inquire.

Our worst fears appeared possible on a 2-week trip in Quetico Provincial Park. On the last portage of the third day, I stepped wrong and rolled my right foot under. I finished the remaining bit of the portage, and we paddled to a site for the night. There Friend Spouse wrapped my ankle lightly in an elastic bandage, which I wore during the day on the remainder of the trip. Luckily, the ankle never swelled much (I had soaked it in the lake as we paddled to camp) and it proved to be no problem for the rest of the trip. It was, however, a sobering experience.

Some veteran campers recommend carrying a whistle in the kit as an emergency signaling device. This idea is particularly valuable if there are children in the party, and, as appalling as the thought might be to some, each person should carry one. There should be a clear understanding in the group that the whistle is strictly for emergency situations and *not* for entertainment.

WATER

It is important to drink enough water every day, and the warmer the day, the more water you'll need. Carry a bottle of water or a canteen for drinking water throughout the day, and drink frequently. (When we are doing a lot of paddling and portaging, it isn't hard for me to drink a full pint at a time.) We each carry a plastic folding cup (the metal Sierra cups are great, too) in our shirt pockets for use.

Re-hydrating and cooking food requires a substantial amount of water, and this counts as an important part of daily consumption. When we start setting up camp, one of the early chores is to get a supply for cooking and drinking. We have long used a 2-gallon collapsible water jug with a plastic handle and spout (sometimes called a Jerry jug). I dislike it intensely as it is very hard to fill. It is easier to take one of the larger pots and fill it.

Prevention of illness is always a pertinent concern. For the canoeist or hiker in the West, one other item in the kit that the Forest Service strongly recommends is some means of water purification. Either use special means of purification or boil *all* the water that you use for drinking and cooking. Water for washing dishes should also be treated. (Using water directly from any lake is not recommended.) The reason is not so much the risk of bacterial contamination but the ingestion of tiny parasites (flagellate protozoans, if you must know) called *Giardia lamblia*. Once into the human system, these microscopic organisms attach themselves to the small intestine. Trouble — in the form of the usual intestinal miseries of cramps, diarrhea, gas, bloating — does not show up immediately, indeed maybe not for several weeks. It — giardiasis, sometimes called "beaver fever" — can last for as long as six weeks. It is treatable, though the doctor needs to be "clued in" that "wild" water may be the culprit.

Basically, there are three methods for treating water, each of which has some disadvantage. You can treat water chemically, mechanically or by boiling. Chemical treatment involves using a halogen, usually iodine (preferably) or chlorine, preparation. This takes care of bacteria, but does not remove foreign matter in the water and will leave a bit of an iodine taste. The chemicals take *at least* 10 minutes to work, and twice as long if the water is very cold, or dirty and discolored. We have used Potable Aqua and Halazone; also there are Coughlan's or Globaline tablets. The chemical products have the advantage of taking up very little space and weight and are quite inexpensive.

Filtration units clean the water mechanically by means of microfilters; they are highly effective in removing particles. The filter type may be a ceramic/charcoal combination, carbon/membrane, or tri-iodine resin. The better ones remove *Giardia* cysts, as well as other contaminants, but generally they will not desalinate water. Several portable water filtration units are on the market, with a price range from $40 to over $725 (admittedly, the latter is heavy-duty, expedition scale). While drinking water from the lakes in the BWCA and Quetico is still generally in good condition, filtering the water removes all manner of particles from it, improving its appearance and taste. (The presence of the obnoxious and objectionable black fly is testimony to unpolluted waters.) Using a filtration unit is an easy way to insure potable water.

While boiling effectively destroys the wildlife in the water, it does nothing to remove other contaminants. It takes time; if you are planning to drink, keep in mind the recommended time for boiling is 5 minutes (and consider the amount of fuel that will be take), and then the water needs to cool before drinking. Having an adequate supply of clean water obviously requires considerable foresight.

Of the three methods for purifying water, the most expensive is filtration. However, it offers more: safety; better taste; appearance, and fairly immediate product. You can filter a couple of gallons in about the time it takes for a chemical treatment. (Remember, too, that you should also be treating the water you use for cooking and cleaning up the dishes.)

You may make a personal choice based on your assessment of the degree of risk and drink the water untreated. It would then make sense to avoid getting drinking water from small rivers, creeks, or lake shore areas; go out to the deeper part of a lake for drinking water. It's unappetizing to get water near the shore, where almost always you'll find twiglets, insect carcasses, and other goodies, which is bad enough. In early spring, when the surface is heavy with pollen, it looks scummy and repellent. (You don't want me to tell you about the times we have found dead moose in the water.)

Our current practice is to filter water to be used for drinking and cooking and to chemically treat the water for dishwashing. After we get camp set up, Friend Spouse filters water to fill a canteen of water and the coffee pot. I put the requisite number of halogen tablets in a large pot of water for cleaning.

Water from one lake may not taste like the water from another, and the taste may not be as pleasing. This was one reason we carried lemonade for daytime drinking. I would put lemonade mix into the canteen before we left camp; the activity of travel would get the sugar well dissolved.

OTHER USEFUL SAFETY TIPS

Every camper should carry some personal identification, particularly if traveling alone or in a small party into more remote areas. Individual "dog tags" can be made at a modest cost, and could be very useful. (See Appendix — Equipment Sources.)

Common sense calls for considerable caution when canoeing alone. The Forest Service and Provincial Parks people indeed advise against it.

HYPOTHERMIA

The beauty of being a warm-blooded animal, such as *Homo sapiens,* is that the creature has internal heat-regulating systems that permit living in a wide variety of climates with more or less comfort. Mankind has enhanced that capacity by devising ways to modify environmental conditions, such as by putting on or taking off clothing, building fires, or inventing air conditioning. We don't very often think about the fact that without these artificial means of maintaining our comfort level, the tolerable range of temperature is not nearly so wide. In fact, in a relatively short time, excessive temperature — either too hot or too cold — can create a dangerous situation.

One such dangerous condition occurs with severe heat loss, or hypothermia, the condition that results when the core, or internal, temperature of the body, drops below the level tolerable for human health and survival. The core temperature, commonly cited as 98.6°F, is the collective working temperature for the brain and internal organs, though specific organs may vary as much as 3 degrees from one another. In an area where wind chill readings are daily topics for winter conversation, it is surprising that relatively little attention is given to hypothermia's potential occurrence in warmer weather. Indeed, people have died from hypothermia: they have essentially frozen to death when the ambient temperature wasn't considered particularly cold.

How can a person get cold enough to become hypothermic? Rather easily, actually, if the air or water around a person is cold enough that the individual cannot get warm or stay warm, and is constantly losing heat to the surrounding medium. We who live in the Temperate Zone, where the temperatures range from -40° to 115° F, seldom give thought to the fact that the ideal comfort range is in the mid-80s. (In the winter, though, Minnesotans dream of the ideal comfort range.) To illustrate, runners racing on rainy days with air temperatures in the 60s or racing on very windy days can become hypothermic, or chilled, as the heat from their bodies is literally washed away by cool rain or blown away by the wind. A temperature of 54° with a 25 mile per hour wind can be deadly to an ill-equipped or ill-conditioned individual.

As individuals, we all have different perceptions of cold: some will complain of feeling cold at a much earlier point than will their companions. One reason for this is that comfort levels — the perception of cold — differ from one person to another. Part of this also is reflected by the human being's other mode of temperature management — the personal fat reserves, food intake, and metabolism.

However, it should be remembered that heat loss or gain, whether a person is getting cold or hot, directly relates to body size. Remember this when you are gathering the clothing to be used by a small camper or a young one. Another point is that generally, women have a higher ratio of fat to muscle than do men. Fat is not only insulates, but it also provides fuel for the body to convert to heat. An enlightening discussion of women's physiology in relationship to heat and cold is in *Hiking the Back Country*, (See Appendix — Useful and Interesting Readings.)

THE SYSTEM

The head, the hands and the feet are particular areas of concern in comfort management. As the site of the brain, the head is crucially important. As with our highly sophisticated computers, the brain requires rather specific temperature conditions for proper operation. Heat is brought to the brain by blood warmed deep in the body. The blood carries away excess heat during times of exertion or fever. This heat transfer process directly affects the other extremities, the hands and feet. When the body begins to get cold, the flow of blood to the hands and feet is reduced, but the head continues to receive warm blood. However, several of the major blood vessels of the head lie just under the skin and consequently lose some of their heat to the ambient environment. If the head is covered, less heat loss occurs. If the head is bare, heat loss speeds up, with the result that the hands and feet get colder, faster. Clearly, then, wearing a cap will help keep your hands and feet warm.

Let's consider for a few minutes how the body's control, or thermo-regulatory, system works. It is in fact a double system: one is the voluntary, or somatic nervous system, which is controlled by the cerebral cortex; the other is the involuntary, or autonomic, nervous system, which is controlled by the hypothalamus. Actually, there is a great deal of temperature variation within the nervous system each day, up to as much as 8 degrees. For instance, a person's temperature drops during sleep. Not only that, but it begins to drop at about the same time each night.

THE SYMPTOMS

When, in response to the environment, a person gets cold, the voluntary and involuntary systems both start up. The conscious, or voluntary, response is behavioral: the person will usually try to change the environment — put on more clothes, close a window, whatever is

available. The autonomic, or involuntary, system kicks in with uncon-
scious responses: the blood vessels constrict to shunt blood away from
the more susceptible extremities. As much as 99 percent of the blood
flow to the fingers can be reduced by this vaso-constriction.

If the chilling continues and becomes extreme, the brain activates
a sort of special "checklist" of priorities for blood, with its heat, to be
diverted from areas of less importance. At the top of the list of course
is the brain; when it becomes too chilled to function, the game is pretty
well over. The heart shares top priority with the brain; they both need
the oxygenated blood. Behind them come the other internal organs.
The limbs are regarded as expendable, and so far as survival of the
organism is concerned, the other extremities — ears, fingers, toes,
hands, feet — are irrelevant.

Physical activity is an important response — whether it is merely
shivering or something more energetic. Either activity is useful
because the body calls on its own fuel supply that is stored in its cells
and converts (metabolizes) it into heat. During this time, a person's
heart is beating faster as blood is diverted away from the cold feet,
fingers and ears, and the individual is breathing faster. During all this
metabolic activity, a good bit of water leaves the body through the
breath. A person can dehydrate in cool temperatures without realizing
it.

As a person gets colder, the body gets a double stress. Not only
is it working against the cold, but the defense effort is also a strain. It
is a bad sign when the cold person has gotten very cold (the body core
temperature is down to 86°) and has stopped shivering. The system
of nerves controlling muscles is no longer functioning. Yet if the core
temperature rises a degree or two, shivering will start up again.

For the canoeist, danger lurks mainly in the lakes. Some of the
deeper lakes never do warm up a great deal, and few of the northern
lakes are popular for swimming, even in August. In water at 80°, a
swimmer must exert himself quite vigorously to stay warm and this
takes energy. In 75° water, a person will begin to chill.

What we are looking at here is the potential threat of lake water
that is 70° or colder. We're talking about a common room temperature in the winter time, a temperature some people consider barely
warm enough. As a reference point, a "good, cold drink of water"
from the kitchen tap will have a temperature of 60° (about 16°C),
which is something to think about when you get a cool drink of lake
water — from the upper, warmer layer of the lake! Obviously these
temperatures are more likely to be colder either late or early in the
season — April, after the ice has gone out, or October, before the
lakes start freezing up. Large lakes of course are slower to warm up
and likewise to cool down than are smaller ones.

Sadly, lakes claim victims each year. Part of these deaths may be due to the inability to swim and the failure to use flotation devices. Swimming and boating accidents probably account for more deaths related to hypothermia than any other single cause. Drowning might not have occurred in maybe half of those events had hypothermia not occurred. Since hypothermia can come on gradually, as on a rainy, windy day, it is important to recognize its signs.

The traditional lore about being thrown out of a boat says to get your shoes off as soon as you can. Dr. Robert Pozos, a foremost scholar of the effects of cold, suggests that in cold waters, such as our northern lakes, it is better to leave your shoes on, as they help you retain body heat for a little while longer. This is another good reason for wearing sneakers or other lightweight shoes; they are not heavy enough to pull you under, as would be the case with heavy hiking boots.

Let us look at a hypothetical situation. A member of your party falls into the lake on a trip in late May. Time elapses before it is possible to get the victim out. (We aren't going to consider the condition of the rescuers at this point.) The victim is wet; the day is cloudy and windy. The conditions are ripe for hypothermia to develop. Let's imaging several scenarios, with the time of exposure varying from a few minutes to more than an hour.

The first scenario, with rescue effected very quickly, will have a miserable candidate. The poor soul will be shivering; the circulation to hands and feet is reduced; most likely and hopefully, he or she will complain of being cold, maybe even of pain. You would notice the breathing is more rapid — perhaps to the point of hyperventilating. Involuntary gasping is a common reaction to cold stress. And maybe, to the victim's eventual embarrassment, there is spontaneous urination.

MEETING THE CRISIS

With any case of hypothermia, prompt action is crucial. Equally important, it should be appropriate. As quickly as possible, get the victim out of the cold wet clothes, dried off and into something warm and dry; a sleeping bag is good. Passive external warming is the term for this technique and it will work in most threatening situations. Remember the risk of dehydration? Warm drinks, and I stress *nonalcoholic,* help. Alcohol dilates surface blood vessels, bringing warmth to the body surface for dissipation, and consequently works against the process of warming the chilled core. Furthermore, alcohol robs the blood of the glucose that provides energy for cellular metabolism.

The second scenario is a little grimmer. The victim has been exposed to cold longer. The victim is confused or irrational, a sure sign that trouble is developing. This is the stage where victims have been known to wander off, shedding their clothes all the while. There is an increasing loss of dexterity; how is the victim's coordination? Another sign of trouble is the slurring of speech, with the irrationality of action perhaps reflected in his talk. Amnesia starts setting in. Clearly, the brain is beginning to opt out. This is now a very serious situation.

The safest trick here is to let re-warming take place at the body's own rate, slowly and naturally, which will occur if the cold stress is removed. The campsite usually will have whatever is needed to keep the victim going. As with the first scenario, the techniques of passive external warming will suffice. Be sure the patient is insulated against heat loss to the ground; a Space Blanket or plastic ground cloth under the sleeping bag is useful. Wrap him (or her) well in sleeping bags, put a cap on his head. A scarf over the mouth keeps body heat in and warms the incoming breath. Keep the head level with the body, with the legs and feet slightly raised. Slowly give plenty of warm drinks such as sweetened (sugared — the victim needs the energy) tea or bouillon. You can test the temperature by splashing a few drops on the inside of your wrist; they should feel just barely warm. With this second stage-type of hypothermia, as noted earlier, the hands are numb and clumsy and will not do a good job of holding a cup, much less a spoon. Someone should hold the drink for the victim. Try to keep the victim awake and talking until fully re-warmed.

The third scenario presents a desperate situation. Here, the victim has quit shivering as the deep nerve response has turned off. The pupils have dilated, a clue of things amiss with the brain. Breathing has become erratic and shallow. The victim is no longer conscious, while the deep tendon and skin reflexes have ended. Now the heart is showing distress. The pulse rate has dropped markedly; since the blood is not circulating well, the skin is discoloring, and the heart beat may be showing frequent irregularities. In very serious cases of hypothermia, the heartbeat may slow to as few as two or three beats a minute, which should not be surprising, considering that the blood has become more viscous, thicker with the cold. However, so long as the victim is ventilating (breathing), the heart can safely be presumed to be beating, and that is a good sign.

I want to emphasize the importance of the effort to determine if there is a heartbeat. In severe hypothermia, it can be very difficult to pick up a pulse. If the heartbeat is very slow or even not detectable and the victim isn't breathing, CPR is the recommended first aid action. This is something of a damned if you do/damned if you don't situation. If the victim is in a state of cardiac arrest, where the heart has stopped, CPR may cause the cardiopulmonary systems to kick back in, and the victim may revive. If the heart is still functioning, CPR can cause it to go into ventricular fibrillation, and then the victim has had it. Furthermore, once CPR is begun, it must be continued until either the patient recovers or until artificial support is at hand. Consider the possibilities of this on a remote lake.

Lake mishaps are dramatic. If a canoeist falls into the water, the urgency of the situation is self-evident. However, rainy days, particularly at the ends of the season or with wind, are potentially as dangerous. There is a detailed discussion of temperatures and rain in Chapter Four. Several hours of being chilled not only are thoroughly miserable, but will sap the individual's energy reserves. Some additional snacking on cool days helps keep those reserves up.

THE RESULTS

Since most of this discussion deals with possible consequences of accidental dumping in the lake, I should mention one other point. That is what happens when someone drowns in cold water. Curiously enough, there is a hopeful aspect. The cold water that chills the person also reduces the body's need for oxygen. Therefore the chances are good that the victim may be successfully revived following immersion of up to an hour's time.

Hypothermia can, for the most part, be prevented. Again, it simply means thinking about conditions: put on rain suits *before* you get wet; wear your life vest on the water (if it covers most of your torso, it will help keep you warm); don't get too tired. (Did you ever notice feeling colder when you are tired?) Take appropriate equipment; plan how you might deal with emergencies before they happen; keep your wits about you in unexpected situations. After all, the idea is to "Stay cool," not "Freeze!"

HEAT DANGERS

Just as the body is not very tolerant of a lowered core temperature, a raised one is likewise a matter of considerable risk. The elevated body temperature is a more familiar situation — we know it as fever and make vigorous efforts to reduce it, particularly when it goes over 101°. We are familiar with hypothermia — fever — when it is brought on by a bacterial or viral onslaught. We do not give quite so much thought to its effects — heat prostration or the more dangerous heat stroke — when brought on by weather conditions or overexertion.

Actually, the tolerable temperature range of the area about us above the golden mid-80s is much smaller than the range below. We find few humans living in those areas where high temperatures of 120° or more naturally occur. Likewise, the internal heat-regulating mechanisms undergo severe stress in maintaining the core temperature of 98.6° when the individual is vigorously exerting himself and the external heat level is high. A high humidity level added to that makes it difficult for the body to cool itself by sweating. The makings of trouble are present.

In the Boundary Waters, it is not common for the temperature to go over the 90° mark, much less stay there. However, on one trip in late May Friend Spouse and I realized that heat prostration is a greater danger than one might think. The temperature had reached 90°; although the humidity was low, so was the breeze. We were double-portaging and double-packing on long portages. We both found ourselves rather severely stressed by the heat, and we could almost feel the energy draining out of us with our sweat. We had both "tanked up," drinking a good amount of water before we started and again at the end of the portage to replenish lost fluid. We also found that it was important, besides being sufficiently hydrated, to take our time on such an effort. Slower movements generate less heat as they use less energy.

Humidity enhances the effects of temperature, whether high or low. Just as cold and damp is more miserable than cold and dry, hot and moist is more unpleasant than hot and dry. What most people do not realize is that the humidity level in the woods, particularly deciduous woods, is higher than the open country because the trees are "working." A tree works by transpiring — where the process of photo-synthesis involves taking in carbon dioxide and giving off water. Thus the humidity level raises the risk level of over-heating on a hot day along the portage trail.

HEAT LAYING YOU OUT?

We all know that someone who is working hard on a hot day not only is sweating, but is also probably red in the face. These are healthy signs. Sweating takes heat out of the body by evaporative cooling. The red face indicates that the circulatory system is carrying off internal heat by means of the blood and is bringing it to the wide area of the skin, dumping its heat into the air in the process called vaso-dilation. If, however, the air temperature is higher than the 98.6° of the body's core, heat will not flow from the body to the air. No cooling occurs. If the humidity is high as well, the sweat will not evaporate, and no cooling occurs. Now problems begin to develop. The person feels tired, and no wonder, maybe a bit faint and dizzy, and grows pale.

These are early signs of heat prostration and should be heeded before the situation deteriorates. What is happening is this. We know that excess heat is carried away from the brain to keep it cool. In the effort to carry heat from the overheating internal organs and to avoid overheating the brain, the blood is pooling in the legs, the most distant point from the brain. Since the blood supply to the head and brain has decreased, pallor and faintness can occur.

Heat prostration is not of itself a life-threatening situation. The object is to get the victim cooled down, sitting down, or better still, lying down in the shade with the feet up, having cool cloths applied to the head, the sides of the neck, and the armpits (cool those blood vessels down!), drinking cool, sweetened drinks — all these are appropriate and helpful measures. Some doctors advise a glass of slightly salted water every 15 minutes three or four times (the salt ratio is 1 teaspoon of salt to 1 quart of water). Bouillon cubes dissolved in water are helpful here.

COMBATING HEAT STROKE

Heat stroke is another matter altogether. As the core temperature rises and it gets more difficult for the body to dissipate excess heat, the heart pumps harder and harder to move the heated blood out to the extremities. The rapid, weak pulse and rapid breathing reflect the growing distress. The skin becomes red, dry and hot. In essence, the victim is in a fever and is literally cooking. He (it is more commonly he) may complain of dizziness, headache, or abdominal discomfort — all signs of systems under siege. As the situation worsens, there may be delirium, muscular twitching or convulsions, and unconsciousness. Unless the overheating is brought down, the circulatory system begins to collapse. If the victim starts developing a gray pallor, he is losing the battle. Prompt hospitalization is vital, not a helpful thought when you are miles from anyone.

PRACTICE PREVENTION

There is really no need for this life-threatening situation to occur if each member of the group is watchful for possible overheating. The aggravating factor of accompanying high humidity is likewise uncommon. (Elevated humidity becomes a problem when the temperature goes over 80°.) That leaves overexertion remaining as the potential cause of heat stroke, and as I have emphasized before, haste and fatigue are at the root of most mishaps.

So if you, or any of your party, are beginning to be affected by heat, take time to cool off. Have a drink of water or juice mixture; make sure your fluid intake is high. Since you normally lose at least a quart of water a day under ordinary circumstances, it should be plain that you will lose more when your body's cooling system turns on. Improve the efficiency of the system by cooling the extremities — indulge yourself by removing your socks and shoes and wading in the water. Bathe your hands and face and neck with cool water. It is refreshing and a good safety practice. Wear a hat to shade your head, thus reducing the heat load on its blood vessels. If the day is slightly breezy, wet your shirt and enjoy the natural evaporative cooling. With a breeze, a loose-fitting shirt can be a good bit cooler than no shirt.

We have been talking about healthy people with no particular problems that warrant continuing medical supervision. However, canoe camping, though a fairly vigorous physical activity, is not limited to the completely sound of body. People with continuing problems, such as heart disease or diabetes, of course should consult with their physician before setting out on an expedition. The level of physical activity and the demands of portaging and canoeing require consideration. People have died from heart attacks that occurred during a trip, though this is a fairly rare occurrence.

The diabetic who relies on daily insulin shots will need to think about temperature requirements for the insulin, and to carry an adequate supply of sugar. So long as the temperatures do not get extreme, and in the BWCA, the summer high temperatures generally are below 85°, insulin may be carried safely for up to 2 weeks. (And there is a trick or two to keeping things cool that can be called into play; what works for food works in other ways, too.) Diabetics do go on camping trips; picking the best time of the season may help, and food selection would be of particular importance, as well as the amount of daily travel. Take along a bottle of short-acting insulin for emergencies. Also a diabetic person is already aware of the importance of food, rest and exercise in dealing with this medical problem, and should be particularly watchful on an expedition.

I gained some insights into problems the summer before I had hip surgery. If the camper has walking difficulties (as I did), it is even more to the point to get topographical maps for planning the trip. Gentler terrain makes life a bit easier. It also became more important to be more efficient in choosing gear and planning food, so that there is not so much stuff to be carried.

Ability varies, whether the members of the party are fully able-bodied or not. Wilderness Inquiry, a Minnesota-based organization serving people with mixed levels of physical capability, works on the philosophy that there are varying degrees of ability. Members of the camping party do their share of what has to be done and that share will, almost of necessity, be based on capabilities. In many accounts of groups of women of their wilderness trips, the dominant note that appears time and again is the spirit of cooperation, and it reveals itself in individuals taking on those tasks that evoke their skills and capabilities.

I should mention that there are at least two programs in Minnesota that make it possible for people with physical disabilities to get a good, first-hand wilderness experience. When I was reminded to caution some people to check with their doctors about taking a canoe trip, I remembered hearing of one group that included a young woman with cerebral palsy, one who was blind, and there were others with problems that in the minds of most people would have kept them at home. It was exciting that such did not have to be the case. Two groups here are Wilderness Inquiry and Voyageur Outward Bound. See Appendix — Canoeing in the United States, Specialized Camping for where to find out more.

Starflower

4

DO YOU THINK IT WILL RAIN?

*There will be a rain dance Friday night, weather
permitting.*
—George Carlin

Weather is always an important consideration with any outdoor
activity. The area I know best, the Upper Midwest — Minnesota,
Wisconsin and upper Michigan — deserves its reputation of bitterly
cold winters. However, the delightful summers, with many bright blue
days and clear air, are not so well advertised.

In planning a canoe trip, several points are of interest: temperatures, precipitation (both affect the clothing taken), and length of
daylight, which affects the amount of travel time per day. Consideration of wind is also of some importance. If you are going well out of
your own region, find out (before you finish planning) the weather
characteristics of the area.

TEMPERATURES

Temperatures for Duluth and International Falls will be used for
reference, as they lie at the outer ends of the Voyageurs National Park
and the BWCA. Quetico Provincial Park lies just to the east of
International Falls and north of the BWCA and generally has weather
quite similar to its neighbors, with temperatures possibly a few
degrees cooler and precipitation a day earlier or a day later than in the
BWCA, depending on the months and weather frontal passages. (The
pattern would be cooling in the north earlier; warming from the south
later.) A look on a month-by-month basis throughout the canoe
season follows. Temperatures for Minneapolis-St. Paul (Twin Cities)
are also listed as a sort of cross reference for those areas where Duluth

and International Falls summer temperatures are not available. Winter temperatures for International Falls are fairly common news items, but the place tends to disappear from the summer maps.

The start of the season of course follows the breakup of the ice on the lakes. In the BWCA, the average date of the last one inch of snow on the ground is April 25. Then things usually begin to warm up fairly rapidly and the ice goes out (a crucial factor for canoeing) about the same time, that is, the latter half of April. May tends to be a fairly consistent sort of month from year to year, with steady warming occurring through the month. However, and this is an important however, in the North Country, wide temperature swings do occur. We made one 10-day trip covering the last days of May and the first day of June, where we began and ended the trip with temperatures in the 40s, but in the middle we had two days where the high was in the 90s. In fact, this sort of variation, with a range of as much as 42° between the highest high and the lowest high temperature during the month holds throughout the canoe season. Like much of the United States, the period between July 20 and August 1 typically has the average dates of the hottest temperatures.

Here is the sort of range to expect. The temperatures given are Fahrenheit. For a reference point, an easy Celsius temperature to remember is that 61°F is 16°C. Thanks to an informative brochure from Travel Manitoba, average highs and lows are available for that province. They could provide some notions for temperatures in the Canadian provinces to the east on the same latitudes.

	AVERAGE HIGH	AVERAGE LOW
APRIL		
Duluth	47.8	29.3
International Falls	49.1	27.3
Twin Cities	55.5	34.7
Southern Manitoba (Winnipeg)	48.0	28.0
MAY		
Duluth	60.0	38.8
International Falls	62.5	37.7
Twin Cities	67.9	46.3
Southern Manitoba (Winnipeg)	64.0	40.0
Central Manitoba (The Pas)	58.0	36.0
JUNE		
Duluth	69.7	48.3
International Falls	72.4	48.3
Twin Cities	77.1	56.7
Southern Manitoba (Winnipeg)	73.0	51.0
Central Manitoba (The Pas)	68.0	48.0

JULY

Duluth	76.4	54.7
International Falls	78.2	53.4
Twin Cities	82.4	61.4
Southern Manitoba (Winnipeg)	79.0	56.0
Central Manitoba (The Pas)	74.0	54.0

AUGUST

Duluth	74.4	53.7
International Falls	75.5	50.9
Twin Cities	80.8	59.6
Southern Manitoba (Winnipeg)	76.0	53.0
Central Manitoba (The Pas)	71.0	51.0

SEPTEMBER

Duluth	64.0	44.8
International Falls	64.2	41.7
Twin Cities	70.7	49.3
Southern Manitoba (Winnipeg)	65.0	43.0
Central Manitoba (The Pas)	58.0	41.0

OCTOBER

Duluth	54.3	36.2
International Falls	54.0	32.9
Twin Cities	60.7	39.2
Southern Manitoba (Winnipeg)	53.0	33.0
Central Manitoba (The Pas)	46.0	31.0

These are *average* highs and lows. While we have seen 90-degree days in the BWCA, generally they are uncommon. Recent years (1988-89) have produced some temperatures higher than normal, and the summer of 1992 was the coolest on record. June 1992 saw near-freezing temperatures in Twin Cities on June 21. Duluth and other points north dipped to about 28°F. It remains to be seen whether they were merely aberrations or are signs of a warming trend.

The Twin Cities expect to have about fourteen days a summer with a temperature of 90°F or above. International Falls, and the inland area generally, will experience a somewhat greater swing between the high and low temperatures than Duluth, where Lake Superior moderates the temperatures. July temperatures tend to have a narrower range between high and low. We have been out when the day was rainy and the high temperature was 58 degrees; it was thoroughly miserable. It is also useful to know that the average daily high temperature in August drops markedly; the end of August is a good bit cooler than the first of the month.

PRECIPITATION

Over the years, it seemed to us that we could expect to get rained on at least once in any trip of at least three days. A look at precipitation data showed that our informal observations actually were sound. The data for the average precipitation for the month and the number of days of precipitation (where 0.01 or more inches fell) follow.

Snow can fall in September and May, and by the end of October, the canoeing season is pretty well ended. Serious snow and freeze-up come in November.

	AMOUNT	DAYS WITH RAIN
APRIL		
Duluth	2.55	11
International Falls	1.67	10
Twin Cities	2.04	10
MAY		
Duluth	3.41	12
International Falls	2.75	11
Twin Cities	3.37	11
JUNE		
Duluth	4.44	13
International Falls	3.91	13
Twin Cities	3.94	12
JULY		
Duluth	3.73	11
International Falls	3.98	11
Twin Cities	3.69	10
AUGUST		
Duluth	3.79	11
International Falls	3.39	12
Twin Cities	3.05	10
SEPTEMBER		
Duluth	3.06	11
International Falls	3.32	12
Twin Cities	2.73	9
OCTOBER		
Duluth	2.30	9
International Falls	1.69	10
Twin Cities	1.78	8

The above data come from the National Weather Service. The average precipitation records are based on data from 1941-1970. However, in the latter years of the 1980s, Minnesota endured an extended period of drought and a couple of exceptionally hot summers. What this will show on updated climatological records remains to be seen.

The BWCA/Voyageurs area, according to Minnesota Department of Natural Resources data, generally averages between 3 and 4 inches of rain each month during the canoeing season (May through September), with June generally being the wettest month. The bulk of the month's precipitation may occur within a particular week. You should be aware that the combination of warmer temperatures and greater precipitation means that thunderstorms may occur, and with some suddenness. Thunderstorms are no occasion to be on the water or in the swamp.

WIND

I grew up in Oklahoma, where the strong and constant wind is a part of everyday life. I hadn't realized how much we took that for granted until we moved to Tennessee, where the air is much calmer. However, Minnesota is more like Oklahoma. (It's part of the reason we Minnesotans pay so much attention to wind chill information.) It is easy to assume that people from other parts of the country will just naturally know we can have many windy days and that indeed, the Weather Service issues small craft warnings for our numerous lakes.

Although data on wind in the BWCA are not readily available, it is worth being aware of the wind for several reasons. The most obvious is the difficulty and potential danger of being on a large lake with a very strong wind. Unless you and the breeze are headed the same direction, paddling on a windy day will be very hard work, trying to keep the canoe pointed generally into the wind. If the wind is very strong, both the paddlers should be strong, too. High winds and their attendant waves present a real danger of the canoe swamping or overturning. (It is a good idea to have a bailing bucket in the canoe.) On more than one occasion we have remained in camp a day because of wind.

Unless our day's route includes a large lake, we tend to pay more attention to the daily *pattern* of winds. (For instance, when we awoke to strong west winds the morning we were to paddle the westerly 15-mile stretch down Quetico's Sturgeon Lake, we decided to go back to sleep. Later in the morning, the wind shifted, so we moved out and zipped down the lake with the wind to our backs.) We have found that mornings tend (notice: I didn't say *always*) to be calm, and the paddling is easier. We hate to lose the easy time by late starts (that is, after 8:30 or 9 A.M.). Likewise, in the late afternoon, around 3:30 or 4, the wind starts picking up, making work more difficult. That is a good reason to have found a camp site and settled in by then. Again, the wind generally drops around 7, about the time we have eaten, cleared up the dishes and tucked the camp in for the night. It's time for enjoying the beauty of a quiet evening on the water!

Wind and thunderstorms are facts of life during the canoe season. Lying in a tent during a wind storm, one begins to feel very small, insignificant and vulnerable. Hearing trees creaking and groaning as the wind roars through them inspires feelings that range from awe to pure terror.

If a storm appears eminent, the Elegant Camper makes preparations to ride it out as safely as possible and with a minimum of discomfort and damage. While we usually rig a tarp for shelter during expected (or actual) rain in the daytime, if it looks like it might be stormy, we have found that it is better to take down the tarp and use it like a quilt, tucking in all the gear under it and fastening it down. We made the change after our experience on Sark Lake, when a horrendous wind storm came up in the night. The tarp flapped and popped until we thought surely it would take off and fly to the far end of the lake. We got up and took it down before it snapped to pieces and covered the gear where it was, on the ground. Happily, there are fewer wind storms than ordinary rain storms.

DAYLIGHT

Until one experiences the change, it is hard for a southerner to comprehend the fact of the tilt of Earth's axis during summer and winter, with the long winter nights and the long summer days. While long summer days may make it tough to get the little ones to bed at a desired hour, they are wonderful for catching a bit of fishing after dinner.

In early May, sunrise is at 6:03 A.M. (Central Daylight Time); by the end of the month, it is at 5:30. It gets light earlier than that, however. By early August, the morning has shortened to 5:58 (CDT), and by the end of the month, sunrise is at 6:33. Be warned that the birds wake much earlier (such as 4 o'clock) and announce to the world that they are ready to take it on. (This is on Minneapolis' longitude; east will see earlier light, west will see later.)

Sunset is about 8:18 in early May, and 8:52 by the end of the month, which gives some 15 hours and 22 minutes of daylight at June's beginning. June has around 15 hours of daylight, then the days begin to shorten. August days see sunset between 8:40 and 8:53 p.m., with day length shortening from 14 hours and 42 minutes down to 13 hours and 20 minutes. By late September, it is dark by 7 p.m. in the BWCA, after about 12 hours of sun time. (These numbers are meant to be viewed for the trend. The point is the *amount* of daylight.) States that link fishing or hunting with daylight hours often publish tables showing sunup and sundown hours. Write the appropriate department (such as the Department of Natural Resources) for a copy.

(The above is Twin Cities data; in going north, the daylight period lengthens during the summer.)

DO-IT-YOURSELF WEATHER FORECASTING

A few weather signs can prove helpful to the camper. For instance, a halo around the sun or moon means that there is an 80 percent chance of precipitation within 36 hours. Falling barometric pressure, a good indication that rain is coming, reveals itself to the observant camper in a number of ways, like the following.

Look at the sky; are there fine clouds, strewn like chiffon veils across? (Some call these clouds "mares' tails.") They are often forerunners of approaching storms.

More gas bubbles rise in the water where there is a lot of decaying vegetation. In swampy areas, you can even smell the gases.

Are the flowers along the portage closed, even though it is mid-day? (But the pitcher plants will open ahead of rain, when everything else closes.)

Smoke particles collect water and become visible, making the camp fire smokier.

Birds get quiet before a storm. Some have observed that the birds seem to sense the duration of a rain. If it is raining early in the morning but likely to clear up later in the morning, the birds wait until it is drier. But if they are out and about in the wet, most likely the rain has set in for the day.

Another useful piece of information comes with the chirping of crickets. Count the number of chirps in one minute's time, add forty and you will get the approximate temperature.

Finally, appreciate the beauty of a mist rising from a pond, not only for its beauty, but for its promise of a fair tomorrow.

LIGHTNING

One of the features of living in the so-called Temperate Zone is thunderstorm season. Thunderstorms can occur at any time of the year (it is weird to get a thunderstorm when there is a foot of snow on the ground, but it happens). However, in Minnesota, the high season of thunderstorms coincides with the favorite months for canoe camping.

Some 200 people a year are killed by lightning in the United States, a deadly score similar to that of hurricanes and tornadoes, though the odds of being struck are on the order of one in a million, or about the same as getting the lucky numbers in a big lottery. In the past 30 years, 39 lightning fatalities have been recorded in Minnesota — a somewhat "safer" place than the Gulf Coast States. Most of those who die by lightning were not in the city; they were outside, enjoying recreational activities, working on construction projects or other open air business. Some of those victims are campers. For this reason, the Elegant Camper would want to know how to keep the odds favorable.

The canoe camper, who spends part of the time on the water and part on the shore, should be aware of the nature of the danger presented by a thunderstorm in either area.

What we are really talking about, of course, is the discharge of enormous quantities of electrical energy we call lightning. All of us are aware of the great flashes of light that leap from cloud to ground, slashing a channel through the air. The beginning of such a flash is called the "leader" stroke. What is not so widely known is that there is a corresponding charge that leaps up from the ground to join with the "leader" stroke. This is called the "return" stroke. The "leader" stroke carries enormous quantities of electrons and creates a very strong electrical field near the ground which initiates the "return" stroke.

Both the cloud mass and the ground are in a highly unstable state, electrically speaking, and a lot of energy is on the move. As the storm wears on, much of the charge is drawn into the ground, and after a time, usually around 20 minutes, the energy is spent and tranquillity is once again restored.

It is one thing to read about all this and quite another to be out in the open air or, oh, horrors, be on the water when these bolts are crashing all around. Yet there are some precautions that can be taken to reduce the chances of being cooked on Mother Nature's great grill.

It always pays to keep an eye on what the sky looks like, especially if you are on the water. Clouds are one thing. But at the first hint of a lightning flash, the prudent thing to do is get off the water as quickly as possible and head for the trees, away from the shore. If you have been happily fishing and haven't noticed a storm developing until the rain starts, get your fishing lines and rods in and onto the bottom of the canoe, make as low a profile of yourself as you can and head for land. On the water, you are at great risk during a storm, and your gear could increase it.

Here's why. A lake presents a flat surface. A lightning stroke could strike anywhere. However, anything that extends above that flat surface provides a base, as it were, from which the "return" stroke can emanate. This protruding object, channeling, as it were, the induced charge on the earth into the return stroke, would be the unwitting canoeist. If perchance, he or she is sitting there with a graphite fishing rod, the result is rather like those cruel "Kick Me" signs kids used to tag on someone they wished to torment.

"*Graphite* is dangerous? Isn't that what pencil leads are made of?" you may say. "Why?" Well, graphite is carbon, an excellent conductor of electricity. Remember all those filaments that Thomas Edison tried before he got one that worked in his light bulb, one that would glow when a current passed through it? That filament was carbonized thread.

Swimming is an even worse idea during a storm. Fresh water, as in our lakes and rivers, does a very poor job of conducting the electrical charge to earth. (Salt water is a much better conductor, though I can't think that swimming in the ocean during a thunderstorm is a particularly smart idea, either.) When a lightning stroke hits, it sends out streamers in all directions that keep going until these streamers ground out either in the earth or on the hapless swimmer. Obviously, there is no protection for a swimmer in the water.

On land, a person has greater chances for safety. In the woods, there is a vast number of objects, usually trees, that stick up further from the surface than a person. Consequently a tree is far more likely to get hit than the person. Conventional wisdom has said, "Don't stand under a tree; if caught out in the open during a storm, one should lie down on the ground."

Lightning study has shown that this is not necessarily very good advice. Here's why. As we have seen, an upright object such as a tree provides a channel funneling a ground charge up to the leader stroke. Lightning may strike a tree, and the charge races down the tree and into the ground, where it may send out streamers which spread over the ground very much as they do in the lake. The tree may serve as the base, but streamers over the ground bring charges to the tree from other regions. A person or animal should be oriented so that he or she can interrupt this horizontal streamer path over a minimum distance. Hence, keep your feet close together, but don't lie down. The longer the path interruption is, the greater the voltage crossing that gap and consequently the greater the jolt received. This is why cows standing out in the pasture during a thunderstorm are frequently electrocuted, while a person standing near by might not be.

The lesson for us is to keep our base as small as possible; stand with feet as close together as possible, and hunker down, reducing the height as much as we can. It isn't comfortable, but, as God told a cranky Noah who was complaining about building the ark in anticipation of the flood (in Bill Cosby's album, "Noah"), "How long can you tread water?"

Certain trees themselves seem to offer more protection than others. There are strong indications that the species of trees with great tap root systems do a better job of conducting the charge deep into the earth than do trees whose root systems are wide but shallow. Oaks have deep tap roots; birches generally do not. All of this is not very comforting: much of the northern forests comprises birch, popple and conifers. The awareness that the rocky, sandy soil is neither deep nor conductive does not raise the comfort level, either.

Live trees carry a charge more swiftly than dead ones, and that becomes plain on considering that a live tree is essentially a great hydraulic system, carrying water from its roots to all parts and sugars from the leaves to the roots. Since water is a conductor, a dead tree would be somewhat safer. Some trees are repeated targets. Watch out for those bearing long scars on their trunks; they could be targets again.

Most campers who were killed by lightning died while lying on their sleeping bags in their tents. By now, it should be clear why this is a dangerous place. A camper really concerned about tent safety and lightning can do one thing. A length of #14 or #12 power wiring, longer than the full perimeter of the tent, can be laid around the test and the ends fastened to complete a loop. This loop diverts those lightning streamers and offers some protection to those in the tent. It is a simple remedy and somewhat effective. The nervous camper who plans to camp in thunderstorm season may wish to check into the space requirements of such a piece of wire, and possibly include it in the necessary basic equipment.

If one of your party is struck by lightning, you may not be able to do much. If the victim is not breathing, but still has a detectable pulse, you can try rescue, or mouth-to-mouth, breathing to get respiration going again. If however, there is no pulse, the only recourse is CPR, or cardio-pulmonary resuscitation, if someone in the group knows how to administer it. It should be remembered that CPR is a first aid measure, which may or may not succeed.

What it all comes down to is this. While lightning deaths are a very infrequent occurrence, people are killed while on the water, while in the water, and while standing in the open. A person who understands why this is so and acts accordingly has made a major effort in staying out of the unfortunate company. It is, I repeat, a minor risk to campers, but knowing what to do and what not to do — and acting accordingly — reduces that risk.

CAMERA TRICKS

If you have your camera along, and if the storm is a big one, you may get some photographs that are truly spectacular. Set the camera on a steady base, a tripod, if you perchance brought one, open the shutter as wide as possible, perhaps facing the lake view — whatever offers the best view of sky and horizon, and leave it open two minutes, then close it and advance the film. Repeat until you are tired of shooting, the storm ends or you run out of film, whatever comes first. If the storm is quite intense, you might want to shorten the length of exposure. You will probably find you have wasted a few shots, but some may be extraordinary.

Many people know the old trick of counting down the interval between seeing the flash of lightning and hearing the ensuing thunder. They count "one thousand and one, one thousand and two," etc., to calculate the number of seconds, and that a count of 5 seconds means a 1-mile interval. If the count gets to "one thousand and ten," then the storm is 2 miles away. What is less familiar is to repeat the count with the beginning of the thunder and count the duration of the rumble. Again, five counts make a mile, and what it demonstrates is the severity of the storm. The length calculated from this second count corresponds to the length of the lightning channel, and the greater the count, the longer the channel and consequently indicates the greater intensity of the storm. More intense storms are bigger; they extend higher into the atmosphere with a longer channel. Neither count will tell you how long the storm will last; generally that is about 20 minutes.

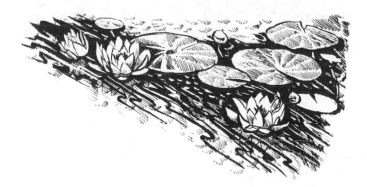

Pitcher Plant

5

WHEN DO WE EAT?

A Jug of wine, a Loaf of Bread and Thou
Beside me singing in the Wilderness...
Oh, Wilderness were Paradise enow!
          — Omar Khayyam

It hasn't been too terribly long ago that eating on a wilderness trip could be a pretty grim business. This is not to say there weren't some men (most of the old-time woods rovers were male) who were really quite good cooks, especially when it came to frying fish, or maybe making a stew, or even doing a bit of baking.

No, the grimness came from the sheer toil of carrying in whatever it was that was slated for the menu. Ernest Hemingway speaks of eating spaghetti and canned beans in his "The Big Two-Hearted River," set in the wilds of Michigan's Upper Peninsula. Canned food was for a long time the reliable source. It could provide quite a bit of variety, but the stuff, as any grocery carry-out boy will tell you, is heavy. What's more, it seems to get heavier on every portage. Nowadays, the idea of carrying canned food is offensive for a second reason: disposal of the metal can. Seasoned campers know that cans (and bottles) are forbidden in some areas, such as the BWCA and Quetico, and discouraged in others.

World War II brought some changes. The technology used in producing the K-rations and C-rations used by American troops was adaptable to camping purposes, though probably without enthusiasm by war veterans who had a great deal of experience with them.

However, the big breakthrough in improving the diet of the woods trekker came from the United States' efforts in space travel. Improved techniques in freeze-drying meant that a wider range of food was available, and better still, it was tastier than earlier products. Even later tricks have produced the so-called shelf-stable products, known to 1990s soldiers as Meals Ready to Eat (MREs).

THAT WAS THEN; THIS IS NOW

Food is a tremendously important aspect of camping for several reasons. Obviously, adequate nourishment is vital for the rigors of the outdoors and for the maintenance of good health. But food is also an important element in camp morale. It needs to be appealing and satisfying. Food planning for a group including youngsters will be different, too. Their energy needs are higher (translated: more food!) They are apt to be rather more fussy about unfamiliar food. In my experience, the more kids involved, the more likely that somebody wouldn't like *something,* no matter what I fixed.

Backpacking, canoeing, and particularly portaging, can be pretty hard work, using up a lot of energy. It takes food to restore those energy levels, and the harder the work, or the more demanding the weather, or both, the more it takes. Life in the wilderness is rigorous enough — no waterbeds, no running water (not counting the creek, of course), or none of the other creature comforts we enjoy at home. Good food, though, is one of the creature comforts that is available, if the planning and preparation have been thoughtful and careful.

The business of food will by far take up more of the time and effort of preparing for the trip than any other single activity, with the possible exception of the length of time it takes to get from your home to the canoeing point. Acquiring and accumulating equipment is a major undertaking, but once it is done, it pretty well stays done. And if you like the elegant approach, once back home you will organize the storage so that it takes a very short time to get it ready for the next outing. Food, however, is something else again, and it must be considered anew for each trip. It does get easier with experience.

In the preliminary stages of planning meals, it is a good idea to pause and consider how much "new" experience is going to happen. If this is a first canoe trip, and you don't have much experience in camping and camp cooking, then it makes good sense to keep it simple. Choose the packaged camp foods; the preparation of them is very simple, and the number of servings is indicated on the label. You can even purchase an entire meal for a group in a single package. It is not a bad way to start. If you have already done some camp cooking, you can be more adventurous.

There are those campers who go trekking with a pretty spartan diet. I have heard of some who took mainly oatmeal — for a week's trip! Others travel light, expecting to make out on the fish they catch. Neither notion is particularly conducive to a happy trip.

However, many wilderness trekkers like to keep a little more control over their diet. They may want something a little different from commercially prepared trail food, or may want to control the amount of salt, or preservatives, or other additives in their diet. They may have some special needs in their food regimen, and here they may find some useful tips.

My philosophy for wilderness cooking is to keep it simple, keep the cooking times to a minimum, and yet try for a tasty meal that appeals to the party. This isn't always easy. It wasn't when we had four children at home: we could usually count on somebody not liking something at any given meal.

Here, the aims are to make inventive use of items available at a good supermarket; to give alternatives to commercially prepared trail foods; to use as short and simple preparation times (on site) as possible; to be fuel-efficient in cooking process; to be nutritionally sound; and to recognize the peculiar constraints of the BWCA or other similar areas.

Whenever possible, the recipes that follow later will call for readily available items. Sometimes it is possible for the camper to dry foods at home prior to the trip and use those items. I have used dried zucchini, eggplant, tomatoes, and peppers cooked with slices of fresh onion, and served with chunks of cheese and pita bread. Not bad! However, not everybody has a food dehydrator or is willing to take the time and trouble to oven-dry foods. (Intending to use home-dried food also calls for considerable advance planning and preparation. It really depends on whether you have the time and inclination to fool with the business.) For this reason, there will not be a great deal of attention paid to that area. However, check out Joanna White's cookbook (listed in Appendix — Useful and Interesting Reading) if you are curious and interested in dehydrating food at home.

SIX CHECKPOINTS FOR FOOD PLANNING

As I see it, there are six points to consider in planning food for the trip. They are nutrition, keeping qualities, personal preferences, space constraints, the actual cooking, and cost. While some count more than others, all are important. Again, here's an area where individual styles come into play. Let's look at each in turn.

NUTRITION

The body, like a machine, needs fueling to function properly. While there is a wide range and varying amount of nutrients — protein, carbohydrates, vitamins, minerals, et cetera — that the body needs and uses, I am going to limit our attention to only three nutrient categories. After all, most people seldom take a canoe trip of longer than two weeks, so careful planning for those three categories will pretty much pull in foods that generally will satisfy the other needs.

The three categories are caloric requirements, carbohydrates and protein. The concern with calories has to do with the overall fuel content. Any food that the body burns gives off heat, or energy. Some foods are more efficient heat (energy) producers than others. Out in the wilderness, you will be exerting anywhere from a fair amount of effort to a downright working your tail off. This is entirely up to you, your party and weather conditions.

There is a simple formula for determining an approximate basic caloric intake need: just multiply your weight by sixteen for the number of calories needed to maintain a fairly active level. The level of activity put forth by a teacher or a mother of small children (not to mention the level of the kids themselves) is considered a moderately active level. If your activity level is highly physical, then change the multiplier to twenty. It is possible to gain weight on a canoe trip. Canoeing in itself does not have to be a terribly strenuous activity, though there are exceptions; a stiff head wind can call for a fairly high level of exertion, as can poling through a marshy or very shallow area. Cool or wet weather demands more energy. Portaging can take considerable effort; this is particularly true if a given portage is rather demanding, and especially if you are double-portaging. Being busy in all that fresh air certainly stimulates the appetite. We have noted on some of our longer, more rigorous trips, though, that as our bodies really got into the routines, our metabolisms became more efficient, and we didn't get as hungry or eat as much.

Actually, most of the caloric requirements can be met by simply planning to satisfy the protein and carbohydrate needs. The place where it is the easiest to get a large number of calories, or hold down the intake, is in snacks. In our early years, when the children were in their pre-teen and teen years, growing rapidly, we happily feasted on Good Old Raisins and Peanuts (or gorp), and chocolate chips. A big handful of that tasted mighty good coming off a long portage or a windy lake. A big snack in the late morning and again in the mid-afternoon will offset a light lunch. However, in recent years, Friend Spouse and I have cut back to a few pieces of hard candy; a little treat is satisfying at the end of a portage. Also, we enjoy coming off a day's trip with a "wilderness daiquiri" and a handful of nuts or some small crackers. Since our lunch is usually little more than a big snack, I try to give Happy Hour some nutritional value as well.

We do need to take a look at the other two components — protein and carbohydrates. Protein is important because it is the material the body uses to keep itself well maintained. It consists of the essential amino acids, in different combinations, that repair damage, refurbish and generally maintain good muscle tone. To many people, protein means meat, and right off we're into some problems.

Now Americans by and large love meat, but including it in the menus of a canoeist presents a major problem, specifically, keeping quality. One answer is to move away from the use of meat and toward other protein sources, such as eggs, milk and milk products, nuts and seeds, legumes and grains. My favorite way to replace red meat is to go out, terrorize the walleyes, and dine on fresh fish. We find that freshly-caught fish once a day is highly tolerable.

But there are other protein foods. For instance, I personally like the various freeze-dried omelet mixtures. A useful assortment — Denver omelets or western omelets or scrambled eggs with bacon — is readily available. Served with crisp cinnamon toast and stewed dried fruit, eggs can make breakfast the best meal of the day. Actually, with a hard plastic egg "suitcase" or even with the usual egg carton, one could take fresh eggs on a week's trip. (More on carrying eggs later.) We don't, primarily because of space constraints. (More on that, too!) Some speak highly of textured vegetable protein (TVP) as a meat substitute. I'd say try it out at home first. Creamettes is one regional brand offering TVP products.

Dairy foods offer several excellent alternatives for protein, though in actual practice many of the dairy foods are hidden. But it doesn't matter whether you see them or not, so long as they are there. Cheese occupies a major spot in my meal planning. Snack packages of cheese and crackers are wonderfully convenient for lunches. Cheese spreads, whether in squeeze packages or small plastic cartons, are marvelous for lunches, and they come in a variety of flavors. The harder natural cheeses such as Mozzarella or Edam can stand wilderness travel rather nicely. As natural cheeses have a fairly high fat content and get greasy, it is important to package them well in a self-zipping plastic bag or otherwise tightly closing container. Mozzarella is more popular with persons concerned with reducing fat content, as it is lower in fat than several other natural cheeses. (Freezer-weight bags are wonderful for camping trips.) Cheese can be stirred into a dish while it cooks, or it can be eaten alongside the finished dish.

Another very useful dairy product is dried low-fat milk solids, or powdered milk. (A useful variant is dehydrated buttermilk.) The beauty of this product is its ability to be an ingredient in making your own baking mix or to mix with the various dehydrated potato products available or to make your own granola. In any of these instances it is no problem to double the amount of milk powder called for and so get twice the nutrient. Calories, too, for extra energy. Dairy foods in combination with certain plant foods complement each other and produce the necessary complete proteins.

Nuts and seeds, particularly cashews, peanuts, black walnuts, sesame and sunflower seeds, also are good protein sources, and particularly so in certain food combinations. One obvious useful item in this category is faithful old standby, peanut butter. (Pack it in a plastic container with a good screw-on lid; you'll regret using a container with a lift-off lid.) Generally, however, the use of nuts and seeds is more apt to occur in snacks and their protein value should be considered when snacks are under consideration. Almonds, pecans and walnuts make fine additions to the baking supplies. Splurge a bit on special goodies such as cashews or pistachios for a special luxurious touch. That will add a bit of elegance while roughing it!

Legumes, peas and the wide range of beans are generally impractical on a camping trip. Most of them require too long a time to cook. Exceptions to the long cooking time include green and yellow split peas and lentils. I prefer to have total cooking time under 20 minutes at most. It's not all that much fun constantly feeding or poking a fire to maintain the desired level for cooking. Likewise when using a camp stove, I prefer short cooking times. I also don't like to have to plan for extended soaking times, either, preferring to keep any preliminary preparation under 15 minutes.

The final protein category is grains (grains are seeds, too), one not often considered, yet replete with possibilities. Wheat ranks highest in protein values, followed by rye and oats. With these come all sorts of options — pasta with cheese, peanut butter sandwiches, bulgur wheat cooked as a side dish, couscous, or oatmeal.

Corn and rice are also useful grains, though with lower protein value. Corn needs legumes to provide complete proteins, and as I mentioned earlier, beans require long cooking. (Corn tortillas and beans are an ancient combination and highly nutritious.) Treating corn with lye converts its protein into accessible form. This is the secret behind the corn in tortillas and hominy. Corn in the form of hominy grits (the instant variety is convenient) is however a practical choice. Grits can be eaten as a cereal with milk, or cooked with garlic and mixed with cheese for a tasty side dish.

Brown rice is nutritionally more valuable than white, but needs about three times as much time to cook. Technically, peanuts are a legume. Eating legumes and grains in combinations enhance the protein. Remember those old favorite bars of rice cereal and peanut butter? Nutritionally, they have a lot going for them.

Some grains are not included in my lists because they take too much cooking time. Pearled barley, for instance, takes about an hour to cook, much longer cooking time than I like to use on an outing.

This brings us up now to carbohydrates, that large group of complex molecules which supply energy and vitamins to the body. Carbohydrates come from the grains, legumes, nuts and seeds already spoken of, as well as from fruits and vegetables. For this reason, carefully chosen breads, crackers, cereals and pasta can do double duty in supplying both desired protein and the carbohydrates needed for the body to do its work.

Pastas are wonderful for camping trips. Their dried forms have excellent keeping qualities. They come in a variety of sizes and shapes, with the flat forms (spaghetti, linguini, fettucini and similar egg noodles) taking up less space. The visually more interesting shells, rotini and the like, hold or attract more sauce. You might like to include the various specialty seasoned pastas — spinach or tomato — besides the traditional paste. Nutritionally, they are all about even.

Add an assortment of dried fruits and dried vegetables and you have the makings of an adequate basic diet. I will elaborate a little later on in this chapter when I discuss food shopping, and that section will include some specific suggestions.

Protein provides staying power; carbohydrates provide energy, and because they are bulky, you feel you've had a meal when you are done.

People nowadays are concerned about fat consumption. Some fat is pleasant, since it carries flavor and provides long-lasting energy; take some butter or margarine, and oil, and goodies like chocolate chips, if you like. Products like Butter Buds are formulated to provide the flavor of butter without the fat. Fortunately, deep-fat frying is generally impractical for wilderness cooking. The nuts and seeds also provide some fat. With all these, as you may suspect, the calories come naturally.

KEEPING QUALITIES

Fresh meat is, to my mind, impractical, at least at this technological point. Summer in the North Woods is too warm for keeping fresh meat safely. (This isn't the only reason for not carrying fresh meat.) There are, however, some dry salamis such as a San Francisco-style that is very good, as is summer sausage, and some of the smoked beef logs or sticks or jerky are safe for short periods of time. I have taken vacuum-packed packages of meat (such as dried beef or Canadian bacon) for use in the early part of a trip, though I am not totally comfortable about doing it if the temperature turns hot. We have encountered people in the BWCA who apparently were carrying ham, hot dogs and the like. Seeing kids carrying unrefrigerated wieners for three or more days gives me the shudders. This is most unwise for several reasons. During the summer months, meats should be kept cold, and it is not only quite difficult to carry enough ice, even in a well-insulated box, it is a pain. A second problem with fresh meat is the possibility of it being an open invitation to bears, which could lead to an abruptly terminated trip. And that's no fun!

We do, though, freeze meat for use in our first night's meal; it's completely thawed by the time we are ready to prepare dinner. We never carry fresh meat for any meal other than for the first night.

The problem of keeping things cool applies to fruits and vegetables. Summer temperatures tend to ripen fruit rapidly, and many vegetables go unpalatably limp. So the Elegant Camper chooses foods that survive well at prevailing temperatures.

Some people feel deprived if they don't have eggs for breakfast, and they mean fresh eggs. This presents a couple of problems. One that I suspect is relatively minor (that is, infrequent) is the risk of salmonella developing in unrefrigerated eggs. The squeamish on this point of course can skip eggs. Fresh eggs can be sealed either by dipping in melted paraffin or by coating them with a sodium silicate (water glass) solution. (You get the stuff from a pharmacist; at one time it was a fairly common means of preserving eggs.) They can then be packed in a rigid carton. One veteran camper uses a #10 can and packs the eggs in sawdust that can then be used as fire-starting material.

Egg shell disposal is a problem. The shells don't burn well. At home, for years now I have thoroughly crushed empty egg shells and tossed them out in the back yard. The critters, birds particularly, pick them up. Calcium is a valuable mineral for creatures, and I suspect that small pieces would not last long. (I don't know what effect wax or water glass would have on the critters if consumed.) If you must have fresh eggs, be sure to dispose of the shells; either burn them completely or crush the shells fine and scatter them well away from the camp site.

Dried foods are dependable. Many freeze-dried meats and meat-dish combinations are available. Some are better than others. One thing we have found is that the stated re-constitution time on meat items is always a good bit shorter than needed for the meat to acquire a reasonable texture. We are not particularly fond of any of the freeze-dried meats, though others may find any or all quite acceptable.

Commercially prepared trail food comes in set portions, both an advantage and a disadvantage. Sometimes the portions are too large (way too large!) and sometimes not quite large enough. Unless you have used the product before, you have no sure way of gauging. It is useful to keep a list of what you buy, the brand name, dish, number of servings it provides, and record your opinion of it. Do this as soon as you possibly can, before you forget. (A log book such as *The Paddler's Planner* is a handy place to keep this information.)

I have watched with interest and have sampled the new vacuum-packed products whose packaging renders them shelf-stable. Several companies have introduced a line of entrees suitable for heating by microwave or by boiling water immersion. We took a couple of them on a trip, even though being essentially table-ready means they are heavy. There are times when the disadvantage of the extra weight is offset by the pleasure the food item itself produces. If you like it at home, you'll love it on the trail.

PERSONAL PREFERENCES

Obviously, about now, the third major consideration, personal preferences, has emerged. A willingness to experiment is helpful. I have found that we like dried fruits better than most of the available dried vegetables. Some of the freeze-dried meats are not particularly appealing. However, the possibilities for interesting and tasty meals are fairly wide. Later on I'll give more details to use in planning meals. But it is important to pay careful attention to preferences and particularly to learn what is not acceptable. Garbage disposal can be a bit of a problem if there is any great quantity. In fact, BWCA regulations specify that garbage be buried quite some distance back from the lake shore. The Canadian parks have similar regulations.

SPACE CONSTRAINTS

Portability is important. Look with an extremely critical eye to see if what is being proposed is really desirable. We could carry fresh eggs in an "egg suitcase." But the suitcase is bulky, and after the eggs are used, it is useless bulk. Dehydrated eggs are quite acceptable, so we carry them rather than the fresh. However that is a matter of taste, and we're back to the point of each camper's own value judgment of what matters. The question one should keep in mind is "How are we going to carry all that stuff?" because it affects weight and space in the camping packs. Again, I recommend against quantities of fresh produce; they are simply too bulky and heavy. We have found that a week's worth of food for the two of us may weigh at least 30 pounds.

COOKING

I prefer to be able to start meal preparations and have the food ready to eat in under 45 minutes, and actually closer to 30 minutes. Also, in planning meals, think about how many pots you will have with you and how many you will need for fixing a given meal. It is all too easy to plan an elaborate, so to speak, meal, and then realize you don't have the equipment to carry through.

Our camp kit consists of one large (8-quart) kettle, two smaller pots, a fry pan, the lid to the large kettle that can double as a fry pan, and the coffee pot. (I don't always take all these anymore.) This generally means at most four vessels, plus maybe a cup, for preparing and cooking. Don't forget that very often you have to mix or hydrate something before cooking, and that unless you are using a heavy plastic bag, that pot is thus out of cooking use. Don't forget about the length of cooking time, either, when planning meals. You may not want to spend forty minutes keeping an eye on the fire to bake something in the coals. If you are relying on a camp stove, short cooking times are very important, as you consider the amount of fuel brought along. Further discussion is coming later in this chapter and in Chapter 6 Skills, Techniques and Tricks.

COST

A final consideration, and no minor one, is what is this going to cost? Generally, you will find that it will cost a little more than what it costs to prepare meals at home and less than to eat out. You can, if you wish, spend a little more on some luxury-type items, such as cashews or pistachios or the fancier dried fruits. The demands and rigor of the wilderness are mitigated if you take a few choice tidbits that you might not ordinarily buy. In the long run, I give less consideration to cost than I do to preferences or portability. Since I do most of the buying at my usual supermarket, I keep the costs relatively low. But this again is a highly individual matter.

FOOD SHOPPING

While we are talking food choices, we should also talk abut source of supply. When we first started our wilderness camping back in the early 1970s, we bought all of our trail food at camping supply stores because they were the only places that carried dehydrated foods. That has changed, and I have found that my favorite supermarket carries a large number of items that are marvelous or suitable for wilderness camping.

A wide assortment of breads or breadstuffs, crackers or basic cookies is available. You can use pilot biscuit (a very dense cracker-like item, similar to what Civil War soldiers knew as hardtack), Ry-Krisp or Wasa Brod, "fancy" salad crackers such as Euphrates or Tucks, bread sticks, whole wheat or stoned wheat crackers. Breakfast breads can include cinnamon toast (not always available), zwieback or rusks. One really nifty item is the Italian "dunking cookie" or biscotto. Almost as hard as rocks, biscotti are tough items, superb for the rigors of camp packing. They are meant for dunking in coffee or hot chocolate, a pleasant and elegant breakfast item. In a good supermarket you can find biscotti in several variations — with almonds, for instance, or chocolate chips.

Because crackers or pilot bread can get pretty boring, I like to have an assortment of breadstuffs for our trips. We enjoy the different textures. Having a good assortment gives contrast to the softness of many reconstituted camping meals.

For the first few days out, it is feasible to use English muffins, tortillas or pita (Near Eastern pocket bread), or even ordinary loaf bread. I think the latter items lose some palatability after a couple of days out. The loaf bread is fine, if you are willing and able to pack it in such a way that it won't get all squashed. Personally, I think it is too bulky for what it offers. The drier bread stuffs likewise need a certain amount of protection from external pressure (it is a rare trip when it has not been necessary for at least one person to crawl over the food pack). Unless the breads are quite sturdy and well protected, they wind up as crumbs. So often, the original packaging was flimsy.

Don't overlook old standbys like graham crackers or vanilla wafers for other meals or snacks.

It is easy to pack some jelly or marmalade into a small plastic jar for your breakfast pleasure. We like the spreadable fruits that have come on the market in recent years. Generally, they have no added sugar in their ingredients, with the sweetening coming from added fruit juices. For pancakes or French toast, these are easier to deal with than syrup.

Commercial baking-mixes, such as Bisquick, are versatile and convenient. You can also find cornbread mixes which are good. The Jiffy brand packs a small box that makes enough for two or three people. You can make your own; I'll give you recipes.

Cereals can be either the individual packs of cold cereal, or granolas, or you can choose from several cooked cereal types — oatmeal, Cream of Wheat, Roman Meal — whatever looks interesting. You can package individual portions, or portions for whatever number you need for a particular meal. The Kashi Company produces a product they call Kashi, the Breakfast Pilaf. Containing oats, brown rice, rye, wheat, triticale, buckwheat, barley and sesame seeds, it is an interesting and highly nutritious dish, suitable for breakfast or dinner, but it takes 25 minutes of cooking time after the water comes to a boil. However, you can bring the liquid and the grains to a rolling boil for 5 minutes, then remove from heat and cover tightly. After warming up in the morning, it will be ready for breakfast. I think it needs a bit of salt either while cooking or immediately after, and nuts or dried fruits added while warming give it pizzazz. Then serve with milk and brown sugar, as desired. One packet makes 3-4 servings.

Pastas come immediately to mind, and this is a rich area. You can pick spaghetti, macaroni, noodles — any of the specialty pastas, "bare" or in prepared meal combinations. Ramen, those oriental noodles with their own dry soup stock, are handy and quite tasty. Lipton, for one, makes an assortment of noodle and sauce dishes. There are several Italian brands that have appeared in camping equipment stores as well as supermarkets, Amare and Vigo being two, of dehydrated raviolini and tortellini (tomato, egg and spinach pasta), cheese-filled and requiring no refrigeration. A seven ounce package serves two. We have eaten them at home and find them quite tasty. This is a sort of acid test for trail food: if it tastes good at home, it will taste good in camp. The converse is not necessarily the case. Often, the prepared trail food is too salty for our taste.

If you are thinking about protein needs, a basic difference between macaroni and spaghetti is that macaroni does not contain egg, but spaghetti does. You will find that some pastas list egg as an ingredient; this is an enrichment, and for camping purposes, a plus. Quick-cooking rice works well as a protein source.

Sometimes, in larger supermarkets, you can find products along the line of the Black Bean Chili (from Taste Adventure). It is packaged in a 5½-ounce container much like a 1-pint milk carton, and makes two good servings. It cooks in 10 minutes, and can be dressed up with chopped onions, grated cheese or bell pepper. Other trimmings can be added according to your camp larder.

Several companies make packaged casserole-type meals that work well for camping. (Kraft calls theirs A La Carte.) These are meals for one, containing a foil packet of a sauce-based dish such as sweet and sour pork or chicken tetrazzini (there are others) and a mesh packet of rice or noodles, depending on the main dish. Both are "boiled in the bag," making it possible for one cooking pot of boiling water to heat meals for two or three people, depending on how big the pot and whether you are preparing four or six packets. We have tried these at home and rate them "not bad."

One disadvantage is that since the main dish has only to be heated and not reconstituted, obviously it is carrying its own water. The weight of a meal runs about 9½ ounces, not unreasonable, but if you were preparing for several meals for several people, the weight would mount up. The Beef Stew in one line comes in an 8½-ounce package and is a bit skimpy for one serving. At 230 calories, it needs company for a trail meal. (Remember, we were talking about a need of over 3,000 calories a day.) Again, this is where individual preferences must be considered. What with the additional possibilities offered, such complete main dishes are not a bad way to go, if they don't have to go alone.

Hormel, among others, also has come up with a line of Meals Ready to Eat (Top Shelf is their brand) that need only to be heated for serving. The packaging is designed for a microwave oven, but can go into boiling water. Like Kraft's A La Carte line, a single serving provides about 250 calories, which is rather meager for a hard day's work. Del Monte has Vegetable Classics, which could be used. Purportedly, the 9½ ounce package will make three servings. Not on a camping trip it won't! The package calls for 20 minutes heating in boiling water. The tray the vegetables are packaged in is recycled paper, as opposed to the plastic microwave dish from Top Shelf. If the pot were big enough, several packages could be heated at the same time.

Potatoes take well to freeze-drying. You can find scalloped potatoes, au gratin potatoes, instant mashed potatoes, or hash browned. I have found that they work very well for the open fire cook. I'll talk about variations in the section on Recipes. One could even convert some of them into a tasty soup, though to my mind, soup is impractical. The usual camp kit does not carry bowls. Consequently, if you really wanted soup, you would need to carry bowls or extra cups or do without a drinking cup. For that matter, the same objection applies to cereals, unless you like them very thick. I do generally carry some bouillon cubes or envelopes for a quick pickup if the day has been chilly and the paddling tough. That's one of those situations where the camp stove proves its worth.

If you happen to be fond of soups, there is a fairly good selection of instant soups, other than simple bouillons, available.

A vegetarian-type main dish is falafel, a Middle-Eastern mixture of dried chick peas and seasonings. It is reconstituted (give it a little extra time to soak), shaped into patties and fried quickly. Several brands are available. I suggest trying them out at home before you take them to the woods. Along the same line are various pilafs — mixtures of rice and vegetables. I found a wonderful one of instant wild rice and vegetables at my favorite supermarket. Some take a longer time to cook than others; check the labels for cooking time first.

Since we don't cook at midday, lunch items include packaged cheese and crackers or peanut butter and crackers that are great for a traveling lunch. We usually eat two apiece; you might want more. Dried beef such as jerky, or the packaged Slim Jims work well for individual lunches. I am particularly partial to convenient lunches: the above mentioned packets, or a hunk of cheese and a package of crackers, or San Francisco-style dry salami. Also very handy is a package of squeeze-cheese — one of those will make a good lunch for the two of us. Several flavors — hickory smoke, garlic or bacon — are available. String, or mozzarella, cheese is marvelous, and it comes in two and four ounce packages. Another excellent possibility is the cold-pack cheese food such as Woody's or Kaukauna Club. The main reason these cheeses are refrigerated is to prevent or retard the formation of mold. Since Friend Spouse and I can polish off one 8-ounce carton in two meals, mold doesn't get much of a chance.

In the gourmet foods section of my favorite supermarket, I have discovered concentrated tomato paste in a tube, a French product. It does not need refrigeration after opening and has excellent flavor. It opens up several additional possibilities in meal preparation.

If you simply must have bacon, cook it ahead of time and package it securely. Sometimes you can find packaged cooked bacon. Or use bacon substitutes such as Bac-Os.

Generally, I find the supermarket has a fine selection of dried fruits — apricots, figs, dates, banana slices, cherries, cranraisins (dried cranberries), peaches, apples, pears, pineapple (delectable if you happen to find it), prunes, raisins both golden and black, and packaged combinations. These can be used as a snack or a course in the meal. I usually take along small packets of spices such as nutmeg and cinnamon, with lemon peel, for flavoring. With some fruits, I repackage and include whatever flavorings I want with them, such as dried apples with cinnamon, lemon peel and a little brown sugar. I sometimes prepare the makings of a graham cracker crust, divide into two portions (since Friend Spouse and I are usually the group), package it and put it with some dried apples or peaches. Be clear on this: do not put the crumbs with the fruit before you cook it. Cook the fruit first, then put it either over the crust or under it — whatever pleases you. Remember, it is nutritionally quite acceptable to serve a fruit dish instead of a vegetable. Many of what we consider vegetables are actually the fruits or seed-producing portions of the plant. (Tomatoes, technically a fruit, were declared vegetables for tariff purposes.) I should also mention that health food stores also offer delectable dried fruit or other nibbling goodies.

Grocery stores, as a rule, have much poorer offerings in the way of vegetables. I have on occasion found dried peas and mushrooms which were quite acceptable. I have found two types of dried corn: one was apparently a freeze-dried sweet corn (not bad!) and the other more like a sun-dried, old-style corn. The latter requires rather lengthy soaking (up to an hour), except for one recipe where the corn was coarsely ground in a blender, then baked for an hour in a casserole. It shows some promise with other techniques. The black Chinese mushrooms with their distinctive taste are an expensive, but pleasant, fancy touch.

Another useful source of supply of good freeze-dried food that may be available to you is the local consumer co-op. Minnesota has a great many of them, but they are by no means universal. It is worthwhile to check out your area for one. Likewise, there is a number of freeze-dried vegetables offered in the camping foods section of outfitters.

Sweets or snack items are plentiful: there are several kinds of granola and milk bars which are handy for lunch desserts. A small pound cake travels well and you can make a delightful little dessert fondue by serving it with chocolate sauce or syrup. Cookies offer great convenience, and for a special touch, try biscotti, those (ahem) durable Italian cookies made for dunking. Then of course there are numerous brownie and coffee cake mixes. Unless you want to go to the bother of carrying fresh eggs, plan to omit them in any of the mixes. As a rule, they won't really be missed. One thing our kids liked to make was make Skillet Brownies. (See Skillet Brownies in the Recipes.) This means you mix the required amount of water in the brownie mix, then turn it into a fry pan (preferably one of the non-stick variety, and cook it over the fire, stirring fairly constantly until the whole mess turns nice and fudgy. One package was worlds for six people. The snacking cake mixes work very nicely for a breakfast coffee cake. One problem with many of these mixes is that a package makes too much for two people.

Instant puddings will work using reconstituted dry milk, though they may not get as firm as with fresh milk. As with the cake mixes, a package makes too much for two. I got around the problem with lemon pudding by simply not using all of it for dessert. I later used the remainder by stirring it in for a thickener with some cooked dried peaches (see Recipes).

Jello will set at temperatures as high as 62°, but it will take more than 3 hours to do it. It can make a fairly pleasant drink. Gelatin desserts that are tasty and set very quickly at ambient temperatures are available from camping food producers. In the Appendix, see Resources — Camp Foods.

Cocoa mixes (there are many available) can be mixed with powdered milk, packaged and mixed with water as needed. You can find an assortment of powdered fruit-flavored drinks, such as Tang, or the newer lemonade drinks. Again, watch the nutritional values: you may have grown up on Kool-aid, but it doesn't offer much. Along that line, recent years have seen a big push toward using artificial sweeteners in drinks for camp. I'm not sure that is really the best idea, and in emergency situations (such as dealing with hypothermia), artificially sweetened drinks simply cannot do the job of providing immediate energy.

Recently there has been a fairly heavy marketing push for fruit-type drinks, ready to use in individual paper cartons. I haven't tried them for taste. They look appealing. A major disadvantage that I see for the canoeist is that old problem of bulk and weight. I might consider them for a weekend trip with a small party. I would not consider them for a 3-day trip for four people.

You can find a number of pleasant instant coffee drink mixes, as well as the plain instant coffee. I have been delighted to find coffee packaged in bags like tea. Tea bags are convenient and a wide variety of flavored or specialty teas is available. Don't forget the possibility of instant tea, either plain or pre-flavored with sugar and lemon.

Finally, for nibbling, check out the varieties of nuts available, or goodies like yogurt-covered raisins or nuts, corn and soy nuts. Fruit leather is also great for traveling lunches. One of my favorite items is a Cotlet or Aplet bar. Individually wrapped hard candies are appealing.

All in all, a good grocery store offers excellent possibilities for camp meals. You should consider certain trade-offs, however. As a rule, the specialty outdoors store will offer a greater variety of packaged main dishes — a greater variety of packaged everything, for that matter. The food quantity is predetermined; your decision is whether to get the package for two or four, or whatever. The packaging is tough, virtually indestructible. Then all you have to do is pack that into the old food pack. Generally, it is more expensive, and you can get a mild shock at the total if you buy it all there. You can save money by buying conventional items, but then you may find that you spend a good bit of time repackaging it into desired quantities. This again is a personal choice. We wind up doing some of both. I always buy freeze-dried eggs, but I make my own baking mix. For the two of us, I may divide a package of hash-browned potatoes, add some dehydrated onion, the proper amount of salt and pepper, and some dried milk to each portion, write the cooking time and amount of water to be used on a plastic bag, and package the works.

In fact, we rely more on grocery offerings than on commercial trail food. We think the taste is superior, with less salt. It must be said, though, that the quality and taste of trail foods are much better, with more interesting items, than they were some years ago. What's more, I am finding that the camping stores are offering more items that formerly were strictly in the grocery store's province. If the trip you are planning is fairly rigorous, you may prefer the simplicity of the ready-prepared trail foods. Again, it is a matter of personal choice, time, convenience, and willingness to try. The point is that the absence of refrigeration need not hamper you. It takes some imagination, open-mindedness and effort, but one can eat quite decently on a camping trip.

FOOD PACKING

There are two stages to organizing the Food pack, and of the two, the meal planning is more critical. The key is to make lists, check and review them. A written list is invaluable in assuring that you haven't forgotten anything. Save those lists for future trips, too.

In the old days, when my daughters and I used to come back from our expedition shopping trips, we would lay out the food packets on the floor, usually with the dinners first. We would then play "shuffle and deal," putting breakfasts and lunches and dinners together in a general attempt to make each day's meals fairly equal over all. That is, if the morning meal looked rather light, then we could put in heartier or more numerous snacks. Then all three meals, plus snacks, went into a single bag, so that we wound up with the number of bags equal to the number of days we were planning to be out. It was then an easy matter just to pluck up a bag and everything was there.

We also counted the evening meal, dinner, as the first meal of a bag. After breakfast, all one needed to do was to remember to put in drinking cups and maybe a knife for cutting salami or spreading cheese or peanut butter or whatever into the bag, and lunch was ready for stowing at the top of the Day pack, or whatever was the most convenient spot for easy grabbing.

I would recommend packing each day's food together especially if your party has more than four or five people or if you aren't terribly sure of pulling together a meal out in the woods. Planning does take a great deal of the uncertainty out of meal preparation, and as a result, it is much easier to feel elegant about it.

One very important point to consider in this matter of planning a meal: Keep in mind the number of pots you have available for meal preparation, and how many you will need for fixing a given meal. It is all too easy to plan an elaborate, so to speak, meal, and then realize you don't have the equipment to carry through.

The other phase of organizing the pack is of course stowing all the meals along with the staples and incidental items. I have used the round oatmeal or cornmeal cartons to hold things like the package of coffee, the seasonings (salt, pepper, lemon juice, bouillon cubes, other spices, etc.) or other such items. Label the lids. The cartons travel very well stacked inside the box liner. Common sense should prevail in packing the Food pack. You can easily put the meals you expect to use late in the trip to the very bottom of the pack. I find that it makes a lot of sense for me to put the baking mix, the oil and margarine (and the rum) toward the top, as those are items I use every day.

There is always repacking, and you'll find that you develop your own procedures, based on the kind and extent of cooking you do. The guiding principle should be to keep it as convenient as possible.

MENU SUGGESTIONS

BREAKFASTS

Now, let's get down to cases and talk about meals.

Breakfasts are generally the best meals. They offer a lot of possibilities for variety, depending on how much trouble you're willing to go to, how much time you have in the morning, and how many pans you have available.

Let's start simple and work up. Put a pot of water on to boil for coffee or tea or hot cocoa mix. Several years ago we started carrying a one-burner Coleman stove and have never begrudged the weight. With it, we could have coffee almost ready by the time the fire in the fire pit is built. Also, we use it for cooking a quick breakfast, with a very easy clean-up. It is also convenient when one is faced with rain and difficulties in getting a breakfast fire going. At any rate, with it, hot water is ready fairly quickly.

For a cold, quick breakfast, how about granola with reconstituted dry milk? For that matter, you could take individual packages of your favorite dry cereal. Packaged breakfast bars such as Pop-tarts really minimize the clean-up.

I must admit such breakfasts do not really appeal to me; I like breakfast! But the Elegant Camper knows that it is shrewd planning to have the makings for one cold breakfast as emergency rations, especially on a trip of five or more days. After all, elegance comes with being able to cope gracefully. (On one trip, the weather was such that cooking a supper did not appeal to me. We wound up having Pop-tarts and coffee in the tent. I then realized the usefulness of having an emergency evening meal, too.)

That said, let's talk about breakfasts that can be more interesting. You can heat more water, or use some that heated earlier for drinks, and cook oatmeal or some other whole grain cereal such as Roman Meal or grits. Couscous also makes an interesting breakfast cereal. This is a good time to use instant-type cereals for their shorter cooking time. If you like a really hearty, one-pot breakfast, throw in some raisins and some nuts, such as almonds, pecans, walnuts or peanuts. Add a sprinkling of cinnamon sugar and a dollop of butter or margarine (a good spot for the butter sprinkle products). Add the dry milk, reconstituted or not, as you wish, and you have a tasty dish that provides proteins, minerals, complex carbohydrates and enough energy-producing calories.

That is a simple, one-pot breakfast. A more elaborate meal could consist of eggs, fruit and toast. Sometimes I like to cook a package of dried fruit the night before, use part of it for dinner and leave the rest for breakfast, which gives the fruit time to soak up the cooking water and "strengthen" the juice. Serve the juice in a cup in the morning and use the pot to hydrate the eggs. Packaged bread such as a cinnamon toast or Holland rusk eliminates the need for a third cooking pan and makes a pleasing texture addition to the meal. And texture, what the food chemists call mouth appeal, is important.

Pancakes are a popular camping breakfast. I don't mind making pancakes for two over a camp stove, but I would hate dreadfully to have to cook for several people that way. Our family doesn't particularly like maple flavor, so we dress our cakes with jelly or marmalade. However, an old friend who is a thoroughly veteran camper tells me he uses an imitation maple flavor product called Mapleine (Schilling also has one) he swears by. He takes the Mapleine and the necessary sugar packaged and makes up the desired quantity on the spot. It has the advantages of being inexpensive, easy to prepare, controlled (your decision) quantities, and to the cook's personal taste. Prices vary widely on the two products mentioned; I suspect it is rather like the bouillons — there are variations and you go with the taste you like.

But to my mind, the best breakfast of all has walleye (pickerel, the Canadians call it) as the entrée. A freshly caught walleye, rolled in baking mix and quickly fried in a mixture of oil and margarine, is superb. With that, I like to cook bread. I use the trusty baking mix, add a little more water than I would if I were making biscuits, and pour the mixture into a heated, well greased (and I mean well greased — use margarine) skillet, and smooth more melted margarine over the top of the dough. Then, covered with foil, it bakes over a slower part of the campfire. With cooked dried apricots, the bread and fish make a most satisfying meal.

Here is a series of meals for a trip of 7 days. Please understand that these are suggestions — combinations that we have used and liked. Obviously substitutions can be made from the possibilities described earlier in this chapter. Likewise, a person should never count on catching fish to provide a meal; the suggestion here is what to have with it if the catching is good.

Day 1:

Scrambled eggs with bacon (commercial trail food)
Cinnamon toast or muffins (home-baked or bakery)
Cooked fruit
Beverage of choice — Coffee or tea or cocoa, whatever

Day 2:

Pancakes with jelly or marmalade
Fruit juice (we generally prefer to have juice as a snack later)
Beverage of choice

Day 3:

Scrambled eggs
Hash browned potatoes
Beverage of choice

Day 4:

Omelet (several varieties are available)
English muffins, jelly
Beverage of choice

Day 5:

Coffee cake, made with nuts and dried cherries
Cooked fruit
Beverage of choice

Day 6:

Oatmeal with raisins and walnuts (or couscous)
Beverage of choice

Day 7: (a cold breakfast)
Granola and milk (or Pop tarts)
Beverage of choice

LUNCHES

As I mentioned earlier, lunch is more of a rest stop with food than a regular meal. No cooking is involved, and the food itself is tucked into the day pack for easy accessibility. Implements for lunch may be only a spreader and a pocket knife.

Day 1:

San Francisco-type dry salami
Stoned wheat crackers
Fruit leather
Drink

Day 2:

Snack packages of cheese and cracker
Brownie bars or cookies
Drink

Day 3:

Snack packages of peanut butter, crackers
Granola bars
Drink

Day 4:

Beef jerky or Slim Jims
Euphrates crackers
Fruit bars (such as Aplets or Cotlets)
Drink

Day 5:

Smoke-flavored squeeze cheese (comes in tubes)
Pita
Chocolate bars
Drink

Day 6:

    Hard cheese (e.g., Colby, Edam, Gouda, mozzarella or cheddar)
    Rye-Krisp or Wasa Brod crackers
    Dried fruit, such as apple slices or apricots
    Drink

Day 7:

    Squeeze cheese (cheddar flavor)
    Pilot biscuits
    Fruit leather
    Drink

Other items that work well are the following:

    Breton crackers, cheddar cheese spread, banana chips
    Crackers & cashew butter, Cotlets
    Banana bread with cheese, smoked almonds, hot lemonade
    Breton crackers with cashew butter, halvah

DINNERS

Dinner is a big meal, and is usually the most leisurely. With the following menus, I am suggesting possibilities and I include commercially prepared camp food, supermarket finds, and some recipe items. As with lunch, the drink depends on group choice. When our children went with us, the beverage was commonly a fruit drink, as none of them liked reconstituted dry milk. We drink coffee; others may prefer tea.

When we go up to the BWCA, where we know we will be camping that night, our first night's meal out generally includes fresh stuff — the sort of things that will tolerate a few hours (the length of the drive) in the cooler, but no more. Meat is packed frozen; by time for dinner it has thawed sufficiently. I have prepared ahead vegetables such as carrots, onions and potatoes to cook with the fresh meat. A pasta salad dressed with oil and vinegar works well, but avoid any mayonnaise sort of dressing.

There are several ways one can prepare boned chicken breasts or legs and thighs. Sauté them quickly in a little oil and margarine. You can then add some water, sliced carrots and onions that have been prepared ahead, bring to a boil, and top with some dumpling mix. Cover, let cook, and you have a tasty one-pot meal. Or you can roll them in a bit of baking mix and sauté them.

I have made beef kabobs on bamboo skewers (that are easily disposed of), which we pan-grilled. The grates are a little nasty for direct grilling. After they are done, de-glaze the pan with a little water, and you have instant gravy. (To de-glaze, put about a half cup of water in the pan, let boil briefly, stir to loosen particles. The pan is easier to wash, and the juice is tasty.) A pasta salad made with bow-tie pasta, blanched broccoli, cauliflower and carrots, onion and green pepper goes well with this. Pita or hard French rolls round out a simple meal, and cookies or pound cake top it off.

Friend Spouse loved the chicken breasts that had been boned and pounded flat and stuffed with cheese and herbs, then rolled in seasoned crumbs and quickly sautéed. (See the recipe in Recipes.)

Another well-received entree was a ham steak, about an inch thick, pan-broiled.

This first night meal can be as simple or as elaborate as you please, and of course it depends on your cooking facilities and when you plan to set up camp. We view it as a sort of celebration of the start of the trip, and I like to make it a bit special.

One last point on planning food for your trip. It is better to have more food than you need — extra meals, or items that can make an extra meal or two. Nothing says you must eat everything you take, and sometimes it happens that you need extra food. However, for a traveling trip, I prefer to plan a little tighter to keep down excess weight. Don't count on catching fish for meals, either. Consider that a bonus.

Day 1:

> Linguine al fresco
> Italian bread sticks
> Raisin bars
> Drink

Day 2:

> Scalloped potatoes with salami
> Green peas
> Skillet Brownies
> Drink

Day 3:

> Falafel
> Pita
> Peach cobbler
> Drink

Day 4:

> Macaroni and cheese
> Lemon pudding
> Drink

Day 5:

> Beef Stroganoff (commercial trail meal)
> Peas and carrots
> Butterscotch pudding
> Drink

Day 6:

> Chili Mac (commercial trail meal) and crackers
> Apple Streusel
> Drink

Day 7:

> Fresh fish
> Frybread
> Cooked apricots
> Drink

Day 8:

> Spaetzle with Gruyère cheese and onions
> Ocean Spray Fruit Relish
> Pound cake fondue

Other dinners have included shiitake mushrooms with bacon bits and onions (see Recipes), one-pot dishes by Uncle Ben and Rice-A-Roni, and Pepperidge Farms' Brussels Lace cookies. Ocean Spray produces Fruit Relish, which comes in several variations on a cranberry theme; while a bit heavy to carry, is full of flavor and great either for dinner or for breakfast. For an opening night, I have prepared and served Steak Diane, tabouli, hard rolls and a pound cake fondue.

Another easy item for a first-night dinner is boned chicken breasts marinated in a mixture of Heinz 57 sauce and honey and then sautéed.

SNACKS

> Smoked almonds
> Pistachios
> Cashew butter
> Hard candies
> Banana chips

BASIC EXTRAS

I commonly use in camp cooking or find convenient to have the following basic items. Useful quantities for our week-long trips are given.

Salt and pepper. You can buy combination salt and pepper containers for camp use or use film canisters . Mark the tops with nail polish to identify which is salt and which is pepper. You can buy salt and pepper packaged in small boxes and keep the boxes in a zip-locked plastic bag. Store them or salt and a small can of black pepper in with the camp gear. Consider including a bottle of Tabasco sauce or a small packet of cayenne pepper. You can store all this stuff in a cornmeal carton labeled "Seasonings" or in a larger zip-lock bag which makes it easy to lay hands on.

Camping equipment stores carry small caddys of assorted herbs and spices for camping. Check to decide whether their tastes agree with yours. Otherwise you just waste money and space.

Margarine. The basic quantity is at least a half pound; more often I take about one pound. I buy margarine in a plastic squeeze bottle, and that is really convenient. If I use the solid variety, I transfer it from the paper wrapper into a plastic jar (the kind that dehydrated onions come in holds just abut one pound, is sturdy and light to carry). I disregard the "keep refrigerated" label on these products, as the aim is to prevent rancidity. On a week's trip, there really isn't time for rancidity to develop. Some people prefer to use clarified butter, which is available through some camping equipment stores.

Oil. For a week's trip for the two of us, I usually take a pint of vegetable oil. If we plan to fish, I increase it to 1½ pints. Just because you have it doesn't mean that you will use all of it, but it is quite an inconvenience to run out. An alternative is ghee, or clarified butter. Its advantage is good keeping quality and the butter flavor. You can buy ghee at camping supply stores or you can prepare it yourself. It involves heating butter to a bubbly state. Carefully skim off and discard the foam that develops. Pour off the resulting oil (the ghee), and discard the milk solids that are left behind.

Butter flavor alternatives. Daughter Jean tipped me off to products such as Butter Buds™, an alternative to butter,which gives the flavor of butter without the fat. Use when you want butter flavor.

Baking Mix. I generally prepare a triple batch (see the Recipes section) or buy a box of Bisquick.

Cinnamon sugar. I carry a 2-ounce jar for making coffee cake or flavoring dried fruit. The precise ratio of sugar to cinnamon is a matter of personal taste. Start with $1/4$ cup of sugar, mix in 1 teaspoon of cinnamon, and test it out by making yourself a piece of cinnamon toast. Add more sugar or more cinnamon as desired.

Coffee. Skip this if you don't have coffee drinkers in your group. Here I am talking about "real" or ground coffee, not instant, which I detest. The precise way to do this is to figure how much coffee per day will be wanted. (The approach is the same for instant.) I plan on making a 4-cup pot for breakfast and another for dinner. This pours as five actual cups. Figure how much coffee you use to make an equivalent amount and multiply that by the number of days you plan to be out. Then, just to be on the safe side, add another half cup of ground coffee. Package in heavy-duty zip-locked bags. For our usual 7-day trip, I take about 3 cups of ground coffee. If you can find individually packaged coffee bags, they are a wonderful solution, precise and tidy, and you don't have "chewy" coffee.

Tea. While we aren't tea drinkers, I usually carry a few tea bags. Tea drinkers can calculate how much they heed to carry by much the same procedure as figuring the coffee needs.

Juice powder. This used to be Wyler's province and Wyler's alone. Now there is a wide assortment of lemonade and fruit drink mixes, complete with their own measuring scoop. We can easily use an entire 30-ounce can in a week; we frequently run short. Thirty ounces makes only 5 quarts, a fact easily overlooked when you are making a daily batch in a 2-quart canteen. (One reason we used so much lemonade was that it improved the taste of the water. A water purification unit with a charcoal filter removes the need for masking water taste.) If you are planning to make "wilderness daiquiris" regularly, you will definitely need to increase the quantity. Read the label for quantities and calculate accordingly. Transfer the contents of the can to plastic bags, and include the scoop. Be sure you know how much it measures. One year I made the mistake of simply opening the can, putting the plastic lid on it, and then putting it into the food pack. Disaster ensued. First the can lost its place in the pack and dumped part of its contents into the pack with a resulting mess. That was the year the bear got the pack and he took care of the remaining drink mix. Since then, I re-pack the crystals into a double bag and then maybe put that into a carton.

Dry milk. I carry about one cup of non-fat dry milk when I include dry cereal for a cold breakfast and instant pudding mix. This is of course a strictly optional item, since its use depends on what else is going along.

Corn meal. This is for fishing trips. I grew up in Oklahoma, where cornbread goes with fried fish and I like to mix a little cornmeal into the baking mix for corn bread, or to roll the fish in before frying. One cup is generally plenty.

Jelly. This could be preserves, jelly or marmalade, whatever the personal preference is. Get a 6- or 8-ounce jar and transfer the contents to a plastic jar. Jelly is easier to deal with on a camping trip than pancake syrup; the packaged syrup mixes are watery when prepared, and the quantity is always wrong for the amount of pancakes. Orange marmalade is wonderful with the frybread.

Bouillon cubes or packets. Bouillon is useful for seasoning or for a quick pick-me-up after a tough afternoon. One teaspoon instant or 1 cube plus 1 cup water will substitute for 1 cup stock. Bouillon brands differ somewhat in tastes: some include monosodium glutamate in their ingredients. Pick your favorite brand and flavor.

These are the standard items in our kit. There are other things that I throw in according to whatever notion strikes me. For instance, if I want to have a sort of cheesecake, I prepare a batch of graham cracker crumbs ready for the crust or top, whichever. Refer to Recipes for particulars.

You might want to include nuts for snacks or cooking. Pecans are a wonderful addition to a coffee cake; walnuts mix well with cooked fruit; cashews, pistachios or peanuts are great for nibbling. Raisins are great in a coffee cake. Pack these collectively in a cornmeal carton or self-zipping bag.

Tomato concentrate paste. This comes in a 4.5-ounce tube; a couple of tablespoons is roughly equivalent to the tomato in a half-cup of canned tomato paste.

Lemon juice. Get one of those juice-filled plastic lemons; you may already have one in the refrigerator. Lemon juice is an excellent flavoring agent for many foods.

Other spices. I make a small packet of "flavored sugar" with a bit of dehydrated lemon peel and nutmeg for flavoring dried peaches. Since I usually split a package of peaches for two people, I repackage with the flavorings with them.

If you happen to have some marshmallows on hand, it doesn't hurt to include them. I did, as sort of an afterthought, and wound up using them with cooked dried fruit, an instant hit.

We also tuck in some rum (in a plastic bottle, remembering the ban on glass) for making "wilderness daiquiris" — that is, lemonade mix spiked with rum. Some may prefer "wild screwdrivers" — vodka and Tang. Daughter Lynne recommends a bit of peppermint schnapps with the cocoa for a very pleasant conclusion to an evening meal.

RECIPES AND TECHNIQUES

Over the years I have developed a few recipes and technique or tricks that work well for canoe camp cooking. Campfire cooking is by no means a precise art. You need to think about what kind of cooking you will be doing and construct the fire accordingly. (I seldom build the fire; Friend Spouse does that for me. He may or may not tend it for me while I cook.) Sometimes wind conditions make a "proper" fire difficult, and so the cooking technique may have to be altered. Some of the recipes are reflections of such experiences. If you use a stove, you have to think about the sequence of cooking items.

Until recently, when we were given a reflector oven as a gift, I never carried a reflector oven or a dutch oven, both of which would widen the possibilities for cooking. Consequently I have had very little experience in using such an oven. Clearly, cooking for two in the wilderness is affected by how much can be carried.

Unless noted otherwise, all the recipes are for two. In all the baking mix recipes, the important thing to notice is the ratio of liquid to mix.

One of the most basic is the old faithful baking mix. I use it for biscuits, frybread, coffee cake, pancakes, dumplings, corn bread, and for dredging fish. I usually make up a triple batch of it and double-pack it in zip-lock bags. It is not uncommon for us to use all of it on a successful fishing trip.

BAKING MIX
1 pot for preparation; 1 pan for cooking

2	cups all-purpose flour
1	teaspoon salt
2	teaspoons baking powder
¼	cup dehydrated buttermilk
1	teaspoon baking soda
⅓	cup vegetable shortening

I put all the dry ingredients into the food processor for a quick whirr before I add the shortening. I like the shortening very well cut in. (This is one recipe; I make it up several times rather than doubling or tripling it.) Package it.

If you can't find the buttermilk, you can make the following changes. Substitute plain dry milk for buttermilk (equal quantities); omit the baking soda and increase the baking powder to 3 teaspoons.

BISCUITS

¼	cup water
1	cup of baking mix (basic ratio)

Combine and stir quickly. Drop by spoonfuls into hot, well greased pan; cover with foil and bake over hot coals. Since there is so much variation in the quality of the cooking fire, the distance above the coals, and the size of the biscuits, it is difficult to give a precise time. You simply have to keep an eye on the process, particularly to see that the bread doesn't burn. I have found that it takes nowhere near the 15 minutes required in a conventional oven, however.

Many books on woods lore speak of bannock, which was a sort of frying-pan biscuit. Eric Severeid spoke of it in his first book, *Canoeing With the Cree.* (See Appendix — Useful and Interesting Reading.) In the wilds of Manitoba, they were told that "Bannock (Cree frying-pan bread) will ruin a white man's stomach in two years, if he isn't careful." I believe my recipe is a little kinder to digestive systems.

FRYBREAD

Frybread is what I make now instead of more conventional biscuits. One beauty of it is that it is already buttered, ready for eating. I add about 1 tablespoon more water (that is, about ⅓ cup water to 1 cup mix) than I would with regular biscuits. I melt a big dollop (2 tablespoons, maybe a little more) of margarine in the frying pan. When the margarine is bubbling hot, I pour in the dough and pat it out with the back of a spoon to a fairly level layer. I use the spoon to distribute the hot margarine over the surface of the dough as thoroughly as the stuff permits. I found that the drop biscuit style would not cook through evenly, and that smoothing over the top makes the baking more even. If the top is well-enough buttered, and the cooking fire is brisk, it is possible to turn the piece over to brown nicely on the other side. When the dough is in the pan and all nicely buttered, you can cover it with a piece of foil. Frybread is tolerant of a hotter fire than biscuits because of the margarine, rather like cooking pancakes, but again, you need to watch the process.

PANCAKES

½   cup water
1   cup Baking Mix

This time, the ratio of baking mix to water is 2 to 1 (one cup mix to ½ cup water for two people). If the batter seems a bit thick, add a bit more water. Thinner pancakes (more like crêpes) cook faster. For pancakes, I generally use vegetable oil in the frying pan, rather than margarine, as the oil will take a higher heat before it begins to smoke. Pancakes will cook rapidly over a brisk hot fire. Turn after several bubbles appear on the uncooked surface. We eat our pancakes with margarine and jelly or marmalade.

For a special touch, you can add dried blueberries or cranraisins (about ¼ cup) as well as a similar amount of chopped or broken walnuts or pecans.

Coffee cake is fun because you can play with several variations.

COFFEE CAKE

1 pot for mixing; 1 for baking

1	cup Baking Mix
1	tablespoon cinnamon sugar
½	cup water
¼	cup chopped or slivered nuts — pecans, walnuts, or almonds (optional)
¼	cup raisins or currants (optional)

Combine water, Baking Mix and 1 tablespoon of cinnamon sugar. Like the Frybread, the dough should be quite soft. Stir in nuts and raisins — whatever pleases you so long as you remembered to bring them along. Plop this into a very well buttered frying pan, again much like the Frybread. You can then take another tablespoon or two of cinnamon sugar, swirl it around on the top, then take a spoon and run it in a spiral through the dough to make a nice streak of flavoring in the cake. For that matter, it works just as tastily if you simply strew the goodies on top. You can do the same with a couple of tablespoons of jelly or marmalade. Cover and bake as for Biscuits.

JELLO COFFEE CAKE

(Serves 4)
1 pot for mixing; 1 for baking

2	cups Baking Mix
¾	cup water
3	tablespoons Jello (strawberry flavor is good)
1	tablespoon sugar
½	cup walnuts, broken

Combine Baking Mix, walnuts and water. The dough should be quite soft. Plop this into a very well-buttered frying pan. Combine the sugar and Jello and swirl it around on the top, then holding the spoon in an upright position, run it in a spiral into the dough, just like for the Coffee Cake. Bake as for Biscuits.

CORN BREAD

¾	cup Baking Mix
¼	cup cornmeal
½	cup water

Combine baking mix and cornmeal, and stir in water. Cook as with the Frybread.

COUSCOUS

1 pot for cooking.

Couscous is good for breakfast, but also serves as a side dish for dinner. You can substitute dried apricots or other nuts that please you.

½   cup couscous
¾   cup water
½   teaspoon salt (optional)
½   tablespoon margarine
¼   cup raisins
¼   cup slivered or sliced almonds

Bring water, salt and margarine to boil in small pot. Stir in couscous, raisins and almonds. Cover and let stand 5 minutes; serve.

GRITS

1 pot for cooking.

¾   cup instant grits
3   cups boiling water
¼   teaspoon salt

Stir grits into boiling water until thickened.

Variations: Stir in cheese and some garlic powder if you'd like this as a side dish for dinner.

Be sure to have a hearty, filling dessert to round this out.

PIZZAS, WILD STYLE

1 container for mixing; frying pan or grill for cooking.

2   English muffins (can use pita instead)
2   tablespoons concentrated tomato paste
2   tablespoons water
½   teaspoon Italian (pizza) herb combinations — garlic, oregano, basil, black pepper
1½   "strings" (1 ounce, approximately) Mozzarella cheese Pepperoni (or other meat, as desired)
½   teaspoon dehydrated onions (or to taste)
½   teaspoon dehydrated green peppers (or to taste) Dehydrated mushrooms, if available (or to taste)

Combine tomato paste, water, seasoning and whatever dehydrated extras you are using. It helps to let this sit for a short time (do this before starting the fire; when everything else is ready, this will be workable).

Tear cheese into small strings, lay on open muffin face. Top with tomato sauce, then add pepperoni.

Cook carefully in frying pan until cheese melts, being careful not to burn bottoms of muffins.

You can bake this in a reflector oven until cheese is nicely melted. A reflector oven makes it easy to cook several at a time.

FRIED FISH
1 pan for cooking; plate or bag for dredging

Our favorite way of cooking fish is the simplest, the old-fashioned way of pan-frying. I do make two major deviations from home-style cooking here. The main one is to use as little oil for frying as I can, as there is no good way to strain and re-use it. What's left after cooking, I burn. The other thing I do is to use a dollop of margarine as part of the oil. It gives a better flavor. Ghee works well, as it has the flavor of butter, but a much higher smoking point. This calls for a brisk fire, a hot pan and a very short cooking time, maybe as little as 3 minutes, as the fish is delicate and should not be overcooked.

Dredge (roll) the fish fillets in baking mix or baking mix with some cornmeal blended in, then place the fillets in the hot oil. Cook till the pieces are golden brown (the baking mix should provide a lovely bit of crustiness) and the fish flakes when poked with a fork.

Most cooks know the trick of cooking fish or meat in foil, but I'll run through it anyway. You need a piece of aluminum foil large enough to fold double, then to fold again over the fish, with enough side room to fold over, making a sealed package. You can cook a whole fish, properly cleaned, of course, or fillets this way. You do have to keep in mind the size and thickness of the pieces in calculating cooking time. Before making the package, lay the fish on the foil, season it with whatever you brought along — salt and pepper, maybe some margarine, lemon juice, onion flakes. If the trip is for fishing, you might include a small packet of dill weed or parsley, whatever you like to cook on fish that will travel. However, the beauty of fresh fish is that it really needs very little seasoning. On a camping trip where the fishing is highly successful, the main reason for additional seasonings is for variety.

FISH, FOILED AGAIN

Fold over the foil and seal the edges as well as you can. Place on the grill (or on the coals) to bake. Turn after about 5 minutes and cook for another 5 minutes on the other side. The ensuing aroma will probably serve as well as a timer to announce that it is done. Open the package carefully; the juices are worth sopping up with a bit of bread. You can test for doneness by opening the packet a bit and carefully poking the fish with a fork or knife at the thickest point. If it flakes, it is done. Like so much of camp cooking, Fish, Foiled Again is an inexact dish, as the size of the fish pieces, the height of the grill and the intensity of the fire all play their parts. A good rule of thumb is to check after about 5 minutes, rewrapping for further cooking if necessary.

This is not a useful recipe for cooking by camp stove.

Since elegance is equated with simplicity, here is a lazy and hence beautifully elegant way to fix a spaghetti meal for two. Adjust the quantity to fit the group. You can substitute macaroni shells or any other pasta that you prefer. I like the smaller, thinner pasta types because they cook faster. The cheeses come in several flavors — port wine, french onion, sharp cheddar, cheddar and bacon, and so forth.

ELEGANT SPAGHETTI

1 pot for cooking spaghetti

In planning to use pasta, it's useful to know that 1 pound (uncooked) serves six; most pasta triples in volume when cooked, and a helpful rule of thumb is to figure 2 to 4 ounces (¼ pound) of uncooked pasta per person.

¼   pound pasta
4   ounces cheese spread (such as Kaukauna Club)

Cook the spaghetti to the preferred state. Drain and immediately stir in the cheese, heating as necessary to melt and be evenly distributed through the pasta.

A dish I developed for camping that has proved popular in our household is Linguine al Fresco. Sometimes I make the pasta myself; sometimes I buy it. It works well either way. It is based on a classic Italian recipe, and using prosciutto stays closest to the spirit of the dish. However, the Italian ham is expensive, rather salty, and not always readily available. Canadian bacon makes an acceptable substitute, as does the dry salami. Please note the salami also tends to be the fattest. This is usually a bit more than the two of us can eat.

I prepare the dry ingredients of the sauce before the trip.

LINGUINE AL FRESCO

1 pot for cooking

¼   pound linguini noodles (can use fettucini or spaghetti)
1   packet of Sauce Mix
3-4   ounces meat, sliced thin (There are several possibilities: prosciutto, Canadian bacon, San Francisco-type dry salami)
1   ounce package dehydrated peas (peas for two)
½   of .04 ounce package dehydrated mushrooms

Bring 4 salted (about ½ teaspoon salt) cups of water to a boil. Add noodles. Boil 3 minutes, then add peas. Boil another minute or two, stirring to make sure the pasta does not stick. Add mushrooms. When pasta and peas are tender, remove from fire and carefully stir in sauce mix, mixing carefully until well incorporated. Add meat and return to fire to cook until sauce thickens and bubbles, stirring constantly. Let the sauce boil about a minute and it should be ready to eat.

Sauce Mix:
- ⅓   cup dry milk
- 1   teaspoon salt
- 3   tablespoons margarine
- ¼   cup grated Parmesan cheese
-       Pepper to taste

Blend dry milk with margarine, pepper to taste, and mix with ¼ cup grated Parmesan cheese. Package.

To serve more people, you can increase the pasta up to ½ pound without altering the rest of the proportions. If you use a full pound of pasta, use more peas and mushrooms, and add more meat. Increase the amount of cooking water, maybe as much as 2 cups. I keep the cooking water to as little as can be managed and thicken it with the sauce mix, since I don't like to waste that hot water (or the fuel to heat it). At home, I would drain the pasta and discard the cooking water.

Pasta al Fresco
Container for reconstituting dried vegetables; 1 pot for cooking
- 1   tablespoon butter
- 3   ounces pasta (broken spaghetti)
- 1   1 ounce package freeze-dried peas
- ¼   cup grated Asiago cheese
- ¼   cup (about 4 ounces) shredded prosciutto
- 2   tablespoons water, mixed with ¼ cup dry milk for sauce

Bring 4 cups water to boil. Check for reconstitution time on peas (usually 10 minutes) and cooking time for pasta. Add each to water according to time needed. When pasta is at desired stage, drain, stir in butter, milk sauce and ham, stirring thoroughly, then stir in grated cheese. Pepper to taste. Serve.

Mushrooms with Bacon, Woods Style
Container for reconstituting dried vegetables; 1 pot for cooking
- 1   ⅝-ounce package dried shiitake mushrooms
- 3   tablespoons Bacon Bits
- 1   tablespoon vegetable oil
- 1   tablespoon instant onions (equivalent to 3 green onions or 1 small onion, minced) reconstituted
        soy sauce (optional)
        salt
        pepper

Reconstitute mushroom. Drain and slice mushrooms. Heat oil, add mushrooms and onions. Stir fry about 3 minutes. Add Bacon Bits and dash of soy sauce. Salt and pepper to taste.

To reconstitute: soak mushrooms 1 hour in warm water (or sherry, brandy or both), then drain. Onions are similarly reconstituted.

Can fry bacon at home, then package in sealed packet.

SPAGHETTI SAUCE WITH ONIONS
1 pot for sauce, 1 pot for cooking pasta

2	tablespoons concentrated tomato paste
2	cups water
¼	cup instant dried onions
¼	teaspoon Italian herb seasoning (or to taste)
¼	teaspoon instant bouillon or salt

The easy way:

Combine and simmer all ingredients 15-20 minutes, if doing the quick and easy way. The onions will be a little crunchy this way, which gives an interesting texture to the sauce. Pour over cooked pasta.
The best way:

Reconstitute onions in ½ cup of the water. Sauté in 2 tablespoons margarine or oil until golden. Add tomato paste, remaining water and seasoning. Simmer 10-15 minutes, then pour over cooked pasta.

POTATOES WITH BEEF STICK
1 pot for sauce, 1 pot for cooking pasta

1	box French's Au Gratin Potatoes
3¾	ounces Reser's Beef Stick, cut into small pieces
⅔	cup water
⅓	cup dry milk

Combine the potatoes with the contents of the seasoning packet, water and milk. Bring mixture to a boil (on a camp stove, this takes about 12 minutes). Cook and stir about 5 minutes, then reduce heat or move to cooler part of fire and cover. Simmer about 5 minutes, add beef stick and simmer about 10 minutes more.

Instant or dehydrated onions (1-2 tablespoons) may be added to this, too, for additional flavor and a few vitamins.

Slowly bringing the mixture to a boil gives a little longer to reconstitute, improving the quality of the texture.

The package says it makes six ½-cup servings. In camp, as a main dish, the above recipe comes closer to 3 fair-sized servings.

RICE AND BEEF STICK
(Serves 3)

1	package (4.2 ounces) Knorr Risotto with Peas & Corn
3	Hormel Beef Sticks (beef sausage, 1.5 ounces)
1½	cups (12 ounces) water
1	tablespoon margarine

In saucepan, combine contents of package, margarine and water, and bring to boil. Cover and lower heat. Cut beef sticks in bite-sized pieces and add to risotto. Simmer 20 minutes or until all water is absorbed.

One more beef stick may be added; however, be cautious about adding additional meat, as more meat gives a saltier taste.

SPAETZLE WITH CHEESE AND ONIONS
1 pot for sauce, 1 pot for cooking Spaetzle

    ½   box Spaetzle (Maggi brand), cooked and drained
    3   tablespoons instant onions, reconstituted
    2-3   tablespoons margarine
    1   cup (2.3 ounces) grated Gruyère cheese

Cook spaetzle and drain. Heat margarine until bubbly, sauté onions and spaetzle until onions are golden. Stir in cheese and serve.

Swiss cheese may substituted for the Gruyère; it is strictly a matter of preference and availability.

TORTELLINI IN BEEF BROTH
1 pot for cooking

    4   cups boiling water
    1   8 ounce package Beef Tortellini (dehydrated)
    3   packets beef bouillon
    2   tablespoons tomato paste concentrate
    3   tablespoons Parmesan cheese (optional)
         pepper (as desired)

Bring water to boil; add bouillon packets and tortellini. Stir in tomato paste. Boil 10 minutes, or according to directions on package, until pasta is done.

Serve in mugs or bowls with cheese sprinkled over.

Different brands of bouillon and soup mix taste different. I like the George Washington Rich & Brown; suit yourself.

This is very easy since it uses supermarket items. This is another way to use part of a 12 ounce stick of salami (for two people).

SCALLOPED POTATOES AL FRESCO
1 pot for cooking

    1   box packaged scalloped (or au gratin, whatever) pota-
         toes (such as Betty Crocker's or Lipton's)
    3   ounces of San Francisco-type dry salami (as desired)
    1   tablespoon (or good dollop) margarine

Mix thoroughly in cooking pot with the amount of water called for on the box, cover and cook over brisk fire. It doesn't hurt for the potatoes to sit in the water for several minutes before cooking. Don't have the fire too hot; if the potatoes cook too fast, they will absorb all the water before they get tender and the sauce will stick and scorch. You may need to add a little water along. I find that the cooking times on the packages are not particularly useful for fire pit cooking. I simply start checking the degree of doneness about 10 minutes before the called-for time.

The contents of one small jar of dried beef may be substituted for the salami. However, first soak the beef a few minutes in clear water to remove some of the salt. Drain, then add.

HASH BROWNED POTATOES

Another packaged potato dish that we like is made from Hash-browns (this is the way they call them). The directions on the box suggest that they can be prepared in either of two ways. One, the "dry" way, simply calls for stirring together into the skillet the potatoes, water (about 2 cups), 1 teaspoon salt (this could be reduced), and 3 tablespoons of margarine. I like to toss in 3 or 4 tablespoons of dehydrated onions and a bit of pepper, too.

Cook uncovered over medium heat until the liquid is absorbed and the bottom of the potatoes is brown, about 9 to 12 minutes. Turn and brown the other side, about another 3 minutes. If you can, use a nonstick pan for this. I never have much luck in being able to turn them as a large single cake.

THE BETTER WAY

They turn out better when you can rehydrate the potatoes (and onions) in very hot salted water for 15-20 minutes before draining and cooking. Then spread the potatoes evenly in 3-4 tablespoons of margarine that has been heated to bubbling over a medium hot fire. Let cook 5 to 8 minutes, until the bottom is brown. Turn with a pancake turner or spatula and brown that side.

Rosamarina is a pasta that looks much like rice. Being small, it has the beauty of cooking quickly.

QUICKIE SOUP

½	cup R-F Rosamarina
4	cups water
3	tablespoons tomato paste
3	bouillon cubes

Add all ingredients except Rosamarina to water and heat to boiling. When boiling, add Rosamarina slowly. Stir occasionally. Cook 7 to 9 minutes.

For variety: add left-over cooked peas, beans or other vegetables.

STEWED FRUIT

You can find a wide assortment of dried fruits — apricots, apples, cranberries, mixed fruits, peaches, pears, plums, prunes and raisins. Any can be cooked for tasty side dishes with meals. The general rule is to cover the fruit with water, and add sweetening. Cover the pot, bring the water to a boil and simmer until the fruit has reached the preferred stage of tenderness. Most need to cook some 5 to 10 minutes until they are tender. You can carry sugar for this purpose, or you can use your fruit drink mix. Cranberries, for instance, are enhanced with an orange-flavored drink mix. Cinnamon sugar (described elsewhere) is wonderful with the apples.

Dried Fruit Variations

1 pot for cooking.

A handful (about ½ to ¾ cup) of small marshmallows tossed into the freshly cook and still bubbling hot fruit (here, use ¾ cup of water to 3 ounces or half a package of fruit) and stirred until completely melted gives a pleasing texture to the sauce for the fruit as it sweetens it. When it has cooled, the mixture is similar to preserves.

Usually, I cook this for an evening meal and we eat half of it then. We have the rest for breakfast, preferably with fresh walleye and frybread, a simply fabulous breakfast!

Apricots Phoebe
(Serves 4)

1 pot for the cooking.

1	6 ounce package dried apricots
½	cup small marshmallows (a handful)
1¼	cup water

In a pan, cover apricots with water and bring to a boil. Let cook 5 to 10 minutes, and just before the fruit is satisfactorily tender, stir in marshmallows until they are fully dissolved and the liquid resumes boiling. Remove from fire. The apricots need to be at the boil when the marshmallows are added so that the cornstarch on the marshmallows cooks. Otherwise a rather unpleasant "graininess" remains.

Dumplings

Dumplings offer several possibilities. Use the basic biscuit proportion of 4 to 1 parts of dry mix to liquid. Dollop spoonfuls of dough into simmering liquid. One pleasant touch is to add a tablespoonful or so of cinnamon sugar (see the Basic Extras list) into the dry mix, and then cook the dumplings over simmering fruit. You will need to add extra water to the fruit when you start — you will need approximately 1 cup of water to 3 ounces of dried fruit. Put the lid on and let cook several minutes. You can speed the process along by turning the dumplings after some 3 minutes. If the fire is brisk, and the liquid really bubbling, it will take only another 3 minutes or so for them to get done. And not to belabor the obvious, small dumplings cook faster than large ones. Start the fruit cooking before you begin making the dumplings. Most of the dried fruits need to cook some 5 to 10 minutes until they are tender.Some people like fruits cooked softer than other people do.

My mother used to make this filling recipe for my father's favorite pie.

FRED'S FAVORITE

1 pot for cooking.

1½	cups raisins
1½	cup water
½	cup pecans
1	tablespoon brown sugar (optional)
1	tablespoon flour (for thickening)

Combine raisins, water and sugar, cover and bring to a boil. Simmer 10-15 minutes, stir in flour mixture and pecans until mixture is slightly thickened. Remove from heat.

PAT'S FRUIT BITS
(Serves 3)

1	6-ounce package (Sun-maid) Fruit Bits
1	cup water
½	scoop (2 tablespoons) lemonade mix
⅓	cup small marshmallows

Combine fruit and water and simmer 5 minutes. Add marshmallows and cook another 2 minutes.

FRUIT MALBERG
(Serves 3)

1	package dried fruit, stewed
½	package instant lemon pudding (small)

Stir dry lemon pudding into the fruit while it is hot. This gives a nice extra flavor and improves the consistency of the juice.

This is particularly good with peaches or prunes, and not bad at all with apples.

A packet of crumb crust mixture is useful to have to put under instant pudding for a cream pie, or you can put it under or over cooked fruit. You can either fix your own mix or buy a prepared crumb mix.

CRUMB CRUST
(Serves 3)

8-10	graham crackers (2 x 2), thoroughly crushed
1	tablespoon sugar
3	tablespoons margarine (you can leave this out or dollop it on when you put the whole business together)

Mix thoroughly and package in plastic bag.

APPLE STREUSEL

1 pot for cooking fruit

A couple of variations are possible here. Both begin with stewing the dried apples with enough water to barely cover. Cover the pot and let them cook awhile. The first variation calls for about a tablespoonful of baking mix stirred in with 2 or 3 tablespoons of cinnamon sugar (suit your own sweet tooth) and then drizzled over the cooking apples. Squirt some margarine over the whole bit and resume cooking until the apples are tender. I usually use a half package of apples for the two of us.

Variation two calls for simply putting a mixture of cinnamon-flavored graham cracker crumbs over the cooked apples.

SKILLET BROWNIES

This recipe is a relic of our daughters' Girl Scout campouts, and is fun to do after the rest of the supper has been eaten. It does require one person's constant attention during the cooking process. Also, the batch is too large for two people to enjoy, a bit much for three, but will nicely accommodate four.

1 pot for preparation; 1 frying pan for cooking

1   box brownie mix (such as Betty Crocker's)
       water, as called for in directions

The box gives directions for cake-like or fudge-y brownies. Use the amount of water for the fudge, and ignore the call for egg. Stir the mix up well and dump it into a very well greased skillet, preferably one with a nonstick finish. Cook over a brisk fire, stirring, especially after cooking signs begin to appear around the edges. The object of the stirring is to prevent the mixture from burning. Keep stirring; after a time, the mix begins to resemble fudge. By the time the aroma is well developed, the stuff can be considered done, and in the language lore of our house, "we'll eat it anyway!"

S'MORES

If you are planning an expedition that includes younger children, say 8 to 10 years old, you might want to include that old kid-pleaser, S'mores. Some people thoroughly enjoy toasting marshmallows over an open fire, which is fine. Just don't cut green twigs for toasting sticks. We used to carry a long-handled (actually telescoping handled) fork, but decided that it was nearly a lethal weapon on trips. If you have such, and want to stick it in your kitchen gear, get a couple of corks to put onto the tines for protection.

I won't talk about quantities for S'mores — other than to mention that the chocolate is supposed to cover, more or less, the graham cracker, and it can take two marshmallows for a graham slat. Place the chocolate bar on a graham cracker slat. Toast the marshmallows and squish them onto the chocolate with a second graham cracker slat.

Graham crackers

Marshmallows

Milk chocolate bars (with almonds, if you want to be fancy)

An elegant variation is to use German sweet chocolate instead of plain milk chocolate. Or you can use dark chocolate, whatever you like.

EASY FONDUE

A pleasant way to end a meal is with a dessert fondue, and this is something that can be as simple or as elaborate as you care to make it.

Basically, you need a sauce for dipping and something to dip. For that matter, the sauce could as well be poured over the other. Pound cake travels well, cuts nicely into cubes or slabs. Any fruit that can be held in the fingers or by a fork dips well, especially banana slices (fresh or dried). Firm cookies such as vanilla wafers or ginger snaps are eminently suitable. Prepared sauces (many now are packaged in plastic bottles) for homemade sundaes work fine.

1 bottle Hot Fudge Topping (19 oz.)

Cookies

Dried apricots or other fruit

Marshmallows

Banana chips

Pound cake

Crackers

Pretzel sticks

In short, take whatever you have that tastes good with chocolate.

Place opened bottle in sauce pan filled with 2 to 3 inches of water. Bring water to boil; reduce heat. Simmer 5 to 10 minutes, or until sauce is warm. Close cap; shake well. Pour into dish or pot to allow for dunking goodies.

If supplies permit, add a tablespoon of rum or brandy to the warm sauce.

One bottle makes a generous fondue for 4.

Can use other topping flavors if desired.

FLAVORED COFFEE

Add 1–2 teaspoons hot chocolate mix to a cup of coffee for your own flavored coffee. In some stores you can find other mix flavorings.

TRAIL MIX

No self-respecting camping book would be without a trail mix recipe, so here is one that we really like.

¾   cup dry-roasted peanuts

1   cup roasted sunflower seeds

1   cup dry-roasted cashews
1   package (small) of M & M candies
1   cup raisins

Mix all these good things together and package in the trusty plastic bags. It is a good idea to package the mix in several bags; for one, the temptation to eat too much at a time is reduced, and because this is one item that really attracts the "marauders" (the chipmunks, mice, and others that will slip into a pack at night and raid).

There are of course several variations that can be played on this snack theme: substitute or add such goodies as sliced dates, or walnuts, or whatever. You notice, of course, that the calories are really taking care of themselves, though otherwise there is a considerable solid food value.

Some would include 1 cup of chocolate or carob chips. The chocolate, with its inherent fat, provides long-lasting energy. I do have some objection to chocolate's tendency to melt in the summer and get quite messy. I am told carob is likewise messy.

Do-at-home recipes

As I mentioned earlier, I like to make our first-night dinner special, to celebrate our coming to the wilderness. We can carry a cooler for the trip to our entry point, which makes it possible to use foods that needed to be kept cold. If the meat is frozen to begin with, you have some additional hours carrying for it, especially if you take pains to pack it so that it doesn't warm too rapidly.

Chicken works very well for these meals, especially boned chicken breasts. Boned thighs, pounded to a uniform thickness (about ½ inch), sauté rapidly over a camp stove or wood fire.

Stuffed Chicken Breasts

2   chicken breasts, skinned
3   ounces Boursin cheese, room temperature
½   cup seasoned croutons, crushed

Place chicken breasts between sheets of waxed paper; pound with flat side of meat tenderizer until the meat is flattened to an even thickness, about ¼ inch. Place 2 tablespoons cheese on each breast piece; fold over meat to cover. The idea is to seal the cheese in. After stuffing, roll each piece in croutons. Wrap individually in plastic wrap and refrigerate or freeze. (Other cheeses may be substituted for the Boursin; it is a garlic and herb flavored cheese on the order of cream cheese. The softer, creamier cheeses are easier to seal and hence are less likely to ooze while cooking.)

In camp, heat margarine or oil to sizzling, and sauté on each side until golden brown.

CASHEW BUTTER

One of the easiest delights to prepare in advance is to take a 12-ounce package of blanched or roasted cashews (pieces are cheaper than whole), dump them into the food processor with the sharp steel blade and process them. It will take 4 or 5 minutes of processing before they change from chunks to grit to smooth, spreadable butter. And that's all there is to it!

SHERRIED DATES

Make this up several days before your trip, and drain off the surplus sherry. You probably won't need all for the trip, as the recipe makes a quart jar full. For travel, pack the desired amount in a small plastic jar or box. Plastic bags are not recommended here.

    2   boxes dates, pitted
         Whole blanched almonds
    1   thin slice lemon, seeded
         a good cream Sherry

Stuff each date with whole almond. Pack snugly, but without mashing or squeezing them together, into a 1-quart jar. Add lemon slice, seeded and slowly fill jar with Sherry, and see that the dates are all covered, and top with at least an eighth-inch of sherry. Cover jar tightly and store in cool place until all the sherry has been absorbed. Add sherry as necessary.

STUFFED FRUIT

    Dates (pitted)
    Walnuts
    Apricots (dried)
    Almonds
    Pecans

Stuff each piece of fruit with a nut. Allow four or five per serving.

HOT STUFF: COOKING TIME

PREPARING THE MEAL

The actual business of preparing breakfast and dinner on the traditional campfire, rather than only the camp stove, is not at all difficult, though I do not recommend a camping trip as the occasion for learning to cook. The Elegant Camper keeps the difficulty level down by getting organized first.

The Number One item on the agenda is the eternal question, What's for breakfast/dinner? If the meals were all planned on a day-by-day basis, the question is settled. The items for the meal can be laid out, along with the pots and whatever incidentals that may be needed. It is nice if there are at least two people to share preparation tasks — one to make the fire and one to prepare the cooking pots. Both are important tasks: if either is done badly, it causes a lot more work.

In Chapter 6, you'll find a discussion of building a cooking fire, but now we'll focus on the cooking.

PREPARATION FOR COOKING

The pot soaping for the trip's first cooking session sets the level of work for final clean-up. Somehow, it seems easier to do a good job on the subsequent rounds if the first went well. Scrubbing all the black off is one of the nastier, more unpleasant jobs of cleaning up at the end of the trip. Outfitters will charge extra (say $5 per pot) for cleaning blackened cookware, and they deserve every bit of it. Prevention is easy. The idea is to apply a film of soap or detergent to the outside only, to any pot that is going over the fire. I never bother with soaping the wire handles. When cooking is done, the well-soaped pot may look dreadful, but it will wash clean with little effort. The same trick of using a detergent film with a fondue pot works equally well back at home.

I used to use bar soap (Fels-Naphtha) to soap pots, but it's easier to pour a few drops of liquid detergent such as Camp-Suds on the bottom of the pot and thoroughly smear it all over the bottom and sides.

COOKING ON AN OPEN FIRE

If I am going to cook with a wood fire, I like a fire pit that has several large rocks around it. These can be shifted (sometimes!) as windshields, very helpful if there is a strong breeze. They also conserve heat and direct it up, making a steadier heat for cooking. I also note whether some of the rocks that are around the fire pit are flat-topped and of a size to use to put pots, spoons, whatever, on while I am cooking. Some of my favorite sites have been favorites because they were so well "equipped."

What's to be cooked of course determines the kind of fire to be built. If the menu calls for cooking a pasta dish and making coffee (one of the simplest kinds of cooking needs — merely boiling a pot of water, though nowhere does it say that you must have a hot drink), then a quick, hot fire large enough for both pots to sit over is required. The prepared pots can go on as soon as they are ready. The job is then to keep the fire fed until cooking is done. If the menu includes baking bread, the fire needs to burn down to coals. If frying fish is included, a wider fire with coals to one side and a livelier area is needed. Maintaining a fire of this sort takes constant tending, and the good cooking areas above the fire bed tend to shift, especially as fuel is added. Locate hot spots by passing your hand over the grate: they are not always where one might think, and this is particularly true on windy days.

Is it windy or calm? Is the fire pit sheltered? It will be easier to make a wide fire for cooking bread and frying fish. Does its grate sit high above the ash bed? If so, a larger fire will be needed unless the ash bed can be raised by adding stones. All of these elements come into play in building and maintaining a fire that will do an adequate job of cooking the food without excessive use of wood. Current philosophy also emphasizes building as small a fire as practical.

If you plan to use several pots to cook, start your fire at one end of the fire pit, building across as the fire grows. This way, heavier pieces, meant to make good coals, can begin to burn down to the desired state for baking, while the other end of the fire can be kept lively for a quick fire suitable for frying or boiling

To the task at hand

With these preparations made, you now can turn attention to the food itself. Once the fire is going well and the pots are ready, it's time for serious cooking. Cooking is a smoother operation if all the items that you are going to need are laid out, ready at hand. This is when you really appreciate a good cooking site.

There is discussion in the Recipes section on particular procedures with individual items, so I won't repeat them here. I will simply make some observations.

Some people make a big thing of brewing coffee over a camp fire. Various tricks are supposed to settle the grounds and clarify the coffee; a classic example involves using an egg. However, that isn't really necessary, and besides, who is carrying an egg? If you are using ground coffee instead of individual coffee packets, bring the water almost to a boil and measure the ground coffee into it. Let the water come to a boil for the desired time (I prefer only a couple of minutes or so), then remove the pot from the heat or over to the side of the grate. You can get the grounds to settle by giving the coffee a brisk, brief stir, then let it sit. This is a lot easier and safer, but much less spectacular, than taking the pot by the wire bail and playing like the pot is a car on the Ferris wheel of your arm for about three swings. The main thing is that grounds left on the strainer during the brewing are moved off and can settle. Or you can simply carry a percolator, which allows you to lift the grounds basket right out. Be careful not to burn your hand when removing the hot basket.

When I fry fish, I use a mixture of cooking oil and margarine, and I use as little as I can get by with to fry the fish. I skimp on oil because I have no good way to save and re-use it. What is left over after cooking, I burn. Do be careful about the fire flaring up when you do this.

A fine way to cook fish is to wrap it with seasonings in foil and bake on top of the grate or on the coals (Fish, Foiled Again). Potatoes can also be foil-wrapped and baked in the coals. They should have been well scrubbed before wrapping, so that the skins could be eaten, too.

After serving the last of whatever was cooked, I clean remaining contents out, put water in it and place it back on the fire to heat for washing dishes.

When you have finished with the fire, make sure that it is quite dead and cold, particularly if you are about to leave the site. However, using the dishwater to douse it is not advisable, especially if there are food particles in the water. They draw flies and small creatures to scavenge, neither of which is at all desirable.

COOKING WITH GAS

Cooking is simpler when you don't have to deal with a wood fire. It does take some practice to become familiar with the intensity of a gas camp stove and to develop the finesse to adjust the flame to a desired heat. You are more restricted, too, on what you can cook without additional equipment. For instance, baking is more difficult.

Earlier, I mentioned a wind screen as part of the equipment. I use one whether it's windy or not.

Don't leave an empty pot on the gas burner — the heat is enough to melt out the bottom of aluminum pot.

Meadow Rue

6

SKILLS, TECHNIQUES AND TRICKS

"This sort of thing takes a deal of training"
W. S. Gilbert, *Ruddigore*

I always enjoy watching an expert work. I like to see the sure moves and focused effort. Skill makes work look easy. It comes from sound technique, which in turn is based on knowing how to do something and practicing it sufficiently to do it without having to think about it. The trick is learning the how-to part. If you are going to feel at ease in camping you'll need to know how to handle the canoe. You need to know how to pick it up safely (without herniating or straining a muscle). Improving the way you paddle the canoe will make travel easier, and being able to pull off a few basic maneuvers comes in handy. Understanding how to load a canoe properly will make the paddling easier as well as safer. Knowing how to tie a few basic knots is very handy. Thwarting bears brings peace of mind.

Following are a few points on how to do a number of things commonly used in wilderness canoe camping. They aren't everything you'll ever need, but make a good base for managing well to start with and to build on as your experience grows.

THE CANOE

We've already talked about characteristics of canoes. Here we'll look at the handling of the craft. Remember that you are placing a lot of trust in your (own, borrowed or rented) canoe, and you should treat it kindly. Present-day materials are wonderfully tough, but that doesn't mean they are abuse-proof.

PICKING UP THE CANOE

At some point, the canoe will have to be moved on land. This means it should be picked up, not dragged along. Never drag a loaded canoe, and don't try to pick it up and carry it. (How would you like to be dragged along on your bottom?) A canoeist's proverb says "Canoes float on the water, sit on the land, or fly through the air."

Usually portaging is a one-person job. The object is to get the canoe overturned and lifted to the shoulders for carrying without risk to either the canoe or the carrier.

There are several ways to do this, some of which are hernia-makers. Some will have you reach across the canoe at its widest point, pick it up and then raise the whole thing, rest it briefly on the knee, then with one great heave, hoist it overhead while simultaneously flipping it bottom-side up.

For those of us in less than top-physical condition, there is an easier way. Stand alongside the rear of the canoe, facing it. Stoop down, and using the arm that is closer to the front, reach across and take hold of the far gunwale. With your other hand, take hold of the near gunwale. You should be grasping somewhere back of the rear seat. (Your thumbs should both be on the inside with the fingers on the outside of the canoe.) Now, with a smooth motion, lift the end of the canoe over your head, rolling the canoe bottom-side up in the process, while at the same time turn to face the front end which is still resting on the ground, so you are not yet carrying the full weight of the canoe. Your arms should be locked at the elbows. The canoe is supported at three points, with most of the weight resting on the ground at the bow of the canoe.

Now, step forward, "bumping" your grip along the gunwales until you are in position under the portage pads. Gently lower the canoe until the portage pads are resting on your shoulders, then allow the nose of the canoe to rise until you have the whole canoe balanced on your shoulders. Now you are ready to move out.

LOADING THE CANOE

A canoe is a wonderful craft: light, agile and generally stable. It is not subject to tipping unless one is foolish about standing up or walking around in it or leaning way over the side. A properly-loaded canoe handles better, gives a better ride, and is much safer.

Nowadays our gear — Big Blue, Miz Blue, the Big Green Honker and Little Blue — makes a pretty good-sized load. And of course it was larger when the children were with us, even with two canoes for the six of us.

The center of gravity, from front to rear, should be near the center. Packs should be well-settled in the middle of the canoe and distributed with an eye to the relative weights of the paddlers. If the paddler in front is smaller, the heavier packs go forward. If the rear paddler is smaller, the heavier packs should go toward the rear. Lay big (tall) packs on their sides or backs; they are not passengers; they do not need to sit up and take in the view. a low profile maintains the canoe's natural stability and gives less wind resistance when the wind is strong.

Haphazard loading also means harder unloading; you do not want cause for regretting sloppy work. Furthermore, at some portages and often over beaver dams, the dry-foot paddler cannot simply step into the canoe; he may have to climb over the gear, which can be tricky if the loading job was haphazard. If climbing over is necessary, one should keep as low a profile as possible, holding onto the gunwales while moving.

Canoe loading gets a little more interesting if there are three in the party, and room has to be made for the third member to "duff," that is, ride without paddling. The duffer usually sits in a somewhat awkward position, with only the skin of the boat between him and the cold of the lake water (you could take along a cushion). On rainy days, it's worse, as rainwater collects in the bottom of the canoe. If somebody *must* sit on a pack, be sure the pack contains nothing that would be damaged by being sat on and won't raise the person above the level of the paddlers. You don't want to risk the person falling out of the canoe or the stability of the canoe itself.

On the positive side, the duffer has the luxury of enjoying the scenery without the responsibility of watching where the canoe is going. Creek stretches are marvelous, especially when the wild iris or pitcher plants are blooming. (One of my favorite places in late May is the upper part of Kelso Lake, a creek, actually. It has, of the creeks and marshes we have visited, the widest range of interesting plants — bog rosemary, leatherleaf, bog laurel, pitcher plants, and on and on.) But, with three, it is a good idea to take turns duffing, if possible.

PADDLING THE CANOE

One of the delightful sights of the North Woods is a well-paddled canoe moving across a calm, morning-bright lake. Sunlight flashing off synchronized paddles lends a special grace and animation that enables the canoe to take a natural place in the wilderness landscape. An awareness that you are paddling in unison with your partner adds to a feeling of harmony with nature.

Learning the theory of paddling a canoe is easy, and being able to move the craft around is not particularly difficult. Paddling a canoe deftly and with authority is one of the simpler skills of the wilderness tripper. Yet few do it really well and novices seem to feel "learning to paddle a canoe" is more intimidating than any other aspect of their wilderness experience. Paddling a canoe across a northern lake safely and with a minimum of effort — hence elegantly — takes learning only a few strokes which can be mastered with a little instruction and a bit of practice. As you grow more adept, you may get interested in finer points of paddling technique and want to read more on the subject. (See Appendix — Useful and Interesting Reading.) Remembering that this is not a treatise on paddling, let's consider a few basics that will ease your travel across a lake or on a river.

In the general scheme of things, paddling is a team effort where the bow (front) paddler provides forward power, while the stern (rear) paddler steers. It is easier and requires much less correction of the heading of the canoe if paddlers are working on opposite sides of the canoe and paddling in unison. What's more, better distribution of the paddling forces make a smoother ride. We once watched a pair of boys work their way up a lake. They were both paddling on the same side of the canoe, changing sides every few minutes, zigzagging their way down the lake and doing about three times as much paddling as was really needed.

On long stretches of lake or river, stroking together also sets up a rhythm that makes the miles go faster. (Work songs originated to develop a rhythm in work, particularly if the work was a combined effort of two or more people. Remember, the old voyageurs sang while they paddled.) You can paddle further if the bow and stern paddlers switch sides occasionally. This gives paddling muscles on one side a chance to rest while you use those on the other. We usually switch about every 5 or 10 minutes. We generally don't bother even call the switch; from my bow position, Friend Spouse can see me make the change and he follows suit. Or he'll call for a switch if I have gotten absentminded about changing.

But back to the paddling itself. The paddle blade is to the canoe like one's hand or an animal's paw is to the swimmer. The wide surface gives power to the stroke as it pushes against the water. Another way of thinking of how a particular stroke affects the boat is to think of the paddle as a stationary pole which you either pull the canoe toward or push it away from. The paddle remains stationary in the water, but the canoe moves. You get a notion of the forces in action when you use your arms to push yourself out of a deep chair. The chair offers resistance, just as the water does.

BASIC STROKES

Essentially, you need to know three basic strokes to get you across the lake from one portage to the next — the forward power stroke, the *C* and the *J* strokes. The first is used by both paddlers and is the one to get you where you want to go. If the bow and stern paddlers do this stroke together on opposite sides of the canoe, they will move it straight ahead. The other two are sweep strokes and they determine the direction the canoe takes.

Forward power stroke. The most basic of all paddling skills is the forward power stroke. Start by taking the paddle with both hands. Put one hand on the *T* at the top of the paddle and the other a comfortable distance down toward the blade, slightly more than shoulder width. Raise the paddle to a vertical position, lean forward, and slice it into the water with the blade perpendicular to the canoe center line. Keep your lower arm straight (but don't lock the elbow) as you dig the paddle into the water and pull.

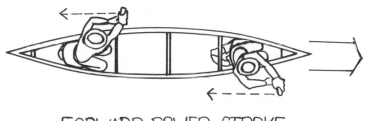

FORWARD POWER STROKE

Let that arm swing from the shoulder and let the other do the bending and pushing. Use the large muscles of your upper body and torso, rather than your arms, to pull the canoe forward. As the paddle comes back more or less in line with your body, slice it sideways out of the water, rotate the blade parallel to the surface, and lean forward into the next stroke. Let your wrists do all the rotating as the blade clears the water and moves into position for the next stroke. If you let the paddle rotate in your hands, you can expect blisters. The opening of the lower hand should be toward the side of the canoe with the knuckles more or less forward.

Short strokes are efficient. You'll find if you complete the power stroke about even with your hip, it takes less effort than when you allow the stroke to continue well past you. Your body, after a time, will complain vigorously if you persist in doing anything more than necessary.

C and J Strokes. Once the canoe is moving, the next problem is making the canoe go where you want it to. In addition to actually turning onto the proper course, small steering corrections must be made merely to paddle in a straight line because the canoe will constantly tend to wander off course due to the dynamic interactions between wind, wave and the relative strengths and techniques of the front and rear paddlers.

On calm, flat water the bow paddler provides forward power by doing a straight-ahead power stroke while the stern paddler steers and makes changes in direction by executing a small pull in or out, or hook at the end of the power stroke.

This small hook at the end of each stroke creates a side force and causes the canoe to turn around a point somewhere about midway between the bow and the stern. Imagine a toy propeller, impaled through its center by a pin on a table top. If you push one end to the left, the other end will point to the right. Conversely, if the back end is pulled back to the right, the other end (the front) will point to the left. This is what happens with a canoe. The strokes to do this are commonly called the *C* and *J* strokes, which come from the basic shape of the hook. Both start like the normal forward power stroke.

Then the *C*, or sweep, stroke starts away from the canoe and makes a small arc or *C*-shape toward the canoe. This pulls the stern of the canoe toward the paddle and causes the bow to turn away from the rear paddle side. (Or to put it simply, with a *C* stroke on the left, the canoe will turn right.)

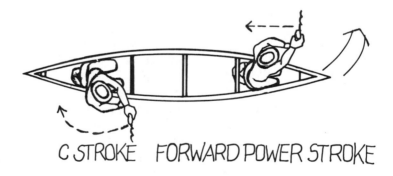

C STROKE   FORWARD POWER STROKE

The *J* stroke is the reverse, starting at the side of the canoe, pulling back in the stroke and ending with a little hook, or *J*-shape, away from the canoe. The bow will turn toward the rear paddle side. (With a *J* stroke to the left, the canoe will turn left.) The size of the moves will determine how drastic or how subtle the change of course will be. Both the *C* and *J* strokes are executed by rotating the lower wrist and pulling in or out slightly, a matter that takes a bit of practice to master thoroughly.

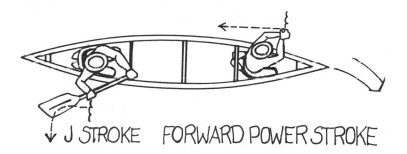

J STROKE   FORWARD POWER STROKE

These three strokes should let you move across the lake with confidence and efficiency.

Friend Spouse likes to pick out a tree or some other landmark on the far shore and head directly for it, keeping the steering corrections as small as possible. On calm water, most of one's energy should go into moving the boat forward.

GOOD MOVES

With the basic strokes for moving forward in hand (as it were), let's look at some useful little techniques for moving in other directions. The strokes described below are not absolutely necessary to get across the lake but may come in handy when sharper maneuvering is required approaching a rock strewn landing or negotiating tight bends in a creek. They are particularly useful for river traveling.

The reverse power stroke. If you want to back up in calm water, or to slow down to land in a fast current (like at the top of a falls), back the canoe, using the reverse power stroke. This stroke, as one might guess, is the reverse of the forward power stroke. The paddle is inserted into the water near, or a little back of the hip. The canoe is pulled backward past the paddle. If both front and rear paddlers do the reverse power stroke on opposite sides, the canoe will back up or slow down, if you're moving with a current.

Reverse power pivot. You can execute a neat pivot of the canoe within its own length if the rear paddler uses a reverse power stroke while the front paddler uses a forward power stroke on the opposite side. The canoe will pivot toward the rear paddle side.

Draw and push-away strokes. When you reach out to the side and put your paddle in the water, blade parallel to the canoe and pull, you make a draw stroke, because it will draw you closer to the point where the blade entered the water. (It will also push the other end of the boat in the opposite direction.)

Conversely, if you place the paddle in the water close to the side of the boat with the blade parallel to the canoe and push, your end will move away from the paddle. This is the push-away stroke.

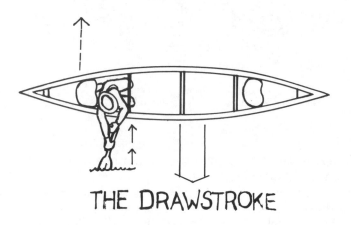

THE DRAWSTROKE

The pry stroke. The pry stroke is similar to the push-away and has the same effect on the canoe, but is more powerful. Use the lower hand and the side of the canoe as a paddle pivot point, or fulcrum, while the upper hand pulls the *T* of the handle toward the center of the boat. (Do this too hard or injudiciously and you can overturn the canoe.)The canoe can be turned virtually on a dime if both paddlers do either a draw or pry on opposite sides simultaneously.

PUSHAWAY STROKE

Stern rudder. A useful maneuvering stroke for going with an active current is the stern rudder. The stern, or rear, paddler trails the paddle behind the canoe. The blade is parallel to the canoe and its edges are vertical to the water.   By shifting direction (to the right or left) of the upper paddle hand,the canoeist can turn the boat in the desired direction. (And by now, you have gotten the hang of how to direct the canoe.) It is a stroke that will get immediate response in the water. The stern rudder stroke provides no forward power at all, leaving it all to the bow paddler. On flat water, the use of this stroke may cause complaint from the front paddler. ("You're ruddering!" an offspring paddling bow would yell at the sibling in the stern.)

Sideslip. When you want to miss obstructions or merely to move to the side, you use a maneuver called a sideslip. I love the sideslip; it's fun. It is a useful technique for easing into a landing or to avoid nosing into gelcoat-eating rocks and gravel.

You can do this a couple of ways. In one, both paddlers reach out on the same side of the canoe and do a draw stroke. This will pull the canoe toward the start of the draw, or to put it simply, the canoe will move sideways. Likewise, both can do a push-away stroke, and again the canoe will move sideways, but this time away from the start of the push. Sometimes it isn't convenient to switch the side you are paddling on. You and your partner can achieve the same effect with one doing a draw and the other doing a pry or push-away on the opposite side. (You do have to be of the same mind about the direction you're going.) With this, the canoe will move toward the paddle doing the draw.

PADDLING ON RIVERS

The better North Woods touring or expedition canoes are designed to track straight across the lake with a minimum of effort since that is what they do most of the time. Because the ability to follow a straight track and turn easily are mutually exclusive in terms of canoe design, most good touring canoes are harder to maneuver in tight spots than are canoes designed for river travel. For this reason, sharper maneuvers require coordination between the bow and stern paddlers. Remember, the current is still carrying the canoe forward, so start your moves early.

Bends. If your route involves rivers, you find that they have bends. In paddling the bends of a river, a good rule of thumb is to paddle near the inside during high water and the outside during low water. Examine a river. You'll see that the main channel generally follows the outside of the bend, and consequently the faster current and the most turbulence are in that area. Since there is more power from the river at such points, the force of the water often not only undercuts the bank but also tends to pile up strainers (downed trees, branches, whatever the water could move). You definitely want to avoid any chance of getting caught up in debris like that; if the current were swift enough, the canoe and canoeists could be caught there finally and permanently. The effect of the power of the water on a trapped canoe is not a pretty sight. The inside of the bend will be smoother and safer.

On the other hand, during low water conditions, the outside bend may be the only part of the river to have enough water to float the canoe.

SLOW DOWN AND TAKE A LOOK

Whenever canoeing, particularly in an unfamiliar area, the watchword is Pay attention to what you are doing! On a lake, this mainly means Look out for rocks lurking beneath the surface. A great many of them are canoe-catchers with silver and color marks on them. If you are barreling along at a good clip and hang on a rock just so, you could very easily tip the whole canoe.

Rivers warrant even more care. Study your maps so that you know something of what lies ahead. Don't go banging along where you can't see what's you're getting into. If you can't quite read the water ahead, slow down for looking by using the good old reverse power (or aft) stroke. This way, you can face forward and survey the river. If necessary, head for shore and scout the river from the bank.

Fine canoeing streams will differ: they will meander in great loops; they will be swift and feisty; they may be interspersed with challenging rapids (the latter two are not for beginners). However, streams in the Boundary Waters and Quetico generally are slow moving and rock-strewn. They often change level by dropping in cascades and waterfalls (and so you portage).

River travel means you will encounter rocks and riffles. Look at a river that makes a drop. The current flowing past a rock in the water will make a wake, much like a boat makes through the water. You'll see that the surface of the water displays one or more V-shapes pointing upstream. The point of the V is from the rock, or upstream end of the V. Where the wake from one rock crosses the wake of another V, they form a V pointing downstream and these downstream Vs are indication of a clear channel. Aim for those downstream Vs. Use the reverse power stroke against the current to maintain position in the river.

For enjoyable and safe canoeing on a river, to all the techniques and moves described earlier, you should add the ferry.

With a ferry, you move sideways in the river with minimum effort and maintain position without going on downstream. Much as a sailboat uses the force of the wind to move across a lake, the canoe uses the force of the water to move sideways. The canoeists paddle against the current with the canoe held at an oblique angle to it.

Upstream ferries. To make an upstream, or forward, ferry, turn the canoe upstream and hold it at an angle of 35 to 45 degrees with the current (that's with the bow toward the side to which you want to move). Both paddlers then use the forward power stroke to hold position while the current moves you across the stream. In short, the upstream end of the canoe should be pointing toward the target bank. The swifter the current, the smaller angle is needed.

Downstream ferry. The downstream ferry is the same as the upstream except that you are facing downstream and are using the reverse power stroke against the current to keep position in the river. Here, the stern is pointing toward the side you want to move. By facing downstream, you can see where you are going and can avoid obstacles that appear. Thus you can slow down and move sideways if necessary

Here's how a sideslip differs from a downstream ferry. The sideslip allows the canoe to move downstream with the current while slipping sideways; the downstream ferry slows the canoe down or holds it at a fixed position with respect to the bank. Additionally, the sideslip is useful in still water. Both techniques are to move quickly to the side to avoid obstacles in the water.

There are other more specialized techniques, especially for the sport paddler and the racer. But these are basic, and will enable you to get where you want to go. The more you paddle, the better you will get at it. As you become more proficient, the easier it will get and the more fun it will be. As with everything else talked about in this book, you will develop a personal style that works well for you, and if you have a regular partner, you'll find that you can become a mighty fine team.

ON THE WATER

I am not going to get into a discussion about using a compass on the lake, but there are a couple of points about navigating that are pertinent. For the most part, the lakes in Quetico and the BWCA are small enough that you can see the far shore. Friend Spouse seldom uses a compass, with exceptions on overcast days and the infrequent very large lake. His usual procedure is to lay out the map, pick out a landmark such as an island or a peninsula out to correspond with the map, and match the islands shown on the map with the land masses. (Sometimes this is easier said than done; gauging the represented size with the actual size gets tricky. Islands become visually three-dimensional only as you near them.) He selects a point and we paddle toward it. Portages will usually be somewhere near a low point on the horizon.

Probably the biggest problem to deal with in lake crossings is wind. Wind is no friend to a canoe. A canoe is not a powered vehicle; it is highly subject to wind, and knowing how to work with the wind when trying to travel across a lake is important. Safety is a foremost concern, and we can break that into three areas for achieving it.

The first is the canoe itself. It is *always* to the point that the canoe load is evenly distributed; that makes for a smoother ride. Put the packs in so that they present the lowest profile. This does two things: it lowers the center of gravity (vertically) and it reduces the wind resistance.

The second area is the condition of the paddlers. Before getting out on a windy lake, take stock of the situation. Are the paddlers' skills and stamina up to the demand? Don't start something you have doubts about being able to finish. Once out on the water, turning back is not really an option. No disgrace rests with the decision to stay put until the wind drops or shifts to a more favorable direction; being wind-bound is a common experience. Again, *wear* that PFD!

The third area is the strategy. Choose places to rest along the way. Hug the shore as much as you can; the idea is to reduce the swim-time that would be needed if the canoe capsized. The lee shore of a lake offers some protection with its wind shadow. Staying close to shore also gives you visual points that you can use to check your progress. This gives an important psychologial edge. It's mentally hard if you are paddling your heart out in the middle of the lake and it doesn't seem as if you are getting anywhere at all.

Try to keep the canoe's nose pointed into the wind. The boat is then more stable, as its length works in your favor, and less likely to tip over. It offers less wind resistance, and that makes paddling easier, too. A canoe going parallel with the waves becomes vulnerable to swamping or overturning.

The steering partner's job of maintaining direction is harder with a strong wind; it is therefore even more urgent that the bow paddler have the strength and stamina for the task at hand.

Friend Spouse notes that waves seem to come in clusters. A series of large ones will be followed by a brief lull.

We were put to the test one time when we were concluding a trip with a paddle up Brule Lake. Brule is several miles long and runs nearly due east and west. We were headed up the lake into a stout east wind. Paddling was tough, and there were few islands on the west half of the lake where we could duck behind and rest a few minutes. Waves were higher than my taste, and at times my paddle only waved at the water. Nonetheless, we persisted and in time made it to our take-out point without mishap.

LANDING THE CANOE

Landing a canoe calls for some thinking about the appropriate approach. On lakes, you do not usually have to deal with the problem of current. The ideal landing spot is one where you can sideslip the canoe up and step out. The reality is that often boulders of assorted sizes are in the water and make the approach more difficult.

If you want to land on a river bank, it takes a little more forethought. One objective in landing is to keep control of the canoe. Go a little ways downstream of your intended landing spot. Make a pivot turn and head back upstream. You can then paddle forward, preferably in the downstream eddy that is produced by an island or a projection along the back. The current will tend to sweep the tail of the canoe into the bank rather than out into the stream.

ALL TIED UP IN KNOTS

This is as good a time as any to talk about one fundamental and extremely useful camp skill, namely the ability to tie a few basic knots.

Camping in the wilderness requires a great deal of tying rope and cord either to itself or to something else. Before leaving home, you may have to tie a canoe to the car or trailer. At the departure point you will want to tie a rope to the bow of your canoe. Once on the campsite there is the cooking tarp to rig, the clothes line to string and the food pack to fly. All of these tasks require some sort of interaction with rope and cord.

Knots that join two ropes together are called bends and those that join a rope to something else, such as a tree limb, are called hitches. There are dozens of different hitches and bends that have been designed for specific applications; however, there are three hitches in particular that will make your camping trip a lot more enjoyable. These are the bowline, trucker's hitch, and the half hitch. Uses of the ones we'll talk about here aren't limited to the campsite, either.

BOWLINE

Use the bowline any time you want a non-slipping loop in a line. This knot is as strong as the line, will not slip and is relatively easy to untie, even with cold, rain-soaked fingers. If you want to tie a safety rope around yourself, tie a loop through the bow ring or a thwart of your canoe or around a tree, use the bowline.

BOWLINE

HALF-HITCH

The half hitch can be used in place of the bowline when hitching to a tree or the canoe but not when tying a safety rope around yourself. This knot can be tough to untie, particularly in the cold and damp, unless the quick-release method is used. Friend Spouse thinks that the quick-release half-hitch loses some security and wouldn't use it in critical situations. For instance, if we were tying the canoe up to the bank and going to remain aboard for a floating lunch, the quick-release half-hitch would be fine, but if we were going to get out and explore the shore, I would use the regular half-hitch or the bowline.

The double half-hitch is probably the most familiar and is a good secure, easy-to-tie knot as long as you don't care if the loop tightens around the hitched object.

SINGLE   QUICK RELEASE DOUBLE

HALF HITCH

POWER CINCH OR TRUCKER'S HITCH

The power cinch, sometimes called a trucker's hitch, is used when you want a really tight line. This is a combination of knots that relies on basic physics to give the mechanical advantage of a block-and-tackle pulley system. Use this knot to secure canoes for road travel or rigging a taut rope between two trees to support the cooking tarp. It is especially useful in flying the food pack. To rig a taut line, loop one end of your rope around a tree and tie off with a bowline. Loop the other end around a second tree and tighten with a trucker's hitch. This same technique also works to get well tightened tie-down cords on the cooking tarp or tent. With the trucker's hitch, you will be able to get any line tight as a guitar string and it will stay that way. The trucker's hitch can also come in handy if you need to pull the canoe off the rocks, lift a heavy food pack off the ground or perhaps move a deadfall off the trail since it essentially doubles the force you can apply to a load.

These three handy hitches will fill most of your camping needs. If you really want to become a knot "expert," see the Useful Reading for Clifford Ashley's *Encyclopedia of Knots* or John Cassidy's *Klutz Book of Knots.* Forget the square knot. Cassidy quotes Ashley to the effect that the "square knot...has probably been responsible for more deaths and injuries than all other knots combined."

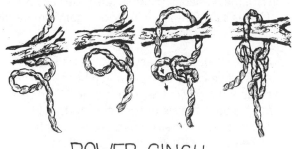

POWER CINCH

CAMP PROTECTION

There several areas, aside from pitching the tent (and that relies on the directions for the particular make of tent) that call for describing some techniques. One is safeguarding your food against marauding bears.

FLYING THE PACK

Traditional wisdom, the Forest Service and Park rangers all agree that the most effective way of preventing a bear from carrying off your food is to fly (hang) the pack. The lore says it should be at least 10 feet off the ground because that is outside the normal black bear's reach. They state that if an average-sized person can touch the bottom of the pack, so can a bear. Likewise, 6 feet out from the tree trunk supposedly is out of range. (In some of the more northern Canadian parks, campers are advised to double those distances. Bears are regarded *very* seriously.) They also point out that bears know how to jump, too. What's more, they are agile climbers, and this system would work well on trees like oaks which have heavy branching habits. However, generally, the tall trees in the BWCA are skinny conifers or birches whose first branches are 20 feet above the ground or with limbs that wimp out at two or three feet from the trunk. Finding a decent limb at the appropriate height and distance is a good trick. In fact, campsites very often have only one or two trees that fit anywhere near those specifications. Consequently, these trees were usually the food pack trees, and it didn't take a college education for bears to figure this out.

The method currently recommended by the Forest Service tries to meet the problem. This involves stringing a rope between two trees some 12 feet from the ground. A second rope is tied to the pack, and the other end thrown over the first rope. The pack is then hauled up and hangs suspended between two trees at the recommended height of at least 10 feet from the ground.

There are two difficulties with this system. One, we have found, lies in locating good trees for flying packs from and in the means of getting the suspension system up without breaking our own necks.

A popular method of getting a rope over a limb is to attach a rock or small stick (to give weight to the end) to the rope and then throw it over the target limb. This is easier said than done. (The light mesh bags that onions are packed in are good for this task.) Agile, athletic individuals may resort to climbing up the tree to get the rope over, and some have fallen and been injured, in at least one instance fatally, while putting up the suspension system. In some sites, campers with not much else to do have managed to put up more permanent suspension systems — they have gotten logs up between two trees from which to suspend the pack. Now, the same camp conditions that prevailed with the first system described were likely to prevail with the second, and the bears have this figured out, too, and the more or less permanent structure reinforces their conclusions.

A major fault with either system is that considerable physical effort is required to raise a 35-to-40 pound pack straight up. The friction produced in pulling up the pack over a limb or rope demands more effort, too. While Friend Spouse had the strength to haul the pack up with my assistance of boosting it up, my help ran out at about six feet.

However, Friend Spouse came up with a system that we have used (happily) for several years. It is easier to set up; it can be set up by people of considerably less than linebacker proportions. Best of all, it solves the basic problem of getting the food pack up away from the marauders and does it without the risks of climbing up two trees to put up the suspension line. It involves a very basic application of the inclined plane with all the benefits of mechanical advantage. All it takes is two stout, 50' ropes, one tall tree and an anchor point such as a rock, a bush or another tree.

It works like this. Follow the advice of the Quetico Park people and select a tree some distance from the tent, a tree that is sturdy and with a high branch. This tree is the base tree. The limb need not be particularly large — two or three inches in diameter at the limb's base will do, and even the stub of a limb will do if it is high enough up. What you want from it is altitude.

Tie a rock or stick to the end of your first line (we'll call it Line A) and throw it over that branch so that you can reach both ends of it. Tie its short end to the base tree. Run the other end of the line through the straps of the food pack. This line is the "track" for running the pack up to safety.

Now, take the loose end of Line A and tie it to a second, or anchor, tree (or bush, whatever) so that you have now strung a sloping line between the two trees. The lower and more distant the end of the suspension line (the track), the less effort it will take to pull the pack up. I generally give the pack a boost while Friend Spouse ties Line A off up shoulder high on the anchor tree. Doesn't take as much rope that way.

Before tying that end off, you need to pull Line A quite taut. Rig a power cinch (discussed earlier in this chapter). With a power cinch, you can remove the slack on the line to an incredible degree. Tie one end of the second rope (line B) to the food pack, making sure that you have it secured well. Throw the other end over the same branch as the first line and pull the pack up the sloping line. When the pack is at a bear-proof height, tie off the hoisting line (line B).

first line and pull the pack up the sloping line. When the pack is at a bear-proof height, tie off the hoisting line (line B).

Useful tip: put your "throwing rock" in a small mesh bag such as onions are sold in and tie the bag to the rope end.

Now comes the beauty part. The pack is hanging from Line A and is attached to Line B. It is ready to go traveling. Pull on the loose end of Line B and the pack travels up Line A until you get it the desired distance from the ground and from other trees. Then, with a couple of half-hitches, simply tie off Line B to a nearby tree. (You can use the base tree, if you like, but a little distance from it works easier. If the ropes are different colors, it's easier to identify which to untie when you want to take the pack down.)

Essentially what you have is the pack traveling up the hypotenuse of a very large right triangle with all the benefits that come from using the mechanical advantage of an inclined plane. It is much, *much* easier to pull an object up a slope than to lift it straight up. With this system, even a small woman can easily haul a 40 pound pack up to safety.

In the North Woods, each campsite comes with a lot of tall trees with a two inch limb 12 or 15 feet up. This means a camper has a wide assortment of trees to choose from for setting up. Finding the food pack tree becomes a bigger, more difficult guessing game for the scrounging bruin. Combined with good housekeeping practice (no food scraps around, care in packing food that might smell super-inviting, etc.), this should help insure a bear-free camping trip.

Friend Spouse and I have been camping in the Boundary Waters country for more than 20 years. We have rarely been successful in finding trees that work with the first system. Infrequently, we have used campsites where earlier campers had constructed some sort of suspension system. We therefore simply parked our food pack on the ground. In all those years, we have had two bear experiences. In one, we saw the bear come into camp. In fact, the bear was closer to the picnic table where our food pack sat than we were. In that instance, we succeeded in scaring the bear away by verbally abusing the poor critter in very loud tones. Bruin did not return.

RIGGING THE RAIN FLY

If you are traveling in unsettled weather, one of the criteria for choosing a campsite is whether it makes it easy to put up a tarp, or rain fly. A well-rigged rainfly is not far behind the tent in adding to your comfort on a rainy day. With it, you can prepare meals in relative dryness, and what a pleasure that is!

To rig the rain fly, you need six trees or bushes, the tarp and lines attached to the corners of the tarp. The first critical point is the location of those trees. You will be putting up the strong rope that will earlier described at a height that is comfortable for working under. Drape the tarp evenly over the ridgepole, and tie the lines to appropriate trees or bushes to stretch it out, using the ever-useful power cinch.

An even better shelter results if you run a secondary ridgepole perpendicular to the first. (This takes another two good trees.) You get a higher, flatter roof line, and more control over the pooling in hollows of the tarp in the rain, which is fine if it is not a blowing rain. With a blowing rain, the single ridgeline is better, as you can have more tarp on one side and pull it lower, for better shelter.

BUILDING A FIRE

You can't cook without fire, and the usual fuel is wood, unless you are using a camp stove exclusively. While more and more the trend is toward using camp stoves, even so, on occasion you may want to have a fire for comfort or for emergencies. There is always the possibility of needing a fire to warm up quickly, so you should know how to build a fire in short order and to keep it going. Usually in the BWCA and Quetico, there is an abundance of decent firewood available for collecting. Some people may be surprised to know that actually rather small sticks and limbs will make quite a satisfactory fire. The problem of finding firewood grows as the season wears on, particularly in the more heavily traveled areas. The Elegant Camper considers those who will be using the site later and refrains from wasteful and excessive fire-building.

FIRE-MAKING

Some people have trouble getting a fire going or keeping it going, once started. As with planning the first camping trip, start modestly. Use small twigs for tinder. A nice piece of birch bark as a base for the fire is great, as it will blaze up readily. Lay small twigs in a loose heap on the bark, then light it. A fire grows in part because the temperature of the combustible material rises. In short, what you do is warm the firewood. Don't waste those pasteboard boxes after you've used the food in them, either; save them for fire starters.

To build a fire, you need tinder, kindling and firewood. Tinder is the starter material; it can be small dry twigs, a piece of birch bark, wads of dry moss, dry paper tissue or the light cardboard from food packaging. Eldest Daughter taught me to carry a piece of birch bark in a plastic bag if we were traveling.

Once we are in a campsite, we do two things to make the fire building process a little easier. We cover the firewood pile at night (good old plastic trash bags!) and we keep a piece of birch bark in a bag, to keep it dry, particularly if we are moving camp on a daily basis. Lynne taught us that long ago, and it is helpful, especially if the traveling day is rainy. Use fallen bark only. Do not remove it from a living tree. Otherwise, later campers may find dead trees. There is absolutely no need to take bark from a living tree; birch abounds in the North Woods. You might have to move out a little way from the site to get some, but if so, move out!

As tinder will burn out very quickly, birch bark's purpose is to burn long enough for kindling to catch fire. Pocket lighters are easier to use than matches, and a lighter with an adjustable flame is even easier. Light the fire from the side where the breeze will do the most good in carrying the flame to the tinder and kindling.

Kindling is heavier material; here we are talking about finger-size twigs or small sticks. Add enough to get a small blaze. When the blaze is well-established, you can start adding larger pieces of wood or fuel. When we carried a hatchet, Friend Spouse used it to split large pieces down into chunks of about an inch and a half diameter. You can get a fire going sooner if you work with smaller pieces as you expose more surface to ready heating. Smaller pieces will burn down faster, too, so you need to be attentive to the fire. Add pieces as needed for the size of fire you need. For a basic cooking fire, you won't need big hunks of wood; it takes too long to get them going.

A good fire makes the cook shine. However, I am convinced that fire-building, like cooking, is an art and not a science. There are too many variables. The kind and quality of wood available affects it. Is the wood dry or wet? Wet wood will burn, if the fire is hot enough. Is it solid or punky? Punky, or partially decayed, wood only sits and smoulders unless it is very, very dry. Is the wood birch, pine, cedar, or what? Each burns well, but has its own characteristics. All the experts agree oak and hickory are marvelous; they are also very scarce in the BWCA.

If there is to be a fire, somebody needs to gather firewood. The Elegant Camper keeps in mind the general principle of minimum impact on the environment, and gathers only wood that is dead and down. That dead tree is home to a great many small creatures. You can pick up downed wood in the forest.

Most lakes have at least a few birch trees, which means that usually you can find nice "beaver logs" which are ideal for cooking fires. A "beaver log" is a piece of wood, generally no longer than maybe 15 inches, usually less, debarked and recognizable by a rather distinctive shaping of the ends from beaver gnawing. New logs, those of the previous winter and the current season, look brighter than old logs, which take on quite a gray coloration. The old will be dryer, unless you fished it out of the lake. Both the beaver and the Forest Service vigorously disapprove of wood being taken from a beaver lodge or dam. Keep that in mind many birds and animals rely on driftwood for their own lives and business.

Get the small pile blazing, and feed it carefully with more twigs and larger sticks as the fire grows. You can use either the "log cabin" or the "tepee" technique, either of which describes the pattern used to lay on the firewood. Sometimes it needs encouragement to blaze, so blow on the coals or fan them with your hat. Larger pieces, of approximate thumb thickness, can be added as the fire becomes established. When it is going well, fairly large pieces can go on if you are interested in getting a bed of coals for baking. Smaller, that is to say thinner, pieces will catch quicker, but will also burn out faster. Wet wood will burn, once the fire is hot enough to warm the piece sufficiently to dry, then burn. Green wood should be avoided. It burns badly — all its moisture must be "boiled" off before it is hot enough to burn. A fire also needs to be able to "breathe." Air must circulate through the fuel as it is put on. Be careful when adding wood; it is fairly easy to smother a struggling fire. It is exasperating when a fire collapses on itself, so that it is necessary to start over, almost from the beginning.

From the evidence at many campsites over the years, plainly a sizable number of people have not caught on to the fact that dry, dead wood burns better and cleaner than green. Pine makes a hot fire, but it should be very dry to reduce the smoky buildup on the cooking pots. Cooking is actually about the dirtiest job of camping when you consider the blackening of the pans and the consequent smudging of potholders and towels. Unless you are camping quite late in the season in a popular area, you can usually find enough good dead wood in the area to provide for several meals. It may be necessary to get in the canoe and canvass further out along the lake and into the woods for your supply. That's a rather pleasant activity, too, as of necessity you are taking closer looks, which sometimes produces delightful discoveries. Likewise, there is nothing amiss with going deeper into the woods around the campsite for firewood. When you prowl the woods, be sure to stay aware of your bearings. Better still, if you know how to use a compass, use it. It is not hard to become disoriented if you are keeping your eyes always to the ground.

Logically, the collected firewood will be dumped within reach for the fire-maker. It should not be so close that accidental ember hops could set the pile afire. Some woods, such as pine, are quite bad about popping sparks, so one should never leave a fire unattended. An elegant pile is one that is sorted for tinder, kindling, and firewood.

It seems more appropriate that the woodpile be just big enough for the needs of the group. We have found some sites with a huge pile of firewood waiting for us. We haven't minded, especially if we have had a hard day of traveling. It does suggest that the previous campers had too much energy and not enough other activities. What I don't like to see is evidence that previous campers had pretty well cleaned the area of good wood and had built large bonfires. The Elegant Camper keeps in mind the guiding rule of being as unobtrusive and non-invasive as possible. Gather only as much firewood as you need to prepare your meals, and keep your fire as small as you can. It is courteous to leave a wood pile, about one meal's worth, for the next camper, if you like, but take your plastic and trash with you.

Corydalis

7

AND WE'RE OFF!

*The Silver Shoes... can carry you to any place... in
the wink of an eye. All you have to do is knock the
heels together three times and command the shoes to
carry you wherever you wish to go."*
Frank L. Baum — *The Wizard of Oz*

At last, the time for the trip approaches. We can start packing,
and later I will talk about selecting a campsite and setting up
housekeeping. I have emphasized having appropriate equipment, and
now you start appreciating your decisions.

The first objective is to have as few individual pieces to stow in the
canoe as possible. By individual pieces, I mean packs and those loose
items which we generally call "trash." I don't mean that they are not
useful items; but "trash" can very easily clutter a canoe and the
portage trail heads when everything is taken out for carrying over the
trail. For us, the trash commonly includes the canoe paddles, the life
jackets and the fishing rods — anything not in a pack. As you see,
these are hardly junk items. However, on portages, we have seen a
truly astonishing and appalling assortment of trash carried by inelegant campers. We have seen a cardboard box, with holes cut in the
sides for handles used to carry food and kitchen gear (it looked as if
they were trying for the kitchen sink) — and we also saw that same box
giving up the ghost. We have seen stuff carried in plastic bags not
much heavier than dry cleaners' bags, with the contents dropping to
the path like Hansel's stones. We have seen, at portages, the favorite
bed pillow (complete with pillow case); we even expected to see the
teddy bear, too, even if the campers were teen-aged boys.

No, if you can't get the item into a pack, maybe you should
consider whether it is really necessary or not. After all, efficiency is

nothing more than a well-orchestrated laziness. Remember, we think of elegance as ease and grace, too.

Consider who is going to carry the packs. Our pack sizes have been geared largely to the carrying capacity of a small woman or a youngster. I think carrying more than one can comfortably and surely manage is dangerous. While some of the portage trails are like garden paths, many are not, and maintaining sure footing is more difficult if one is overloaded or vision is obscured by double-packing. Furthermore, double-packing can get uncomfortably hot!

ORGANIZING THE PACKS

Essentially, we use four packs: the food pack, the housekeeping pack, the shelter pack and the day pack. The carrying capacity of our various packs determines who carries which on a portage. We generally try to keep each pack weight under 40 pounds, which is about as much as I can easily carry on a portage of any length; the general principle is to gear to the weakest of the party. One shouldn't lose sight of the size and strength of the people who will be carrying those packs. If there are younger campers in the group, there is the risk of ruining the experience by overloading them. Young or inexperienced canoeists, not necessarily the same group, don't need to be treated delicately, but it is sensible to consider the strength and fitness level of all the party and load packs accordingly. Canoe trips should give a person a chance to extend oneself a bit, yet be able to enjoy it. With the paddles and life vests, the whole load of gear in the canoe weighs about as much as a person.

PACK LOADING

In loading a pack, do not use the grocery bagging rule. You *don't* want the heaviest stuff to the bottom. Backpackers understand this "body-loading" well. Even with a pack frame, the lowest part of their load is barely below the waist. However, the height of the load may extend a little above the packer's head without adding difficulty to managing it. The weight of the pack, as well as the bottom of it, should be above the carrier's tailbone. If the heaviest part of the pack is below that point, it creates a greater strain on the back, shoulders and legs; it is much harder to carry. Shortening the pack straps also moves the load higher where it is easier to carry. This is the problem that the newer packs address so beautifully. They have a hip belt and a chest strap as well as the shoulder straps which makes it possible to fine-tune the adjustment of the straps so that the load rides as easily and comfortably as possible.

If the pack (of the Duluth variety) is like a huge cube, the packer will have trouble getting up with it and balancing. Just imagine an enormously pregnant body in reverse.

While originally writing this book, I discovered that most of the books having to do with hiking and camping were written by men who were not thinking about women taking up the activities. They had a marked tendency to recommend larger packs and loads than are really feasible for most women, and totally out of the question for young-sters. For recreational camping, with a fair amount of canoe traveling, and hence portaging, a pack should weigh no more than one-quarter to one-third of the carrier's weight. I don't care if the voyageurs did sometimes carry 200 pounds at a trip. That couldn't have been fun, and they wore out well before their time. Likewise, the matter of bulk should be looked at. The contents of a #3 pack may not be terribly heavy, but a small person has less length along which to distribute the bulk. The distance from neckbone to tailbone is less. The newer equipment is much improved over the old time stuff. Designers are developing packs similar to a backpacker's pack, but better adapted to canoe travel. More companies now are designing packs meant to fit women, too. (See Appendix, Equipment Sources for a more extensive discussion of packs and pack manufacturers.)

Let's look at what goes in each pack.

THE FOOD PACK

We long used our old faithful #2 Duluth pack for carrying our food, and it is quite roomy for a week's supply for two, which runs about 35 pounds. The food pack, is, at least at the beginning, the heaviest. I would hesitate to use a #3 for the simple reason that fully loaded, it would be too heavy for me. Miz Blue, the internal frame pack I carry, now is the food carrier and has a greater capacity than the #2 Duluth. On trips, as the food supply goes down, I shift food preparation articles into it to even out the loads to be carried. The Duluth pack comes into service for longer trips when a second food pack is needed.

Actually, there are two stages to organizing the food pack, and of the two, the meal planning — deciding what is going into the pack — is more critical. The key is to make lists, check and review them. A written list is invaluable in assuring that you haven't forgotten anything. Save those lists as reference for future trips, too.

In the preliminary stages of planning meals, it is a good idea to pause to consider how much "new" experience will happen. If this is a first canoe trip, and you don't have much experience in camping and camp cooking, then it makes good sense to keep it simple. Choose the packaged camp foods; the preparation of them is very simple, and the number of servings is indicated on the label. You can even buy an entire meal for a group in a single package. It is not a bad way to start. If you have already done some camp cooking, you can be more adventurous.

In the old days, after my daughters and I came back from our expedition shopping trips, we would lay out the food packets on the floor, usually with the dinners first. We would then play "shuffle and deal," putting breakfasts and lunches and dinners together in a general attempt to make each day's food intake fairly equal. That is, if the morning meal looked rather light, then we could put in heartier or more numerous snacks. Then all three meals, plus snacks, went into a single bag, so that the number of bags equaled the number of days we were planning to be out. It was then an easy matter just to pluck up a bag and everything was there.

We also counted the evening meal, dinner, as the first meal of a bag. After breakfast, all one needed to do was to remember to put in drinking cups and maybe a knife for cutting salami or spreading cheese or peanut butter or whatever into the bag, and lunch was ready for stowing at the top of the day pack, or whatever was most convenient for easy grabbing.

I still make menu plans before I go grocery shopping, but I don't necessarily follow them when we're out.

Packing each day's food together is a good idea especially if your party has more than four or five people or if you aren't terribly sure of pulling together a meal out in the woods. Planning does take a great deal of the uncertainty out of meal preparation, and as a result, it is much easier to feel elegant about it.

One very important point to consider for planning a meal. How many pots do you have along, and how many will you need for preparing a given meal? It is all too easy to plan an elaborate, so to speak, meal, and then realize you don't have the equipment to carry through.

The other phase of organizing the pack is stowing all the meals along with the staples and incidental items.

First of all, I line *all* our packs with heavy plastic liners, heavier than the usual garbage bag (this is insurance for wet days, water in the bottom of the canoe and small critters in camp), and insert a cardboard stiffener to give shape to the pack (a large detergent box or heavy cardboard box works well). An internal stiffener makes getting at stuff in the pack easier, and it also makes it possible to carry food items that otherwise might get all squashed out of shape. A #2 Duluth pack takes a box that is 15" x 9" x 16" deep. It is not the easiest box size to find; you may have to cut one down to size and tape the seams with heavy tape. An empty 40-pound detergent, though a little small, will do nicely, and I hear a beer case fits a #3 pack quite nicely.

I have used the round oatmeal or cornmeal cartons to hold things like the package of coffee, the seasonings (salt, pepper, lemon juice, bouillon cubes, other spices, etc.) or other such items, but now I am more likely to put such stuff into a gallon-size zip-locking bag. (Unless they are really messy, I put emptied self-zipping bags to other use.) Label the lids. The cartons travel very well stacked inside the box liner. Common sense should prevail in packing the food pack. You can easily put the meals you expect to use late in the trip to the very bottom of the pack. I find that it is more practical for me to put the bulk items — baking mix, the oil and margarine (and the rum) toward the top, as those are items I use every day. Packing snack items in small batches reduces the potential damage from the "marauders" getting into the food.

For the daily repacking, you'll find that you develop your own procedures, based on the kind and extent of cooking you do. The guiding principle should be to keep everything as convenient as possible.

THE HOUSEKEEPING PACK

Big Blue, the masculine version of our internal frame packs, carries the housekeeping gear. At the beginning of a trip, this pack holds the tent, ground cloth, tarp, first aid kit, all the cooking and eating equipment, rope collection, repair materials, and the saw. This will generally start out as the heaviest of the lot, weighing in at some 42 pounds with our current gear. (Big Blue can hold much more, but we try to keep the loads smaller.)

Remember to pack the first aid kit high so you can get at it easily if needed. We pack it in Big Blue rather than in the day pack; we find the need for it more likely arises in camp rather than on the trail.

THE SHELTER PACK

Over the years, we have varied our procedures regarding the personal gear. Currently, we each have a stuff sack that holds spare socks, etc., clean clothes and our sleeping garments. Those stuff sacks go into the shelter pack along with our sleeping bags, a small toiletries kit, mattresses and inflatable pillows. The Space Blanket goes into that pack, too. (Because we like some comforts, we also take canvas camp seats, and they go in here, too.) The Big Green Honker, the #3 Voyageur pack, holds it all nicely.

Some tents have their poles in sections that live in a small bag. This used to be the storage place for our camp saw. We used to have to carry the tent bag separately, but it now has a home in Big Blue.

THE ODDS AND ENDS

The day pack holds items you want handy — lunch, the canteen, camera gear and perhaps rain garb. This can easily run to about 15 pounds. This is the best pack for shared items such as insect repellent and sunscreen, and for the miscellaneous items like personal medications. I have accumulated a "bag of tricks" with such items as extra bungee cords, the compass, some string, a few Band-aids and towelettes, and the like.

"TRASH DISPOSAL"

Friend Spouse says that wearing his life jacket on portage gives a bit of cushioning under the canoe portage yoke if a canoe does not have good (comfortable) portage pads. However, now he pokes both his jacket and mine under the front seat. In some canoes, the paddles can be secured in the canoe. (In the "olden days," the paddles were placed in so that they formed the portage yoke.) We have made progress with handling our fishing rods. Originally, on the first day out and the last day coming in (thus bracketing the fishing opportunities), the rods were usually broken down to carry in a small case. During the trip, they were at full length, making them a little more awkward to carry. Then we found bungee (shock) cords work well to secure fishing rods to the underside of a canoe seat or thwart. Friend Spouse glued Velcro strips into the canoe to hold the rod butts and an extra paddle. I have since seen some commercial versions of this idea, which is definitely a winner. The important thing with loading the canoe with such items is to insure the canoe's balance while being carried. Properly done, the carrier needs only one hand to keep the canoe on an even keel while making the portage.

The point? It is desirable to keep at least one hand free while walking a portage. It helps in balancing and in shooing bugs. It is even nicer if both hands are free.

Since double-portaging is so routine for us, we have found it helpful to designate — in our own minds, at least — what goes together on a trip. For instance, on my portages, I carry the loose stuff. The object of this little exercise is to reduce the likelihood of something being left behind on the wrong end of a portage. The Elegant Camper keeps an alert eye on the gear.

THE EXTRAS

The number of persons in the party will have some effect on the number of extras, or "toys" that are taken, though the number of canoes needed must also be considered. Since commonly there are only the two of us, we tend to take as little as we can. Once you have the food and the housekeeping stuff organized, the rest is really fairly simple. More people in the party are additional "mules" who do not significantly add to the amount of housekeeping gear, other than tents and sleeping bags. A party of four will generally mean at least a second canoe and one more pack. The cooking equipment is the essentially the same (for us) for six as it is for two. Extra food may call for an additional pack, depending on the number of people and the length of the trip.

If you can, rehearse your packing before you make the trip. If you are renting a pack, this is inconvenient. Load it and walk around with it a while to get the feel of it. One suggestion: when double-packing (if you feel you must), put the larger pack on first; this is the rear pack; then put the smaller pack on to the front. The idea is that if it becomes necessary to drop a pack, it's easier to do the front one first. One the trips where I have double- packed and double-portaged, I made a point of carrying the smallest pack (usually the day pack) in front on the first trip so that I easily see what problems the trail might offer. Carrying a #2 pack in front does tend to block the view, and some trails are trials.

LOOK BACK, THINK AHEAD

It is helpful to the habitual camper (one who goes year after year or oftener) to keep a basic collection of items together in the housekeeping pack. I make it a point, at the end of a camping trip, to replace missing or consumed items such as insect repellent, matches, etc., so that this basic pack is always ready for a trip. It also makes sense to check for needed repairs and tend to them immediately on return, before you forget what the problem was.

ON THE MOVE

Before we get into a discussion of portages, let me re-emphasize the value of including a map such as those discussed in Chapter 2 among your equipment. I can't imagine anything more ill-advised than to go into the wilderness without maps. I don't care if you have gone into a particular area before. It is absolutely incredible how much a lake can seem to change on a foggy or rainy day, not infrequent events, and a paddler can easily become thoroughly disoriented.

MAPS

BWCA and Quetico maps not only show the waters of the particular area, but where to find the portages and where campsites are. Also, BWCA maps tell the length of portages (in rods; remember there are 16½ feet per rod and 320 rods per mile). The Appendix includes a conversion table listing the equivalents of rods, meters, yards, miles, acres and kilometers. The newer maps, such as those described in Chapter 2, show contour lines, helpful information in looking for a portage. Look to the horizon in the direction of the area the map says is the portage location. The skyline generally droops, thus indicating a water course. The portage will usually be quite close by. (For map sources, check the Appendix — Sources.)

At one time, each BWCA portage had a sign — a simple post bearing the name of the portage and its length. Some wilderness enthusiasts favored letting these portage markers completely disappear, and that is what has happened. In Quetico, there are no portage markers. Sometimes a portage can be very difficult to locate, even with the post marker. Rainy weather makes it even harder.

VIVE LA DIFFERENCE!

Of course, what the maps do not tell you is what the portages are like, other than that they go through steep or gentle or marshy terrain. Portages are as individual as people. Some are inviting, picturesque, and cheerful. Others are foreboding at their ends, but hold unexpected delights along the way. Each portage has its own unique combination of flowers, trees, and shrubs. There are virtually countless ways in which they differ. Let me give a few examples. In the eastern BWCA, Alton Lake is at the end of a 30-rod (165 yards or 150.9 meters) portage. At either end, the landing is friendly and convenient for loading and off-loading a canoe. The path itself is wide, nearly six feet across, fairly free of rocks, and relatively flat. If it were completely flat, Alton Lake and Sawbill would be the same level. As it is, a small creek flows from Alton down into Sawbill. It is a fine portage for people who come up to do a little fishing but are really not up to heavy-duty camping and portaging.

The next portage, from Alton to Beth Lake, expects more, but still reflects the fact that it is fairly close to an entry point. A portage of 140 rods (under half a mile), it used to have three canoe rests, or points where the canoe bearer could pause and rest with the canoe propped up. (There were no such rests for the "pack mules.") I long suspected that the number of canoe rests on a portage was determined by a formula based on the difficulty of the trail, its length, and how close the portage is to an entry point. Further out from entry points, canoe rests seemed to be generally at 70-rod intervals on long portages, and a portage, unless it is very difficult, had to be at least 110 rods to qualify for a rest. (I use past tense in describing canoe rests; in 1993 the Forest Service was in the process of taking them all down. They will be missed.) The Canadians don't provide canoe rests.

In contrast to the nearby portages, the less-heavily used Hazel portage is narrower, in spots quite sunny. It has a wonderful feeling of wilderness, until about half way across it, the trail is crossed by the wide swath of an old logging road, a jolting reminder of human use.

Long (200 or more rods) portages pose a bit of a problem if there must be return trips (for us, that is a given). Don used to carry the canoe straight through, but as we have gotten older, we carry half way and stop at a canoe rest. We then go back to get the rest of our gear. Then we tackle the second half of the portage in the same way. A variation on this works well if the party has an odd number of packs. One can carry the canoe all the way through while the second brings one pack to the half-way point. Both then re-trace, with the first picking up the pack at the half-way point and the other bringing on the gear left at the trail head. Some veterans prefer to take a pack through first in order to check out the trail.

Keep in mind that it is potentially very dangerous to overload. A carrier needs a good clear view of the trail, especially if it is an unfamiliar one. I have spoken about the problems that would arise with a leg or ankle injury. Injuries are more apt to occur when a person is over-tired or is trying more than his or her capabilities allow. Finally, to emphasize that this is a real judgment call, think about the specific capabilities of each member of the party. Remember part of the fun of canoeing and wilderness camping is the opportunity to see how much one can *comfortably and safely manage,* not to create an ordeal.

In Chapter 6, I spoke of loading the canoe; now that well-organized gear is ready to load. If there is not a light line, or painter, tied to the bow of the canoe, put one on before you start out. You'll find it handy to tie up the canoe to a tree or rock while you enjoy a floating lunch. Some call it a dingle string and find holding it helpful in balancing the canoe on portage. If we anticipate needing to "line" a canoe through a portion of a stream (either because the water is too shallow to carry canoe and us or the stream is too swift to paddle against), Friend Spouse ties leader lines to both ends of the canoe, all bundled up and secured to the thwart with a bungee cord.

The best loading sites are those where you can pull the canoe up alongside and unload. However, they aren't all alike. At some portages, gear must be handed forward (or back, depending on whether you are loading or unloading) and that is much more work. Then you begin to appreciate the Duluth pack's "ears" — those upper edges of the flap — as you haul the pack around. They make helpful handles to grab, and if someone has been properly crafty in loading the canoe, the straps and buckles will not be on the side where they would hang up when the pack is being dragged out.

Once out on the lake, with luck or skill and cunning, you suddenly realize that not only can you move the canoe, but you are paddling in efficient harmony with your partner. The physical effort, at least for a time, feels good, and the soft sound of the water burbling past the nose and along the keel of the canoe is pleasant. Your spirit lifts with hearing bird calls from the forests along the shore, punctuated occasionally by the rowdy calls of the ravens or the calls of frogs, or the underlying hum of insects. Surrounded by a heightened sense of the wilderness, it no longer seems right to be noisily human, and the Elegant Camper finds him- or herself lowering the voice, to be less intrusive.

But pleasant as the lake may be, for the traveler, a portage is the goal.

PORTAGING

Portage. The word is a French one, referring to a carrying place. We use the word in confusing ways. Out on the lake, we look for a "portage." That is, we are looking for the end of a path or trail that is also called a "portage." Then we "portage" or carry our stuff from the portage, or trail end, to water again. We do this because the Boundary Waters area is dotted with lakes, the remains of ice blocks from the last Ice Age (and some would swear they are not much warmer, either). Water needs places to drain, and so there are many creeks, and bogs, and marshes. Some of these are not big enough or deep enough for canoe travel. At certain seasons, too, the water level is lower than at other seasons, making water travel difficult or impossible. In places, ridges separating one lake from another have low points. It is such places where a person or an animal can find the most favorable path for getting from one lake to another. I have often speculated as we portaged, who started this particular path? Was it an animal, in company of its kind, seeking an easy route? We know animals do have their habitual trails. Was it an Indian, searching for food? I suspect that many were indeed originally animal trails, followed first by Indians, sometimes later by the old fur trappers. Some trails are modern, built as the Forest Service people shift traffic from too-heavily-worn areas or from trails flooded by beaver projects. It is not an important question, but thinking about it gives texture to the experience.

THE FAIR SHARE

The Elegant Camper tries to insure that he or she is doing a fair share of the work. On portages, this involves getting all the gear from one body of water to the next with minimum effort, but with a reasonable amount of effort by all concerned. Personally, I cannot carry a 75-pound canoe alone, though our 110-pound daughter could for short distances. However, I am a good walker, and I have no objection to making two trips on a portage to carry two packs. (I seldom double-pack.) If one has the strength and stamina to carry 50 to 80 pounds over a long portage, that of course will get the job done faster. For me, and perhaps for many others, it is less wearing to carry smaller loads twice than one huge one once. In packing for a trip, it is smarter, to my thinking, to pack gear into two packs that may be carried singly or double-packed, rather than into one large one.

One should avoid the sort of situation we saw at one portage. A couple had been fishing; they had the canoe and what appeared to be a #4 pack, plus an assortment of hand-carried fishing gear items (what we call "trash"). They unloaded the canoe, and he headed down the portage with it. She slipped the straps of the pack on, but was unable to get up with it; the center of gravity was too far back. She said she had carried it before, and quite possibly she could have this time if she had help in getting up. But she left it for her partner to come back for while she took the hand stuff. This is not elegant! Her partner was compelled to carry an outsize share of the load, and this should never have been necessary on a routine basis. They would have done much better to have divided the gear into two packs, perhaps one as large as a #3, which she could confidently and consistently manage, and a smaller one that possibly could be double-packed if the situation warranted.

MANAGING LONG PORTAGES

Long portages pose a bit of a problem if there must be return trips (for us, that is a given). I don't like to leave our stuff widely separated, but there are several ways of dealing with it. You can carry a load about half way, then go back for a second. Take it all the way through, and then go back to pick up the other. I like this because it gives a bit of a rest between loads. This is particularly good if everybody has two trips to make. A variant on that it is for one to take a load half way, while the partner is going on through with his first load. On the return trip to the trail head, the first person picks up the remainder and goes on the full trip with it. The partner goes back to the half way point to pick up that first load. This makes an equitable distribution of walking and load.

Keep in mind that it is potentially very dangerous to overload. A carrier needs a good clear view of the trail, especially if is an unfamiliar portage. I spoke about the problems rising from a leg or ankle injury. Injuries are more apt to occur when a person is over-tired or is trying more than his or her own capabilities allow. Finally, to emphasize that this involves a real judgment call, think about the specific capabilities of each member of the party. Part of the fun of canoeing and wilderness camping is the opportunity to see how much one can manage, but not how much one must manage. It is supposed to be fun. It should not be an ordeal.

UNLOADING

Having found the portage, you unload the canoe. Try to keep the canoe supported by water so long as it is loaded. Dragging a loaded canoe across the ground is hard on the craft and should be avoided. We prefer standing on the shore or on a rock for unloading. At some portages — not many, it is possible to pull the canoe alongside the shore; then it is easy to pull the packs out before removing the boat from the water.

An alternative method in loading or unloading is the so-called "wet footing" method, favored by most experienced canoeists (but not this one) and those with Kevlar (expensive) canoes. As its name suggests, one steps into the water to load or unload the canoe. A disadvantage to this manner of loading is that wet feet bring water into the canoe. I don't like that.

Sometimes it happens that another party is coming from the woods. Since there is not very much room at a portage and two canoes cannot work at the same time, one should think about the courteous and practical thing to do. If the other party is simply carrying gear at this point, unload your canoe and get it out of the water as soon as possible to make room for the canoe that is coming. Keep your gear to one side and all together to reduce possible confusion. Some parties travel with an incredible assortment of stuff. One time a party of six fishermen came up behind us on a very long portage. Along with all their fishing paraphernalia, tents, food, etc., one man was carrying a beer keg — the hard way, in his arms like a baby. Their canoe carriers were following us fairly closely, so they could not put their boats in the water until we got out of the way.

Having completed a portage, you may feel a snack (such as a piece of hard candy) is in order. Depending on how bad the bugs are, or whether the portage was crowded, you may choose to enjoy it while still on shore or out on the water. Then it's off to the next portage.

HOW IS THIS PLACE?

After all the effort of determining a route, getting gear together, planning food, and finally making a day's trek, the prospect of a pleasant campsite grows in importance. In some wilderness areas, such as the BWCA, the designated campsites have been selected, marked, and prepared for campers by experienced people. Even so, some sites are better than others, and some are better at one time rather than another. After a trip or two, you will find that you are already becoming something of a connoisseur in considering sites.

The management of wildernesses may vary on what is called a campsite or what will be found at one. Follow the appropriate regulations, and follow the general principle of making minimum impact on the site you choose.

We like island campsites. Possibly it's because of the sheer poetry of the notion of staying on an island in the wilderness; possibly it's because there is a greater feeling of privacy there, though that's not necessarily the case. If you feel that an island site is more apt to be safe from bears, you should know that they actually are competent swimmers. However, I feel that a bear would be rather loath to swim a considerable distance just to check out an island that had had little to offer. This is not to say that we avoid or dislike shore sites; we don't. Shore sites have their own special qualities.

ASSESSING THE SITE

Weather may have a major effect on your choice of site. (This assumes you are in an area that leaves room for choice. Lakes on popular routes on rainy days may have every site occupied.) You'll think about wind direction for orienting the tent. If rain seems likely, you should consider the feasibility and ease of putting up a tarp where you would enjoy it.

While at first you may find yourself noting only the beauty of a site, it isn't long before you begin almost automatically noting the assets and deficiencies of a place. You notice the character of the landing area: how easy is it to load and unload a canoe there? You note the fire pit. Authorized campsites in the BWCA have a steel fire grate; in fact, it is illegal to make a fire in any place other than in one of these prepared fire pits. While it is not particularly a problem in the BWCA, as the rocks there are most frequently granites and gneiss, some rocks are porous and may explode with their own internal steam produced by the heat of the fire. However, in recent years I tend to use camp stoves almost exclusively for cooking, but the grate still is the cooking area and the degree of protection it has affects the ease of work.

However, in 1984, the U.S. Forest Service announced that tracts on eight lakes in the BWCA would be taking on a more primitive character with the removal of the fire grates and latrines. The affected areas being managed for primitive camping comprise about ten percent of the federal land in the BWCA and generally are deeper in the interior of the Area. (See Appendix — Canoeing in Minnesota.)

Quetico campsites are more spartan; there is no fire grate nor latrine. However, long custom has led to the presence of fire pits (sometimes more than one at some sites).

You can expect "sitting" logs on two or maybe three sides of the fire pit area. Once in a while, you will find a picnic table left from the Forest Service construction era of the 1950s and '60s that has been overlooked by those who would keep the wilderness experience as primitive as possible. A table with benches is luxury!

Another point to check out in the first inspection of a campsite is where the tent pads are. They are easily recognizable as an area with a rectangular and generally smoothed surface. If you have a free-standing tent, the task of erecting the tent is simpler, as you do not have to rely on tree placement for erecting it. You do want to pay attention to the direction of the prevailing wind since you want to orient the tent in the direction that will provide the most comfortable ventilation and will let the wind blow the bugs away from your door. Sometimes it is pertinent to notice whether the tent site is protected from the wind or rain. Another consideration is how level it is. It is not always possible to pick a site that offers a completely level tent pad. Consequently, you have to think about where you propose to put the head of your sleeping area. It is not particularly restful to sleep with your head on the lower end of a slope.

It makes sense to check for rocks and roots, particularly if you are not using any sort of mattress. We have rejected one or two campsites because a hill of large ants was in the tent pad.

When we are checking out a campsite (whether we propose to camp there or whether we are stopping for lunch or just to make a pit stop), after giving the main area the once-over, we check out the necessary facilities — the latrine.

THE FACILITIES

The matter of latrines is rather interesting. In the BWCA, this is part of the basic equipment for the authorized campsites, with its location carefully chosen by those experts who selected the campsites. The latrine must meet certain legal specifications, most notably the distance (at least 150 feet) from the lake or stream. The object of course is to prevent pollution of the native waters, but it has resulted in some curious locations. The facility itself is a simple structure. The earlier sturdy wooden box throne with a lid is being replaced. The replacements are plastic, frequently lidless, and made to look rather like tree stumps. In short, what you have is a basic throne over a pit latrine, and that's all there is. It is reached by a trail from the campsite.

Now, as I say, the first concern in locating the latrine is the "safe" distance from the lake or stream. Apparently the second consideration is whether it is possible to dig a latrine in that area. Privacy is obviously a third and minor consideration, probably because in the summer the trees and undergrowth are expected to provide screening. It is not at all unusual for the throne-sitter to have an absolutely spectacular view of the lake. I remember one site where we stopped while out on a day-trip. I no longer recall whether the site was marked on the map, or whether we spotted it and went in. The site looked unused, even unfinished; I suspect that it was abandoned before completion because the site-choosers decided they had made a mistake. However, I found the expected trail and followed it. It made several bends through the brush, and each bend took a steep turn up. finally, puffing and panting, I got to the top of the trail and found the throne. Even then the climb wasn't finished; it had been necessary to put a couple of small log steps in place before the seat was accessible. However, the spot offered an incredibly beautiful view of the lake.

In Quetico, latrines, like steel fire grates, are not a part of the site equipment. I have mixed feelings over which arrangement is better. A major problem with provided latrines is that people all too often have used them as disposal units for all manner of things — plastic bait cartons, schnapps bottles, underwear, even running shoes (running shoes? yes, running shoes!). The warm season when all the organisms of decay are most efficient is not really very long. It is expecting far too much of the organisms to think they can dispose of plastic bags or metal, and there is no way they can deal with glass.

One point cannot be over-emphasized. The latrine is there for one purpose and only one, specifically the disposal of human bodily waste. Certainly the latrine is not meant for anything not readily biodegradable. They are not garbage disposal units. What's more, bears aren't squeamish about where they forage for food. Yet there are those clods loose in our forests who apparently think their wastes and trash will all miraculously disappear. It's enough to make an Elegant Camper develop an elitist attitude.

On the other hand, the absence of a designated place for human waste provides its own objections. On our first trip into Quetico, I kept seeing funny little white mounds short distances back into the woods. It dawned on me that the white stuff was toilet paper that had been rained on a few times. Seeing those papier-maché-like artifacts made me aware that a walk in the woods could provide one with a nasty little surprise. The inclusion of a backpacker's trowel should infer that it will be used.

Kathleen Meyer, in her excellent little book of forthright and provocative title (See Appendix — Useful and Recommended Reading) addresses the larger issue of responsibility for human waste by all who engage in outdoor activities and its proper disposal. When the urge hits on the trail, and believe me, it will, you will do what any animal does, but choose your animal carefully. The cat is a good model: it likes a bit of privacy while relieving itself, and it scratches a cat hole (what else?) for use and then covers it up. A hole about six inches deep is deep enough for the soil bacteria to get at wastes to be decomposed. Replace the top soil and duff to conceal your work.

The sheer numbers of people taking to the outdoors make a cogent reason for learning how to dispose of one's wastes properly and considerately. Consider: river-running canoeists in other parts of the country are advised to take a can (covered, one would hope) for storing used toilet paper to be burned later. A winter resident of the Florida Keys has a holder, resembling a suet feeder for birds, and matches at hand for burning used toilet paper. It is fastened to the tree by his "ladies' facility." (It is one of the rules of his island: Burn the toilet paper.)

LOCATION, LOCATION, LOCATION

These are the most important points for consideration at a new campsite. You also want to note what exposure the site has to the wind and whether at the given time that is what you want. There are various factors to be considered. One of the most important, I think, is the direction and strength of the wind. I spoke about the tent site's relationship to wind. Equally important is the fire pit's relationship. If you have a spot that on that particular day is quite windy and the fire pit is open, rather than having a rock shield, you may as well forget about baking biscuits over a slow fire. You had better shift the meal plans to use as few pots as you can and be prepared for constant vigilance and some frustration. You'll have as much difficulty with the stove, as the wind blows the heat away. If the day is windy and cold, pick a sheltered spot, or barring that, look for trees that can be used as points for putting up the tarp as a windbreak.

I always check out the trees around the immediate site area with a thought to basic housekeeping. Where am I going to string my clothesline? Do we need a couple of trees to string line to put up the tarp? Is there a good spot to put up the hammock (if we brought it)? For the bear-wary, where is the best place for flying the food pack?

Other things to think about are bugs, rain and sun. A good breeze to keep bugs at a distance can make all the difference in comfort. If the weather looks like impending rain, we look for trees from which to rig a rain fly. Conditions will dictate exactly how the fly or tarp is rigged. You may want to rig what is essentially a roof. This works fine for misty days. Or you may want it with a long slope from the ridge, where it can not only deflect wind, but also drain away rain water, instead of allowing it to puddle on the tarp. (Actually, it is very difficult to prevent some puddling.) In cool seasons, a sunny site is a joy. On a hot day in high summer, that same site could well be a hot-box.

A characteristic that can enhance a campsite is the nature of the landing area for the canoe. Can we land alongside the shore or do we have to step out at the front and pull the canoe up for the rest of the unloading? How easy will it be to get the packs in and out? What will the job be like when it is time to pull the canoe up on the shore for the night? Since contemporary (non-metal) canoes are lighter than their older counterparts, they are much more vulnerable to being blown about on land. The same characteristic that makes them slip through the water also makes it easier for them to slide off a slope. If a stormy night seems likely, take especial care to see that the canoe will stay where you put it.

SETTING UP CAMP

Good housekeeping is the hallmark of the Elegant Camper. By "good housekeeping" I refer to the handling of all those matters that have to do with getting on with life. The Elegant Camper works to achieve a comfortable and pleasant home in the wilderness, be it for one night or for two weeks, which is the time limit for staying at any one site.

Let's talk about several aspects. Once the site has been selected, it is time to settle in. The canoe is unloaded and secured up on the shore (there are few things more inelegant than one's canoe escaping, especially from an island); the gear is all brought up to the site and (usually) dumped. If we have been traveling, we prefer to stop in the middle part of the afternoon, say about 2:30 or 3, set up camp, relax a bit, prepare an early supper and then go fish for a couple of hours before dark. When the children were young and along, we didn't fish; generally we traveled each day, and we found an early stop was pleasant. Then after supper we would explore the area around that particular site.

Even now, this is always a delight for me: each lake is different, with its own character, its own particular plant life and animals, and I never tire of the variations. The recollections of some campsites are enriched with the memory of the bird that sang us to sleep each night. (I later learned it was the gray-cheeked thrush.) As the darkness deepened, his calls came further apart and seemed more reluctant, as though he were listening to some other voice telling him he had to get in x-number more before he quit for the night, until finally he got his quota in.

Getting the tent up is the first order of business. Then I like to get the sleeping bags opened out to the air, especially if we traveled that day. The personal gear goes inside the tent. The old practice of digging a little trench around the tent with the object of draining away rain water is not only thoroughly outdated, but vigorously frowned upon. Trenching damages the area, leaving it highly vulnerable to erosion. The soil of the forest floor does not go very deep.

Then we turn our attention to the "kitchen" area. I look around for large flat rocks or log sections that would serve for a surface to set things for food preparation. It is much more esthetic to set pans or packages on a rock that you can clean off than on the ground. It's more convenient if there is a couple fairly close to the fire pit. A few sites in the BWCA actually still have tables, but don't expect them. The food pack and the housekeeping pack are deposited in the kitchen area. Then I select a couple of trees to string the clothes line and I hang out the towels to air.

We select a tree for flying the food pack. The lore of the North Woods is full of stories of tents ripped and packs shredded by marauding bears. (In Florida, raccoons are the major offenders.) Campers tell tales of seeing Miz Bear instructing her cubs in the ways of acquiring a hapless camper's food supply. Some swear that the bears have maps showing all the campsites. (The canoe outfitters also urge flying the food pack; what's more, they charge for rented packs that are lost to bears.) Need I remind anyone about the hazards of having food in the tent?

Over the years, bears have gotten quite sophisticated about recognizing packs or other containers that might hold food, particularly if the contents were fresh and sweet. It hasn't taken very many ursine generations to learn that campsites mean campers, and that campers mean that food is available, and that food tends to put it in the same spots. As all the lore goes, bears adore bacon, peanut butter, candy and lemonade mix (we know this last from experience).

Thwarting hungry bruins becomes a preoccupation, even an obsession. Scheming campers have devised various techniques and systems to try to insure that the camper can depend on enjoying future meals. Bears are creatures of habit and conditioning. They routinely check out campsites. If a site is frequently used, the odds are that the food pack has commonly been put in one particular place, usually hanging from one particular tree. One ploy some use is to put the pack somewhere else, even on the ground, some distance away from the expected place. One long-time resident of the area writes that he puts the pack under the canoe, a practice that gives other veteran woodsgoers the shudders. If the bear smelled food, he would not be reluctant about moving the canoe to get at it. (Apparently this practice dates from the times when wilderness trekkers commonly carried guns to deal with the wild life.)

The canoe can be brought up to the campsite and overturned so that the bottom becomes a makeshift table. At least, that's what a lot of writers say. We've tried it, and it is much more trouble than it is worth.

RAINY DAY PREPARATIONS

On more than one occasion, we have made camp either with rain falling or threatening. The first thing we did to settle in was to rig a rain fly so that we could keep gear dry while doing the rest of the setting up.

This involves running a stout line between a couple of trees. The rain fly should provide you shelter while you prepare meals (but it should not be over the fire).

A rain fly or tarp involves a simple concept, with several variations for adaptations to circumstances. Basically, it is a large rectangular sheet of material — plastic, coated fabric, whatever — thrown across a ridge line, with ties fastening down the four corners. As with many simple concepts, the execution is not always so easy. finding good tie-down spots can lead to a less than perfectly beautiful rain fly.

If there is wind with the rain, you may prefer to hang the tarp with a longer side to block the wind. After all, no rule that says you must have that ridge line exactly in the middle.

If the weather threatens a stormy night, we have found that rather than leaving the rain fly up, with the packs all under it, it works very well to simply take the tarp, cover the packs, and tuck it under. The packs stay much cleaner and dryer.

READY FOR THE NIGHT

Veteran campers develop routines for settling down for the night. The food pack must be secured away from all marauders. The kitchen area is put in order. The campfire, if there has been one, is out and the ashes cold. The canoe has been brought up out of the water and turned over for the night, tucked away from the wind. The light weight of many of the modern canoes makes it imperative to guard against the wind blowing it away. Part of our settling routine includes a hunt with the flashlight for any mosquitoes that may have gotten in the tent with us. Spending a few minutes doing this is worth the effort. (We repeat this if either of us has to go outside in the night. We both wake up when one gets up, and since we are awake anyway, we may as well kill intruding mosquitoes.)

HOME IS WHAT YOU MAKE IT

As a part of good housekeeping, the Elegant Camper tries to keep track of whatever he or she has brought along. It helps to develop a sense of place and routine at the campsite and to observe it, at least in your own mind. "This is the housekeeping area. Here is where we set up the work area for food preparation and cooking. Here is where we park the pack that has all those outdoor items we'll need within convenient reach — matches, toilet paper, soap and towel, cooking pots, cords — all the stuff that is in the housekeeping pack. The tent is the personal and sleeping area. That's where we keep whatever extra clothing we have brought along, personal gear, sleeping equipment." By having this sort of mind-set, and by returning items to their appropriate area after use, you are not so likely to lose anything. Life in the woods may be casual and primitive, but it does not need to be slovenly. Routine ways of doing things and locating items reduce the amount of time necessary to spend on routine activities. Being at least somewhat systematic makes repacking for the next move of the trip a little easier.

LEFTOVERS?

Food, as I have mentioned before, is of great importance. If you have calculated the quantities to an incredibly accurate point (translate that into *everything* gets eaten at each meal), this next point is of no real concern. However, sometimes miscalculations are made; appetites are smaller (something that can happen well into a longer trip); the meal in question was less than favorite; whatever the reason, you find yourself with surplus food, or garbage. What to do with it? How you deal with this is important. My feeling is that if meat — anything of animal material — is involved, to be careless in disposing of it around your campsite is to invite trouble. Maybe not trouble for you, but trouble for anyone who uses that site after you. As has already been pointed out, bears have a very keen sense of smell and are attracted by the scent of meat or meat products and by sweets. They are not foolish, either. If a site proves productive once in their rounds of checking out their territories, they would very sensibly put it on their lists for subsequent checkouts. If they have had no reasons for foraging around a campsite, it is foolish to provide them with any.

Okay, then. What to do? You bury the remains way back in the woods, some distance back from the water and from the campsite and do a good job of it, too. (The Forest Service says at least 150 feet back.) The recommended depth is 6 inches, as this seems to permit the most rapid decomposition. Apparently below that the soil is essentially sterile — devoid of organisms that cause decay. It is a depth that a trowel can handle. It is likewise consistent with the minimum-impact camping that is stressed in Canada as well. The same with fish entrails; they should either be buried back in the woods or cut into small pieces and placed on rocks, well away from campsites and portages, for the gulls to eat. These spirits of the air make an attentive audience for the fish-cleaner, and they are very possessive of the area. We have been greatly entertained by the acrimonious screeching set up by the first gull on site when others show up. "Those goodies are mine, by gully!" is the message.

Burying also reduces the lure for annoying flies. It is particularly important that care in these matters be observed on lakes that are closer in to entry points; those are more heavily trafficked areas, and problems compound rapidly. An Elegant Camper considers those who will be using the site at later times.

Small quantities of leftover food can be burned in the fire pit, but get a fairly hot fire going first so that you do a quick and thorough job of it. The smell of burning food is not particularly pleasant and you don't want any scraps left in the fire pit. This matter of burning or burying garbage is a major reason why I don't like to take fresh eggs or vegetables that require peeling. Any of that sort of garbage attracts creatures scavenging for food — mice, chipmunks, crows, ravens, jays and such. If you choose to burn out foil in the fire pit, have the goodness to pack out its remains. It is disgusting to find foil remains, cans, scraps, whatever, in the fire pit. (At home, I have found that finely crushed egg shells are consumed by calcium-needy birds. The need for calcium is also a reason you seldom find old deer antlers or moose racks.)

The old BWCA rules limited the number of persons to a site to ten. This was an excellent rule. (The Canadians went it one better: their limit was nine.) A larger group puts considerable strain on a site. Not many of the sites have two or more good tent pads. If cooking with wood, a larger fire is needed for cooking and cleaning up. Then, too, a big bonfire may often be an entertainment. The rules are being reconsidered, with an eye to fewer per site, per entry point, and fewer canoes permitted.

GATHERING

While on the subject of gathering, I should stress that the Elegant Camper restricts the gathering or collecting to three areas, namely firewood, food and fish, gathers enough for the party's needs, and quits. This means don't pick the flowers. Some kinds, such as the orchids, are rare and protected by law. Although many, such as the cornel berry or Canada dogwoods, are abundant, leave them alone. It is a pity to pick them only to find that they very quickly droop and fade. Many plants provide the basic fare for numerous animals — leaves, flowers, fruit or roots. Knowing that blueberries in season are an important staple for bears, I feel I am robbing them of sustenance by picking them. After all, I am quite unwilling for Bruin to eat *my* food. Try to leave an area as though you hadn't been there.

TALKING TO THE ANIMALS?

One of the greatest pleasures, and yet often one of the greatest causes for anxiety in a beginning wilderness camper, is the presence of creatures. Some are very quiet as they go about their business; others, such as the moose, have absolutely no regard for the niceties of quiet. What animals you see may have little relationship to what you hear.

WHAT WAS THAT SOUND?

Many people on their first night in the woods find it difficult to sleep. The sounds are strange, mysterious and therefore disturbing. Any new place to sleep — a motel room, a relative's house, a new home — can cause this. The mind identifies what it can and the imagination takes over the rest. It is the sort of response that has kept the human species alive for millennia. If you hear a noise that unsettles you, and you think it is a critter poking around camp, make your own loud noise; the forest critters are just as unsettled by unfamiliar sounds as you are.

However, the fact that tent walls are essentially transparent to sound means I can listen to the sounds of the night and enjoy them — the humming chorus of mosquitoes (which stops when the air cools enough), the late evening birds, the occasional owl, an alarmed loon. As the night passes, you may hear the small dramas of life and death, as predator finds prey, and one small life goes to feed another.

Over the years I have found it interesting to watch for animals. Sometimes we see very few, which is always a surprise and very much a disappointment.

We can usually count on seeing beavers. Like the loons, they are a quintessential part of the water scene of the North Woods. When we go out on the lake in the evenings, it is delightful to spot the broad wedge-shaped wake that marks a beaver in passage. We have learned the booming tail-slap is not necessarily because of our presence in the area, especially when we hear it in the night. One occasion we have been treated to seeing a beaver moving about on the shore, selecting evening tidbits. We think of our fat cat and are impressed with the size of the beaver, which can weigh as much as sixty pounds.

We have been charmed by otters. On one trip, one appeared in the river just in front of our canoe, swam ahead of us, pausing from time to time to look back to see if we were following him. He seemed to be encouraging us to follow him, and we found that we indeed had, right up into a little bend of the river, while the main part of the stream went on in a different direction.

On a more recent trip, we were fishing along the base of a small bluff when a large otter suddenly appeared. He was not happy about our presence; he threatened us with strange hissing noises and charged at us in short bursts of fury. We would not have been surprised if he had come even closer to the canoe. Instead, he swam around to another side and threatened again. His partner then appeared alongside the bluff. We decided we had disturbed them quite enough and moved away.

Another denizen of the woods and creeks that we have seen more frequently in recent years is the moose. A moose is, as the French say, a "serious" animal. A small cow moose can weigh 800 pounds, and the bull is even bigger, as much as 1800 pounds. Neither is an animal to trifle with. While they aren't what you'd call aggressive animals — one is not likely to take a notion to hunt you out — they aren't so shy that you'd never find any trace of them. One the contrary, the evidence of their presence — "moose berries" — lies piled all around. Once, while we were camped on an island, Don was on the trail to the latrine and came up on a cow moose and her calf. They all looked at each other momentarily, then mother and baby turned and left. We think it was the same pair we had seen earlier swimming up to the shore of an island opposite ours. Moose are strong swimmers, and we have seen the baby riding on mother's back as she swims.

On a more remote site, we have heard moose walk through the camp at night, and we have known them to bed down close by.

In contemplating a moose and its potential danger, remember that old saw that says the difference between a hero and a coward is the direction he is pointed when the adrenaline hits. That applies to moose, too. Consider the size and weight of the moose in motion and respect accordingly. Assume that a moose on the move has the right of way. Be polite, prudent, and try to avoid startling the animal if you should come across one. Bull moose get particularly testy during September and October as they go into rutting season. They are likely to charge if suddenly met face to face. The best course of action is to put a tree (the bigger, the better) between you and him and stand still. It is a marvelous experience to hear them bellowing, crashing and banging around in the woods during the rut.

Some years ago, Eldest Daughter was camping with us. It was raining fairly steadily as we came off a portage onto the Temperance River. Lynne was leading, and she suddenly realized that the very large stone a short way out into the river was actually the back of a cow moose browsing for underwater goodies. Not wishing to startle her into abrupt moves in our direction, we began talking to the moose in calm but strong voices, telling her how much we admired her, what a splendid creature she was, and didn't she have an appointment to be somewhere else at that time? After we had carried on like that for a while, the moose moved on, quite deliberately, into the forest, leaving the river to us.

Prudence of a different sort is called for in encounters with smaller animals such as chipmunks, squirrels, ground squirrels and mice — the Marauders, I call them. One can gauge with some accuracy whether a particular campsite is heavily used by less-than-woods-wise campers by the behavior of the chipmunks and red squirrels. Close-in or easily accessible and frequently used camps will have remarkably brazen small animals. While I have yet to see a chipmunk actually lift a lid on a cooking pot, some are not all reluctant to check out supplies that may be laid out for preparing a meal, even with people not 2 feet away. On one of our earliest trips, we were all busy getting camp set up. A little red squirrel (we always think of them as "little red") was watching us. He then bolted down the tree to our food pack that was sitting loosely opened on the ground, sort of in the middle of things, grabbed a nectarine, and dashed up another tree — one long smooth continuous motion. He than sat on a limb, clutching the nectarine and swore at us. We all stood open-mouthed with amazement at his audacity.

A tiny mouse boldly checked out our breakfast table one morning (a site with a rare table), though we sat there. He even climbed onto the camera when Friend Spouse attempted to photograph the little rascal and was not easily shaken off.

Critters get this way when opportunities have been productive. We have not seen much of this kind of behavior on the more remote sites. Over the years, people have been entertained by having them around: chipmunks and squirrels are cute and appealing. People have fed them goodies. People have been careless about leaving food in the fire pit or just casually tossed back in the woods. The distance between scrounging for tossed tidbits and helping oneself in the packs isn't that great for the small animals, and the morality of the matter doesn't enter their furry heads. Don't feed them, deliberately or unintention-ally. You might enjoy them at the moment, but you are creating or extending a nuisance for later campers.

In fact, the small creatures, especially the mice, have given us more trouble with our food pack than bears have. If you don't want to "fly" your food pack, you can transfer stuff to your cooking pans. Be sure to put fairly heavy rocks on the lids.

Some people have porcupine problems (and a sticky business that is!). It seems porcupines like salt and will chew on canoe paddles for the sweat residue. We have never had the problem and cannot say whether that is due to an absence of porcupines or absence of sweat on the paddle handles.

We have lost fish on stringers to otters, mink and turtles.

THE BEAR FACTS

I mentioned bears. Some people get very nervous about bears being in the woods. It is comforting to remember that the odds of being killed by lightning are twelve times greater than those of being killed by a bear anywhere in the U.S. (And lightning deaths are rare.) These are so-called black bears (Euarctos americanus), not grizzlies. Grizzly bears are quite another matter. Black — which may be cinnamon rather than black — bears are dangerous to food packs, not usually to people. They like things such as blueberries, honey or sugar, and margarine even better than meat, though they are fond of bacon. In all the years that we have been going out, we have had a bear situation only once. The nature of that situation is enlightening, too. It was the first night out; I had cooked our supper, which included fresh chicken (no bones); we had eaten and cleared up things afterwards. Then we had set the camp in order for the night before we went out for an evening of terrorizing the walleyes. We fished for about an hour, but decided to call it quits because it was rather windy and the fish weren't biting. When we came back to the campsite, we discovered the food pack, which, according to our custom, we had left on the ground by the housekeeping pack, was no longer there. Immediately we had visions of a grossly curtailed camping trip. However, we noisily started on a search of the area, and very quickly picked up the trail of items dropped from the pack. We succeeded in retrieving the pack, undamaged, — with one of the three straps unbuckled — with a loss only of a package of Italian bread sticks and half a can of lemonade mix powder. The cardboard can and lid were marked with unmistakable teeth marks.

It was an unsettling experience. That night we "flew" the food pack from a tree limb, something we almost never did. We took the added precaution of putting the forks and spoons into the coffee pot and hung that from the bottom of the pack as a sort of alarm system. All was quiet that night.

Now several points about the matter were pertinent. As I said, we had never before had a bear encounter. However, this site was on a lake that is heavily used, being the next lake over from an entry point. This lake enjoys the reputation of being an excellent fishing lake. Popular lakes, generally not far from entry points, often have resident bears. There is a National Forest campground near this lake, with inevitable garbage accumulation because it is a popular spot, and it attracts bears. The Rangers, as at other similar spots, have run a veritable travel agency for panhandling bears. Consequently, bears are not uncommon around Sawbill and the other lakes closest by. Our site was on one of those lakes.

By the evidence, the problem was aggravated when earlier occupants of the site had cleaned fish a short distance from the site proper and had left the heads and spines on a rock at the lake's edge, at that time a rule violation. This is all but offering an invitation by special delivery. Further, we found that other garbage had been simply discarded in the woods close by the campsite.

There is absolutely no excuse for this sort of thing. The distance from this site back to the entry point can be covered in something like 45 minutes, and that includes 15 minute (or less) to make the portage. I do not understand the mind- set of people who are too lazy or so indifferent that they do such things. I am outraged by such behavior. Ignorance is no excuse, either.

The whole North Woods is bear country. That should be kept firmly in mind. Any outfitter could give you a count of the number of packs lost to or ripped up by bears each summer. There is the tale, probably apocryphal, of the camper who came back to his campsite just in time to observe Mama Bear holding up the tent flap for Junior to carry out the pack. More likely, she would simply slash the tent to get at the goodies. Bears are smart and they are strong. So far though, they haven't put together the means of getting a pack that is properly flown.

The Quetico Park Service has a policy that campers in that region should hang their food every night. The Canadians advise campers to move on if they find signs of bears in the proposed camping area. The Hansens at Sawbill believe that a similar policy will eventually apply in the BWCA. The bear problem is really a people problem. Campers can save themselves a lot of grief by prudent action.

Another point to observe is the importance of good housekeeping. Frank Hansen taught me years ago about the value of maintaining a tidy camp, with a minimum of fresh foods with alluring odors. I think a second factor may have contributed to our bear encounter. In making the portage, the container holding the lemonade mix had come open, spilling part of the sugary contents into the pack. I had not succeeded in getting all that out. As it happens, not only are bears very fond of sweets, they have a keen sense of smell, and apparently he had smelled the sugar. When we retrieved our pack, we found the container and it had been swabbed clean! So the lessons are (1) select a clean campsite away from established bear country; (2) don't carry fresh meat or any other food that will send invitations; (3) maintain a tidy camp, and (4) fly the food pack.

SHOULD BOWSER GO ALONG?

Some people like to take their dogs along on a canoe trip. Certainly the dogs, at least some of them, seem to enjoy it. The literature for the Canadian parks forthrightly advises against taking a dog into the wilderness. Personally, I don't like to meet strange dogs on portage trails, particularly if they are unleashed. I think a dog in the wilderness is inappropriate and intrusive. Some people think a dog provides better protection against bears, mainly as an early warning system, I suspect. However, another school of thought believes that a dog in the area could enrage a bear.

The animals deserve to be left alone. Sometimes people blunder along, not realizing consequences of their actions. One year we were sitting in our campsite, enjoying the evening and the view of the lake. It was fun, sitting there watching a gull and her three big gray chicks as they paddled around between a pair of islands not far from us. A pair of campers appeared, paddling their canoe, also enjoying the evening, and they passed between the two islands, just idly cruising the lake. The mother gull immediately led her chicks around one island, out of our sight, to get them away from the interlopers. The canoeists disappeared from the scene; the gulls returned from around the island, but one of the little ones was missing. We watched for quite a while, but it never reappeared. What happened to it we could only guess — a turtle, perhaps. It was a bit sad. True, the world won't miss one gull. Perhaps something eventually would have gotten it, but we have always felt that careless intrusion cost a small life, and it wasn't necessary.

The main point to keep in mind is that we who go into the wild areas are, in a sense, intruders. It behooves us to make as little impact as we can, and since upwards of 200,000 people a year (essentially the population of the city of Tulsa, Oklahoma) the Boundary Waters alone, never mind the other wild areas of the country, there is bound to be cumulative impact. We should not develop exotic tastes among opportunistic animals — they don't really need to learn to like marshmallows, and we certainly don't need to encourage them to take advantage of human visitors.

It is worth noting that while the winter climate is grimly severe, and the woods are not unduly generous with food goodies, there is compensation in that the North Woods have no poisonous snakes or poisonous insects. I used to think there was no poison ivy, either, as we had never seen any in the eastern portion of the BWCA where we usually went. However, we have seen it in the western reaches and have found several places in Quetico where it grew abundantly.

HOME, SWEET HOME

There is something enormously satisfying about a properly set-up and tidy camp. How can I describe the pleasure that comes from a lake view that is all your own, for the time, with your tent tucked away under sheltering conifers, the wonderful woods scent, a cozy kitchen area, and around meal time, signs of food preparation.

Equally satisfying is to look around the campsite as you prepare to depart and find that you have left no particular signs of your stay. The ashes are cold in the fire pit; no foil, no plastic, wire ties or other rubbish have been left in it (some Elegant Campers have been known to pack out foil or other debris left by earlier clods). No live tree in the area has suffered cuts or bark pulling. No nails have been pounded into trees. No garbage or other trash remains in the area. No belongings have been overlooked and left behind. Satisfied that the site is in good order, you can depart.

NOW THE TRIP IS OVER

So now the trip is over, and you are no longer a rank beginner on planning and carrying out a canoe trip. However, there is still a little more to do, and it is as important to being an Elegant Camper as the rest.

Usually, the one thing that takes the top priority on completion of a trip is a shower. Maybe you got one before you made the trip home; maybe that's the next thing to do after unloading all the stuff and leaving it in the middle of the floor. That's fine: it is a most commendable action.

However, the really important part comes with dismantling and putting away all the gear, and that is no small job. This is the time when you begin preparations for the next trip. Surely there will be another trip! The guiding principles here for the Elegant Camper are two: put stuff away clean and in good repair, and replace equipment items that have been used up or are otherwise deficient. Make it easy to get everything together for the next expedition.

It helps to set certain priorities. If there is anything in the food pack that would benefit from refrigeration, tend to it. The next, and really more important, matter is getting bedding aired. Most likely, the sleeping bags were stowed shortly after being vacated, and so are probably still damp from body moisture. If the bag is not aired, mold or mildew may form, and from then on, the bag will have an unpleasant musty odor. If you have an outside clothesline to hang the open bag over, that is excellent. Balcony deck rails work well — fresh air and sunshine are the best ways to keep the bag healthy. A clothes dryer is effective, too. A sleeping bag should occasionally be cleaned (washed). Just be sure to use the correct method for your particular bag. If you use some sort of a mattress, be sure it is dry before putting it away. Check the manufacturer's instructions for storage.

Likewise, the tent needs to be put away clean and dry. This of course applies only to your own or a borrowed tent; outfitters tend to this themselves. Friend Spouse does this. He takes the tent outside and without setting it up, unfolds it and with the garden hose, he washes off the bottom of it. When it is good and dry, he sets it up, carefully cleans the interior with the whisk broom (just as he does whenever he packs the tent for the day's move) and lets it air out for several hours in the sun. He usually washes out the inside, too, if we have had rainy weather on the trip. *Don't* wash it in the washing machine. That will damage the coating to the fabric and ruin its water repellent.

If there are tent pegs to be replaced, or repairs to be made on the tent, do so as soon as possible, and leave the tent (folded up again) where you will trip over it until the problems are corrected. Over the years, our tent acquired numerous pinholes in the floor and side, which were patched with ever-dependable duct tape.

Depending on the material of your tent, you may choose simply to stuff the tent back into its bag, rather than fold it. This prevents creases from persisting always along the same places that will eventually weaken the fabric in that area. It doesn't feel as tidy as to fold the tent carefully, and may be a bit harder to get into its bag.

While you are in the process of getting the sleeping bags out in the air, you are undoubtedly also faced (nosed?) with the pile of dirty laundry — the towels, pot holders, the socks, the underwear, the pants and shirts. Put them to soak in cold water. If you are really fastidious about the appearance of this laundry, you can give it a spin and then a second soak. Let the wash cycle thrash a bit to loosen up the dirt. When you come back to finish this task, use hot, not warm, water for washing, and you can feel perfectly justified to include a shot of bleach. Very little of it will be totally satisfactory in the whiteness contest, particularly after these items have been used for a few trips, or made a single jaunt through swampy water. Remember I said I reserve this stuff for camping only? Now you know why. At least it's all clean. When all is clean and dry, I put the basic underwear and socks into a bag, one for each of us, and return them, the towels, pot holders and scrubber to their respective packs.

Now you can turn your attention to the cook kit stuff. If before cooking over a wood fire, you were careful about thoroughly soaping your pots, they probably aren't too grubby. Usually a little ammonia in the hot dishwater will make the scrubbing with the Scotch-Brite or a soap-filled Brillo pad fairly easy. I have tried filling the largest pot with water and some dishwasher detergent, putting in the pots that I used, and bringing the whole batch to a simmer. Then I turned off the heat and let them sit and think about it. When I came back to scrub them, it didn't take much effort. If you use a camp stove, cleanup is easy. At any rate, all the dishes, pots, utensils, and chow kits that went on the trip are washed carefully and thoroughly dried before being put away.

Clean out the food pack. This is always a bit of a job, because for one thing, while on a trip, I stow the foil and trash that are to be packed out in a bag in the pack. Too, we generally have food left over. Separate stuff like the baking mix from the stuff that is packaged for long-term storage, such as the commercially prepared trail food. This is a good time to note what you have and store it together, if it is appropriate, for the next trip. (Here is where those commercially packaged meals really shine.) Just as I make lists each time of what all we take with us, I now make note of what we used. A good place to keep those notes is with the Housekeeping stuff. I keep my menu notes from one year to the next (they turned out to be very useful while I was writing this book). This is the time, for instance, to itemize the foods that went over well, and more particularly those that did not. A notebook or book such as The *Paddler's Planner* is handy for this.

Keeping detailed notes requires some effort, but the payoff is worthwhile. Review the trip, what the astronauts call "de-brief," and make notes about what should have been done differently. Recall the good parts. Put the notes with the equipment so you can easily find them next time.

Once everything has been carefully cleaned and checked for repairs or replacements, put it all away "where it belongs" (the Elegant Camper Comes Home!), ready for another time.

If you took pictures, get them developed and re-live your trip. I hope it was a good trip, and the next one should be even better!

Cornel Bunchberry

8

WHY ROUGH IT?

We use the word "wilderness," but perhaps we mean wildness. Isn't that why I've come here? In wilderness, I seek the wildness in myself—and in so doing, come on the wildness everywhere around me because, after all, begin part of nature, I'm cut from the same cloth.

Gretel Ehrlich, in *Montana Spaces*

Having read this far, you may be wondering, What is the point of all this effort? Is it worthwhile? Why should anyone go through all the trouble? People who have never gone on wilderness trips often see and hear only the absence of comforts — the sleeping on the ground (well, nearly), the bugs, the labor of carrying everything from one water spot to another, the fickleness of the weather. They listen to descriptions of horribly rocky portages or steep climbs or paddling on windy days. They wonder why one would do this, and question whether it could possibly be any fun. Well, yes, at such times, the question, Are we having fun yet? does occur. But those are single events. Quite honestly and forthrightly, wilderness camping isn't to everyone's taste, and that's fine. The French have a good phrase — *"chacun à son goût* — each to his own taste," they say. However I can give you some reasons and tell you why I find it worthwhile.

WHY ROUGH IT?

Re-creation, a re-building of one's inner resources and balance — the change of activity from one's normal life pattern — is a valid use for wilderness, especially with the enjoyment of wilderness for sake of outdoor experience.

Re-creation is a strong and compelling reason to head to the wilderness. Camping in the wilderness is not particularly arcane or difficult, even though a great deal of physical energy is expended. But the pace is not, or does not need to be, demanding. Setting up and taking down camp is a busy time; meal preparation and cleanup are busy. The very matter of doing all the things to be done is, over all, relaxing. Canoeing and camping demand constant attention: watch for rocks that lurk; the water is almost hot enough to put the coffee in; is that really a fish nibble or is the lure just bumping bottom? The concerns that absorbed us at home recede to the backs of our minds, displaced by the activities of the moment.

Even when Friend Spouse and I go on leisurely fishing trips, we don't spend all day at it. Instead we loll around in the afternoon. By about the third day, my mind feels quite refreshed by its vacation from usual activities. Now, if I want to consider long term goals or projects, priorities seem to have sorted themselves out, and useful possibilities present themselves. Friend Spouse and I agree that these trips are physically and mentally invigorating. The wilderness is a source of re-creation. There one can refresh one's spirit and soul by absence of usual activities and influences.

SENSE OF ADVENTURE

Ask campers why they like to head for the woods (or the desert, or the mountains, or the river), and they will tell you that it is "because it is something different," or that they were seeking adventure, or that they "wanted to get away from it all."

A desire for adventure impels them to seek out wilderness. What constitutes adventure lies in the eye of the beholder. In its root sense, *adventure* means a coming upon, something that comes up to one. What is tremendously exciting to one may be strictly ho-hum to another. My sense of adventure is satisfied by moving through unfamiliar territory. Bumbling off on the wrong portage is quite enough.

But the best part of adventure for me is new places and what's there. Wilderness presents prime opportunities to watch creatures going about their business of making a living.

EXPERIENCE THE NATURAL WORLD

Every trip has something special. Generally the wilderness grants a singular gift each trip, and these gifts are magic moments. We were thoroughly enchanted by the otter that seemed to be leading us back to his home — to the point, we discovered we had turned away from the true river channel. Fascinated, we watched the pair of falcons circling lazily overhead when suddenly one apparently spotted something of interest on the ground, and abruptly plummeted with dazzling speed. The other circled a bit more, then flew on off.

Once in Quetico, I came back to the tent and found Ms. Spruce Grouse and family out foraging by it.

Again in Quetico, after seeing bits of wings from luna moths, we came across a live, intact moth. It was the first time either of us ever saw the great moth, pale green, exquisite, with delicate trailing wings.

One of my greatest pleasures comes from the abundance and variety of the spring flowers that make early trips a special delight. It seems the flowers of the early spring are dainty and white. In late summer, the dominant colors become purple and gold. The quantity of kinds of flowers continually astonishes me.

Always, I learn something.

TREAT THE IMAGINATION

The imagination can fully occupy itself. You can speculate on the life of travelers in the region (whether the BWCA or some other area) one century, two centuries, one millennium before. You can look at the rocks and try to visualize the immense ice sheets that covered the country, and the sounds of ice moving, grinding, compressing. At night, you can watch the ghostly fires of the aurora borealis, something hard to do in our light-polluted cities and towns. You can think what of the streams of colors have meant to people who have seen them before you.

After a trip, the canoeist never again sees the world in quite the same way. I first realized how the mode of transportation affects the view of the scenery when I rode behind Friend Spouse on his motorcycle. The vantage point of a motorcycle is vastly different from that of an automobile. A car is closed; a motorcycle is open. From a car, you see fields; from a motorcycle, you see fences. You see things; you hear things; you smell things that you were not likely to in a car. You *experience* the countryside. A bicyclist will tell you the same.

Like bicycling, canoeing is low-tech: you move by your own physical exertions and those don't take you very fast. You have time to look around you and see what is there. Furthermore, the view from four feet above the water level is quite different from the everyday point of view.

When you get to know an area, you begin to see changes that occur over time. You become aware, in time, of "the fundamental interdependence of all things."

SOLITUDE

One of the best parts of a wilderness trip is the opportunity to enjoy solitude and the tranquillity that accompanies it. On one of our best trips, we went more than two days without seeing another person or party, an experience that sadly has not been repeated in trips of the past seven years. I like to lie all snuggled into my sleeping bag and listen to the night. The sounds vary: sometimes what I hear is the drone of mosquitoes; sometimes it is the anvil chorus of frogs. There may be an occasional small cry as a creature moves from living to dinner. Occasionally, I wake in the night to a stillness that is complete and wonderful.

It is one thing to see shoe tracks on a muddy portage trail. It is another to encounter party after party along the way. (It is to avoid this that party size and number are restricted, a policy I wholeheartedly endorse.)

Do I look different?

The wilderness becomes a doorway through which we can discover ourselves and our capabilities. The successful completion of a challenging wilderness trip brings great satisfaction, and success breeds subtle changes in a person. Certainly this is no secret to all those who have done it. For many men, this sort of achievement is familiar from athletics. For many women, and let's hope that today's young women take advantage of the opportunities, that sort of experience has been much less common.

I am, as I said, a woman with grown children. The whole business of highly physical, outdoor activities came relatively late in life for me. I have been astounded and elated at learning that I can organize and set up a comfortable camp, plan and prepare pleasant meals, that I can carry my share of gear over whatever portages may present themselves, that I can maintain a reasonable pace, whether paddling or portaging. The discovery that I am physically fairly competent has greatly enhanced my confidence, an enhancement that carries over into my workaday world. Add to that a growing awareness and knowledge of the natural world that has enriched my life no end. Best of all, an increasing number of women behind me in years are finding this out.

Values shift

It takes some discomfort to appreciate the comforts of modern life. In *Moby Dick,* as Ishmael settles himself deep under the quilts on a cold night, with only his nose sticking out, he reflects that to appreciate being warm, some part of you must be cold. A different set of perspectives emerges. It is hard to maintain an inflated sense of self-importance in the violence of a summer thunderstorm.

We nearly lost it

In far too many places in this country, we nearly lost the opportunity for the wilderness experience.

To begin with, the woods and waters were sources of food, shelter and transportation for the native tribes. They believed the resources of woods and waters were gifts of the Great Spirit and were careful not to exhaust the supply of whatever they were using. If they were about to kill for meat, they first would ask forgiveness of that animal, and they gave thanks for what they got.

Newcomers to the continent saw the wild country as a boundless resource to be exploited. Fur traders relentlessly trapped animals for fur and skins, only occasionally for food. When the animals diminished in numbers, the trees became the object of interest. Those who came later saw the vast forests as sources of wealth. In northern Minnesota, northern Michigan, Maine, and the mountain regions of the West, lumber barons made huge fortunes from the cutting down of the forests. Even today, a concept of "harvesting" timber and animals remains. In Minnesota, some of the consequences were quite severe: denuded areas were vulnerable to erosion, and the Mississippi began to carry away Minnesota soil.

In time, tourist trade, a newer form of exploitation, became important, as the call of the wild has echoed down through the years. In fact, the tourist or visitor in the wilderness who went to get away from it all saw the woods as a place to exploit. They went to fish, to hunt — not just to satisfy immediate needs of hunger, but to catch the greatest number of fish, to bag the trophy animal. The attitude that the land was to be used is quite evident in the writings of Hemingway, Rutstrum, and others — even those who loved the special qualities of the wilderness. They would cut spruce boughs to make beds, chop down a tree for temporary furniture, and so it went. To many, the wilderness was a place for really cutting loose and having a good time — drinking (and leave the bottles around), eating (leave the tin cans, maybe take a little time to bury them; feeling free to cut loose to do one's own thing (loud partying, firecrackers, etc.) "Wreckreation" is a fairly apt description of the attitude demonstrated in the extreme behavior of some people.

Farsighted people believed that it was important to preserve and maintain stretches of forest, keeping them safe from timbering. From the work of dedicated visionaries in time came the Boundary Waters Canoe Area and Quetico Provincial Park in the great North Woods of northern Minnesota and southern Ontario. Battles were and continue to be fought over unique wilderness areas in other parts of the continent. Now the arguments rage who will use the remaining wilderness areas and what uses are acceptable.

I would raise my small voice to insist that wilderness should be wilderness, and not developed. We need, not only in this country but in this world, places where one can go unpursued by the high-tech world of late twentieth century America. I want to get away from the sounds of contemporary life — the noise of engines, the crowds —

and hear instead the quieter sounds of the forest — the birds, the wind in the trees, the gurgles of the water.

I do not know how to account for it; as I said earlier, all I know is that when I go into the wilderness, the trip restores my soul.

WILDERNESS IS VITAL TO OUR WORLD

Reports come weekly about the loss of forests, alarming reports, to our widening perception of the importance of the world's forests and wilderness areas for keeping the air we breath fit to breathe. We so often tend to disregard (or "un-regard") air. Something I read once, though, comes back to haunt me. Argon is a rare gas. Inert, it simply passes in and out of lungs, remaining unchanged, neither increasing nor decreasing. The haunting comment was to the effect that perhaps the argon we breathed in yesterday had been a part of the breath of Julius Caesar, or Genghis Khan, or Marie Antoinette.

Equally sobering is the awareness that the water of this planet likewise circulates not only through the earth, the oceans and the air, but also through time. The waters of the lakes we paddle on have been used before and will be used again. Will they be fit for future use?

It is tremendously important that the remaining wilderness with its rich diversity, whether in the northern United States or in the rain forests of southeast Asia, survive. So little is known about so many of the creatures and plants on this earth — only a portion of life's creations have been recognized and catalogued — yet many are disappearing without a trace. Wilderness should be a reminder of our responsibilities to our country and to the planet. Repeated trips make a conservationist. For the novice, one trip is not enough for full appreciation of the values of the wilderness — there is simply too much to learn.

All in all, what it amounts to is this. The more you put into a trip — careful planning, thoughtful acquisition of equipment, keen observation, and later learning what you saw, a wholehearted effort in doing — the more will come back to you in the forms of refreshed outlook, widened perspectives, keener appreciations, and enhanced confidence.

The Elegant Camper prepares to cope and is then free to respond to what the wild world deals out. The end of every trip begins with the departure from the last camp site. As you finish your trip and return home, you can reflect on the entire experience.

And we may as well rough it elegantly — simply, efficiently and appropriately.

CANOE CAMPING IN THE UNITED STATES

Several states still have areas suitable for canoeing with a wilderness character. I have not included whitewater rafting opportunities as that is a rather different type of undertaking.

CONNECTICUT

This tiny state has numerous lakes and streams for canoeing. Write the Connecticut Department of Environmental Protection, Office of State Parks and Recreation, 165 Capitol Avenue, Hartford, CT 06106 for information. Three of its state parks feature camping in primitive riverside sites with fireplaces, pit toilets, water supply and tent ground sites (tent pads). Write Manager, Gillette Castle State Park, East Haddam, CT 06423 for reservation information. Can also contact Connecticut Tourism Division, Department of Economic Dvelopment, 210 Washington Square, Hartford, CT 06106 , or call 203/566-3948.

FLORIDA

Florida has extensive opportunities for canoeing. Canoe camping in the Everglades National Park and in the Ten Thousand Islands Region just north of the Everglades will provide wilderness experiences quite unlike those found in northern regions. You can travel along the 99-mile Wilderness Waterway that runs from Flamingo, at the very tip of peninsular Florida, along the west coast up to Everglades City. Canoeists planning to travel the length of the Waterway are advised to allow at least eight days. Park officials recommend against one-day round trips, other than just day trips around Everglades City or Flamingo.

Florida is generally rising from the sea, and new islands emerge when mangrove trees succeed in establishing themselves. Further, the underlying sand shoals shift under the action of wind and tides (some stretches are very shallow, and during low tides will be impassable). Planning for trips in these areas includes provision for fresh water (you must carry all fresh water you will need), nautical charts for route planning and navigation, and current information on tides. Arrangements for shuttle must also be considered, no small matter since the drive from Flamingo to Everglades City is about 125 miles.

Permits are mandatory in the Everglades. As with the Boundary Waters Canoe Area Wilderness, the aim is to regulate flow of traffic so that a a good quality wilderness experience is possible and to keep down the strain on a fragile environment.

Persons planning to canoe in the Ten Thousand Islands Region should be aware that some of the channels in the region are open to motorized traffic .

For information on canoeing the Waterway, get the "Backcountry Trip Planner." Write Information, Everglades National Park, P O Box 279, Homestead, FL 33030, or call 305/247-6211. At the Visitors Center, the Everglades Natural History Association sells publications about the Park. Write the Association (at the above address) for their catalog. One book that would be very helpful when considering a trip in the region is Dennis Kalma's *Boat and Canoe Camping in the Everglades Backcountry and Ten Thousand Islands Region* (Florida Flair Books, Miami, Florida, publisher of several useful books). Kalma gives a good overview, with attention on preplanning, route planning, campsites, emergencies, several suggested routes, and sections on the natural and human histories of the region.

William Truesdell's *A Guide to the Wilderness Waterway of the Everglades National Park* ($14.95) (see Useful and Interesting Reading) focusses more on the actual trips and routes.

The Florida Department of Natural Resources (Marjory Stoneman Douglas Building, 3900 Commonwealth Boulevard, Tallahassee, FL 32399, phone 904/488-6327, has a brochure describing designated canoe trails.

Another area of interest is the J.N. "Ding" Darling National Wildlife Refuge, established as the Sanibel National Wildlife Refuge. Some 2,825 of its more than 5,000 acres are designated wilderness. For general information call the Lee County Visitors and Convention Bureau, 800/237-6444.

MAINE

Maine is literally freckled with lakes formed generally from the same processes that shaped northern Minnesota and the Upper Peninsula of Michigan.

The crown jewel is the Allagash Wilderness Waterway, a 92-mile corridor surrounded by a vast commercial forest. Contact the Maine Department of Conservation, Bureau of Parks and Recreation, State House Station #22, Augusta, ME 04333. For information in May-October, call 207/289-3821; November-April: 207/723-8518.

Other wilderness canoe camping opportunities include Mattawamkeag Wilderness Park, which is operated by Penobscot County. Contact Reservation Clerk, Mattawamkeag Wilderness Park, Mattawamkeag, ME 04459, or phone 207/736-4881.

Can also contact Maine Publicity Bureau, 97 Winthrop Street, Hallowell, ME 04347, or phone 207/289-2423; Director, North Maine Woods, Inc., P O Box 421, Ashland, ME 04732, or phone 207/435-6213.

MASSACHUSETTS

Massachusetts has several state offices for information; two pertinent ones are the Department of Environmental Management, and the Division of Forests and Parks, both at 100 Cambridge Street, Boston, MA 02202.

While several parks provide camping facilities and canoeing is possible at many, only two State Forests and Parks give opportunity for wilderness camping and canoeing. They are the sizeable East Branch State Forest, near Chesterfield, and tiny Tully Lake Recreation Area, near Baldwinville.

MICHIGAN

Michigan also offers splendid canoeing opportunities. One contact is Travel Bureau, Michigan Department of Commerce, P O Box 30226, Law Building, Lansing, MI 48909. Michigan claims to have more than 70,000 campsites (this is for all sorts of camping), 11,000 inland lakes and nearly 18,000,000 acres of forests.

The United States Department of Agriculture Forest Service supervises several forests that provide excellent opportunities for wilderness canoe camping. They include Ottawa National Forest, Hiawatha National Forest, and Huron-Manistee National Forest. The headquarters office is 272 North Lincoln Road, Escanaba, MI 49829.

The Ottawa National Forest offers arguably the best opportunities for wilderness canoe camping, with river canoeing rather than lake. It is located on the western-most end of the Upper Peninsula. Write the Ottawa National Forest office for its River Information Digest. It identifies river sections and describes section lengths, facilities (e.g., livery operators, canoe landings, etc.), character of the river and surrounding countryside, and the fish of the area. The Ottawa National Forest has 27 campgrounds for a wide spectrum of camping experiences. All campgrounds include picnic tables, tent pads, fire grates, and toilet facilities. There is a daily user fee; check for the current rate. The Forest Service Contacts listed are for areas with considerable canoeable rivers.

Get a map if you plan to visit: 40 percent of the land within the Forest is privately owned. Detailed maps can be purchased at Ottawa National Forest offices. The Forest Supervisor's Office (ONF, East U. S. 2, Ironwood, MI 49938) has U. S. Geological Survey maps of the Forest for purchase (see also Sources — Maps). Selected topographic maps are available at District Ranger offices.

The Sylvania Wilderness, located within the Ottawa, offers a special primitive camping opportunity in gorgeous surroundings. Travel to the area's interior is by hiking or by canoe only (and there are more than 3,500 acres of pristine lakes. There are special regulations pertaining to camping and fishing in Sylvania; get information at the Visitor Information Station at the entrance to Sylvania, the Sylvania Visitor Center in Watersmeet, or at the Ottawa National Forest Offices. Call 906/932-1330 for additional information.

The Hiawatha National Forest covers much of the rest of the Upper Peninsula, and between it and the Ottawa lie some State Forests. Contact points in Hiawatha National Forest (call 800/999-7677 for general information) are as follows: St. Ignace Ranger District, 1498 West US 2, St. Ignace, MI 49781 (906/643-7900);Sault Ste. Marie Ranger District, 1500 Business Spur I-75. Sault Ste. Marie, 49783 (906/635-5311); Munising Ranger District, 400 East Munising Avenue, Munising, 49862 (906/387-2512); Manistique Ranger District, Manistique, 49854 (906/341-5666).

The Huron-Manistee National Forest lies in the Lower Peninsula.

MINNESOTA

Minnesota has many, many other places to canoe and canoe-camp besides the BWCA. The Minnesota Office of Tourism has a booklet, "Explore Minnesota Canoeing, Hiking and Backpacking." This 16-page brochure is a beauty! It contains a brief survey of Minnesota weather, a general state map showing canoe areas, a discussion of canoeing generally and specific sources for particular canoeing areas (not just the BWCA, but the whole state). Also included is a list of canoe rental and outfitters with addresses and phone numbers. For those interested, the brochure also covers hiking and backpacking trails. In the metropolitan Minneapolis-St. Paul area, call 296-5029, or toll-free 800/657-3700 outside the metropolitan area. The address is Minnesota Office of Tourism, 375

Jackson Street, 250 Skyway Level, St. Paul, MN 55101. Other booklets in the series are "Explore Minnesota Fishing Guide," "Explore Minnesota Resorts." The Resorts guide identifies those resort owners who feature canoeing.

In Minnesota, *all* watercraft, including canoes, must be licensed. Licenses from those states requiring them are valid. Write Department of Natural Resources, License Center, 625 North Robert, St. Paul, 55101. (A license may be gotten at the Deputy Registrar's Office, Grand Marais, Ely, Duluth, or Virginia on weekdays only.)

Forest Service Contacts. The National Forests of the Upper Midwest offer many delightful opportunities for experiencing a bit of wilderness without the rigors that accompany the canoe camping in the BWCA. For those with young children (say under the age of ten), it is a good place to start. Robert Beymer describes the possibilities to be found in the Superior National Forest (it surrounds part of the BWCA), in his book, *Superior National Forest.* National Forests also often have hiking and bike trails that add variety to the experiences.

The Superior National Forest Service is the agency that controls the use of the BWCA; permits to travel in that region come from the Forest Service. Write to the Forest Supervisor, Superior National Forest, P O Box 338, Duluth, 55801, or call 218/720-5324 for additional information.

Permits are required for any visitors traveling in the BWCA between May 1 and September 30. Entry quotas have been established for overnight campers. Reservations are strongly suggested for high summer and holidays. Beginning in 1994, a Maryland company is handling them. Call Biospherics (800/745-3399) or write, BWCAW Reservation Service, Box 450, Cumberland, MD 21501. Written requests must include the name of the party leader, desired entry point, desired entry date, estimated exit date, estimated party size and a $9 non-refundable payment. Payment may be made by check, money order, or VISA or MASTERCARD. Any changes in reservations cost an additional $7.

If the agency handling reservations changes after 1995, get information by calling 218/720-5440 or by writing BWCA Reservations, Superior National Forest, P O Box 338, Duluth, 55801. Or check out the World Wide Web page (http://www.gis.umn.edu/bwcaw/) for the latest information.

After reserving a permit for overnight visitation in BWCA, trip leaders will receive a letter confirming that a reservation has been made for them. The letter will instruct them to pick up their permits in person within 24 hours of their trip at a Ranger District Office (RDO) or an outfitter or business that is an official issuing station.

The change allows Forest Service and issuing stations to make face-to-face contact with BWCA visitors and provide the opportunity to inform them about wilderness ethics and minimum-impact camping procedures. The Forest Service recommends viewing a video, "Leave No Trace: A Wilderness Ethic," prior to entering the BWCA. (It's a beautiful video: you can buy your own copy. Send a check for $15, made to the Boundary Waters Education Consortium, to the Duluth Forest Service office listed above.)

Visitors who wish to obtain their overnight or motor permit on a walk-in basis will be able to do so within 24 hours of the time they wish to enter the BWCA, providing quotas have not been filled. Walk-in permits will be available at all RDOs and at official issuing stations.

Information on camping and canoeing also can come from the Chippewa National Forest, Supervisor's Office, Cass Lake, 56633, or phone 218/335-2226.

Since the original publication of this book, the Forest Service has designated a number of sites in the BWCA as ultra-primitive. These sites do not have fire grates or latrines. Inquire if you are interested in a more challenging experience.

Voyageurs National Park. Voyageurs National Park, Box 50, International Falls, 56649, or phone 218/283-9821. The brochure "Area Services" gives information on outfitters, resorts. The brochure "Voyageurs" gives a detailed map of the area, with general boating information.

Licenses are required for fishing. Outfitters can usually sell them.

NEW ENGLAND

The Appalachian Mountain Club (5 Joy Street, Boston, MA 02108) has some flatwater canoe suggestions for Massachusetts, Connecticut, Rhode Island, New Hampshire, Vermont and Maine.

NEW HAMPSHIRE

Contact New Hampshire Office of Vacation Travel, P O Box 856, Concord, NH 03301, or phone 603/271-2665.

NEW YORK

New York State Office of Parks, Recreation and Historic Preservation, Agency Building 1, Empire State Plaza, Albany, NY 12238, or phone 518/474-0456 for information on state parks.

Map Information Unit, NYS Department of Transportation, State Office Campus, Building 4, Albany, 12232, or call 518/457-3555.

The Department of Environmental Conservation (DEC) administers the state's forests and maintains the 54 public campgrounds in the Adirondack and Catskill Forest Preserves. Write Recreation Operations, DEC, 50 Wolf Road, Albany, 12233-0001, or phone 518/457-3521.

New York State Department of Commerce, Box 992, Latham, 12110, or phone 800/225-5697. General source for tourism.

Southern Franklin County , in northern New York's Adirondack country, has numerous lakes, and its St. Regis Canoe Area is billed as the only Wilderness Canoe Area in the northeast. Contact Franklin County, Department of Tourism, Malone, 12953, or phone 518/483-6788. This huge state park still has many pockets, or in-holdings, of private property. Canoeists may need to get permission to travel in some parts of the park.

Please note: this is mountain country, popular with skiers. Topographical maps of the target area are *essential* for persons unfamiliar with the area. The U.S. Geological Survey Quadrants include St. Regis (this covers the wilderness area), Saranac Lake, Long Lake, Santanoni, Debar and Loon. Lean-tos are scattered along canoe routes. See Useful and Interesting Reading for Paul Jamieson's book on Adirondack canoeing. Write the Adirondack Park Agency, DEC, 50 Wolf Road, Albany, 12233-0001, for more information. For traveling in the Five Ponds area, contact the U.S. Forest Service, 317 Washington Street, Watertown, 13601, or phone 315/785-2236.

While not particularly applicable for wilderness camping, it is of interest to canoers that New York has a system of canals dating back to 1817, with parks located at points along them. Canoe races are still held on part of the Erie Canal. Write the New York State Department of Transportation, Waterways Maintenance Division, 5 Governor Harriman State Campus, Albany, 12232, or phone 518/457-1187 for maps and information.

VERMONT

Vermont's canoeing is mainly on rivers, with little opportunity for wilderness canoe camping. Contact the Vermont Department of Forests, Parks and Recreation, Agency of Natural Resources, 103 South Main Street, Waterbury, VT 05676, or phone 802/244-8711. Send a SASE for their brochures "Vermont State Parks & Forest Recreation Areas" or "Vermont Guide to Primitive Camping on State Lands."

The U.S. Department of Agriculture Forest Service, 151 West Street, Rutland, 05701 (802/773-0300) has available a Recreation Map and a Secondary Base Series Map, $1 per copy (1993 price). Inquire for price of topographical maps of the entire Green Mountain National Forest.

Can also contact Vermont Travel Division, 134 State Street, Montpelier, 05602, or phone 401/277-2601.

WISCONSIN

Wisconsin likewise has a National Park Service office which supervises the beautiful St. Croix National Scenic Riverway. Write the U. S. Department of the Interior, P. O. Box 708, St. Croix Falls, WI 54024, for general information about the Riverway (very popular for canoeing) and maps of the surrounding area.

National Forests in Wisconsin include the Nicolet National Forest, with contact through Florence Ranger District, Nicolet National Forest, Route 1, P O Box 161, Florence, 54121, or phone 715/528-4464.

Wisconsin's Department of Tourism, Department of Business Development, P O Box 7606, Madison, 53707, has an 80-page booklet covering all attractions with detailed information.

Wisconsin's Department of Natural Resources (P O Box 7921, Madison, 53707-7921) publishes a brochure, "A Guide For the Mobility Impaired," prepared by a paraplegic using an electric wheelchair. The brochure identifies state parks, forests, and recreation areas accessible by people with mobility limitations. Write the same address for general park and forest information.

SPECIALIZED CAMPING

People with disabilities now have more options than used to be the case. At the time of the first edition of this book, I knew only of the Minnesota organizations. As the following list shows, opportunities have appeared all across the country for people with disabilities. It should be noted that the primary focus for some of these groups is the acquisition of water sport skills, not necessarily camping skills and opportunities.

Since the passage of the Americans with Disabilities Act, considerable work has begun to make campgrounds accessible. I know first hand of several Superior National Forest campgrounds with ramps to fishing docks.

The American Canoe Association kindly provided information about the following organizations that do work similar to Wilderness Inquiry, and who certify canoeing instructors across the country.

American Canoe Association, 7432 Alban Station Blvd., Suite B-226, Springfield, VA 22150-2311 (703/451-0141).ACA serves as a clearing house for unique information on adaptive equipment, as well as sources of instruction and training. The people atACA are happy to respond on an individual's particular needs, as well.

Challenge Alaska, P O Box 110065. Anchorage, AL 99511 (907/563-2658). They organize sea kayak trips.

Cooperative Wilderness Handicapped Outdoor Group (C. W. Hog), Idaho State University Student Union, Box 8118, Pocatello, ID 83209 (208/236-3912). University-based adventure programming. A broad program which encourages adventure to each individual's limit.

Environmental Traveling Companions (ETC), Fort Mason Center, Landmark Building C, San Francisco, CA 94123 (415/474-7662). Able/disabled day and overnight trips in the San Francisco area only.

Maui Sea Kayaking, P O Box 106, Puunene, HA 96784 (808/572-6299). Contact Ron Bass. Sea kayaking and canoeing instruction and able/disabled trips.

Nantahala Outdoor Center, US 19W, Box 41, Bryson City, NC 28713 (704/488-2175). Instruction for able and disabled in whitewater kayaking, including Eskimo roll.

Pacific Water Sports, c/o Tim Davis, 16205 Pacific Hwy South, Seattle, WA 98188 (206/246-9385). Water sports for people with disabilities.

Shared Adventures, Inc., c/o Kent Winchester, 76 Eastland Avenue, Rochester, NY 14618 (716/442-8104). Able/disabled canoe and kayak trips in the Adirondacks and Canada.

SOAR (Shared Outdoor Adventure Recreation), P O Box 14583, Portland, OR 97214 (503/238-1613). Sea kayaking instruction and tours on Oregon rivers in August and September.

S'PLORE (Special Populations Learning Outdoor Recreation and Education), 699 East South Temple, Suite 120, Salt Lake City, UT 84102 (801/353-7130. Flatwater canoeing and whitewater rafting.

Vinland National Center, 3675 Ihduhapi Road, Loretto, MN 55357 (612/479-3555, voice or TTY). Located just to the west of the metropolitan Minneapolis area, Vinland focuses on health sports for persons of varying abilities. Such activities are aimed to improve physical, social and emotional fitness, thereby improving one's health, quality of life and employability. Wilderness camping is not a primary focal interest. Like Camp Northland, participants are housed in dormitory style, with shared baths available. Canoeing and camping are only two of the physical fitness, sports and recreations skills training provided. A summer conference is held for persons of varying physical abilities.

Voyageur Outward Bound School, 10900 Cedar Lake Road, Minnetonka, MN 55343 (phone 612/542-9255 or 800/328-2943 for non-Minnesota residents; fax number 612/542-9620). Voyageur Outward Bound, another Minnesota-based operation, also has programs for the physically disabled and hearing impaired. According to their literature, persons disabled with multiple sclerosis, cerebral palsy, muscular dystrophy, paraplegia, limb deformities, and sight and hearing impairment have successfully completed their courses, which run 14 days. These Outward Bound courses are offered in conjunction with Wilderness Inquiry.

Wilderness Inquiry, 1313 Fifth Street South East, Suite 327, Minneapolis, MN 55414 (612/379-3858). Wilderness Inquiry has pioneered outdoor adventure programs for the physically disabled and hearing impaired. Mixed in range of physical abilities and disabilities, age and place of origin, groups usually consist of eight — four able-bodied and four disabled — and take part in courses and canoe trips ranging in length from 5 to 14 days in length.

This non-profit group offers canoe trips ranging in locale from the St. Croix River (fairly close to St. Paul, MN), theBWCA, Ontario, and the Arkansas Ozarks. Trips have included individuals who were confined to wheelchairs, blind, afflicted with cerebral palsy, etc., and range from long-weekend trips to 2 weeks. Special clothing, other techniques and equipment have been devised to facilitate matters. For the really adventurous, the Wilderness Inquiry people also offer wintertime dog sled trips or a 28-day trip to the Yukon!

The Forest Service people and the Wilderness Inquiry people have developed a "Disabled Visitor's Guide to the Boundary Waters Canoe Area Wilderness." Its focus is on the more accessible canoe routes in the BWCA, and would be helpful for persons or groups planning trips involving people with mobility impairment. Write to the Forest Service at the Duluth address listed earlier.

Other organizations cater to individuals with special needs in established camps, including the following:

Camp Northland, 1761 University Avenue, St. Paul, MN 55104 (612/ 645-2136). (Summer address is 3606 North Arm Road, Ely, MN 55731.)

Camp Northland is a complete program and retreat owned and operated by the St. Paul Area YMCA. It can accommodate groups of up to 100 during the summer and forty-five during the other seasons. Elderhostel programs are held at Northland during the summer.

Wilderness Canoe Base, 940 Gunflint Trail, MN 55604 (218/388-2241, voice or TTY). Winter Camp Office, 2301 Oliver Avenue North, Minneapolis, MN 55411 (612/522-6501).

Wilderness is an Outreach of Plymouth Christian Youth Center. Its focus is more on an organized group camp experience with a Christian emphasis. A note from the Camp Program Director informed me that they serve the mentally handicapped population more than the physically handicapped. Their brochure lists camping sessions one or two weeks in length through the summer. Wilderness camp includes rustic cabins for family camping, canoe camping for groups of four to nine. Rock climbing is also an activity.

Investigation in your own area may reveal other opportunities.

CANOEING IN CANADA

Canada offers many opportunities for more adventurous canoeing or camping, be it white water or "real" wilderness. She has National Parks, and the provinces also have parks, analogs of our State Parks. Saskatchewan, Manitoba, Ontario and Quebec have many lakes and rivers which call to the canoeist with opportunities for wilderness canoe camping. See Sources for addresses and phone numbers to get information. All costs for Canadian materials quoted here and elsewhere are in Canadian funds.

Of the provinces, Ontario has more parks easily accessible to Americans (that is, close to the border) and it is the province with which I am the best acquainted. Hence the bias on information.

In addition to the park lands, where camping is regulated, usually by permit, there are Crown lands where camping by non-residents may or may not be permitted. These are government lands, corresponding more or less to our Forest Service lands or other government reservations. Restrictions and fees generally are applied, but vary somewhat from province to province. Hunting and fishing license outlets or the province's Natural Resources office can fix you up.

It is truly wonderful that Americans and Canadians may pass between the two countries with so few restrictions.

ONTARIO

Ontario alone has 260 Provincial Parks. These are classified into six types: Recreation, Natural Environment, Nature Reserve, Waterway, Wilderness, and Historic. Historic parks and Nature Reserves are generally not for camping. Recreation Parks may or may not have camping facilities. Wilderness and Waterway Parks are not always accessible by road, though rail, air or water access may be available. Some parks are described as "non-operating," which means simply that facilities have not been developed. Some of these "non-operating" parks such as Woodland Caribou are nonetheless popular spots.

The spring and peak seasons for Ontario Provincial Parks generally begin on May 24 and end with Labor Day (like in the U.S., the first Monday in September. Reserved camping dates are May 24 to September 1.

Numerous Wilderness or Waterway Parks are available; five of them have come into the Park system since 1980; several of them lie well to the north, and all call for considerable skill in canoeing and camping in them. If this book is a sort of elementary course for wilderness canoe-camping, these Provincial Parks call for a college seminar (this holds true for the other provinces discussed here).

Seven of the eight wilderness parks are of interest to canoeists: Kesagami, Lady Evelyn-Smoothwater,Temagami, Opasquia, Wabamimi, and Woodland Caribou.

As their name implies, waterway parks (there are 29) generally follow rivers and may involve rapids (Class III or more) that are beyond novice skills. Some of interest here are Chapleau-Nemegosenda, French River, Lower Madawaska River, Mattawa River, Mississagi River, and Winisk River.

The National Environment parks, which share some characteristics of American National Forests, are more developed with a wider range of recreational facilities and opportunity for motorized vehicles (RVs and motorboats, for instance). However, some do have interior sites and motorboat restrictions, two qualities appealing to a wilderness canoe-camper.

Parks that fit the qualifications of having interior sites and motorboat restsrictions include Algonquin, Bon Echo, Charleston Lake, Esker Lakes, Frontenac, Halfway Lake, Killarney, Murphy's Point, Silent Lake, Sleeping Giant (formerly known as Sibley), and White Lake. Some parks are clustered, at least administratively.

The majority of interest here is located in the southern part of the province.

Algonquin Provincial Park, the largest and oldest, is just slightly due east of Michigan's Upper Peninsula on Ontario's eastern border. Algonquin offers some 3,000 square miles (or 7,600 square kilometers, 1,870,720 acres) of lakes, streams, forests and bogs. It is within a day's drive from central New York state.

The Friends of Algonquin Park produce several publications about this park, and one of the most informative is the map/brochure, "Canoe Routes of Algonquin Provincial Park," priced at $2.25 (1992).

Algonquin differs from Quetico in some respects. It does have designated campsites, which are classed as either regular or low maintenance sites, with box latrines (the "thrones"). Likewise the portages are differentiated by low or regular maintenance.

Ontario uses a zoning system to designate the type of use a particular portion of a park may get. Algonquin is a mixed use park, with nearly nine percent of its land designated as Wilderness Zones, and there are three Wilderness Zones. These are equivalent to the interior zones of Quetico.

Then there are 70 Nature Reserve Zones, amounting to four percent of the area. They generally lie outside the Wilderness Zones. However, the bulk of the park (75 percent) is designated Recreation-Utilization Zone. Here logging is permitted on a highly regulated basis.

The Friends forthrightly state on their map that canoeists do have a harmful impact on the environment, and that regulations are therefore necessary. Like other wilderness parks, entry into the Interior areas is regulated.

As of 1992, Interior camping permits were $3.04 per night per person ($1.64 for ages 12-17). Permits to enter are regulated, much like the BWCA. Call for reservation application forms. (The reservation service fee is $4.50.) You must use VISA or MASTERCARD if you are making a reservation by phone.

Quetico. Atikokan, Ontario, is a gateway of sorts for some 3500 square miles (or 9,065 square kilometers) of splendid canoe country, most notably Quetico Provincial Park to the south. Another wilderness area for canoeing is White Otter Wilderness Area, northwest of Atikokan.

Quetico Park officials also accept VISA or MASTERCARD for annual vehicle and camping permits and for Quetico interior reservation fees. (This is true for other parks as well.) Park personnel also accept phone reservations using credit cards, but the actual card will be needed when the party reserving enters the Park. They will not accept personal checks drawn on American banks.

Quetico is unique among Canadian Parks in that it borders an American park. In fact, some 80 per cent of Quetico's visitors are Americans. There are some 22 entry points into Quetico, three from the American side, and they are open only for certain periods of time each year. If entering from the American side, everyone — U. S. or Canadian citizens — must stop at a Canadian Customs Station before reporting to the Quetico Ranger Station before entering the Park, and must have a valid BWCA wilderness permit. To camp overnight in the interior (wilderness), a visitor must purchase a Wilderness Camping Permit at the Ranger Station. As with the BWCA, Ontario uses a quota system (the Visitor Distribution Programme) in regulating usage of her wilderness areas. Entry permits are limited and may be reserved. Party size is limited to six.

Quetico has two types of campsites: those in an established camping area (Dawson Trail Campgrounds) and wilderness (interior) sites. The fee for wilderness camping is $2.00 *per person* per night. A campsite permit in the Dawson Trail Campgrounds costs $6.75 (1993) and allows vehicle and occupants to occupy a designated campsite until 2 p.m. the following day. (Other parks have similar and maybe higher fees.)

Campsites in the wilderness interior parks may have a horizontal pole privy or a primitive box-type toilet. Note the word "may." Neither may be present. You may have to dig a facility of your own. In Quetico, there are no established latrines. Please note that this calls for more skill and greater care in finding and setting up suitable campsites. Actually, the campsites in the Park are properly not "designated" campsites; they are more on the order of traditional sites, places people have used for years for camping. Occasionally, you will find sites where previous campers have constructed other fire pits.

Write the District Manager, Quetico Provincial Park or phone for reservations and Quetico Park Rules. For remote border crossing permits apply to Canada Immigration, RR 7, Hwy. 61, Thunder Bay, Ontario P7C 5V5.

The Atikokan Chamber of Commerce will gladly send information on accommodations and resorts in the area. The Chamber is also a source for area resorts, campgrounds, outfitters and flying services. Generally, an inquiry about a park to the appropriate tourism office will also produce information about accommodations, resorts and other activities in its area.

For traveling in Quetico Provincial Park or other points in Ontario, write for "Wilderness Outfitters Guide" which is available through the Ministry of Natural Resources. Cost is $9.95 plus $1.00 for postage and handling.

Killarney. Killarney Provincial Park, approximately 150 miles east of Sault Sainte Marie on the north shore of Lake Huron, also is easily accessible for Americans. An interior camping reservation service is offered at these parks. Reservations can be secured by contacting the Park directly.

The Ministry of Tourism and Recreation publishes a booklet called "Wilderness Outfitters: Canoe, Whitewater Rafting and Backpacking Excursions," which is loaded with useful information. Not only does it list all of Ontario's canoe outfitters and the services provided, it gives additional sources of information other than listed here, the addresses of the various district offices for specific information on canoeing in a particular area, and useful publications.

Two other sources of general information on canoeing or kayaking in Ontario are the Ontario Recreational Canoeing Association (with a $2.00 charge) and the Canadian Recreational Canoeing Association.

For general information on non-Canadians' travel in Canada, contact District Manager, Revenue Canada, Customs & Excise, 301 Scott Street, Fort Frances, ON P9A 3M9 (807)274-3751,or Manager, Canada Immigration Centre, 204 First Street East, Fort Frances, ON P9A 1K6 (807) 274-3815. (Obviously, these are immediately pertinent to Ontario; they will have counterparts the length of the national border.)

Ontario fishing license regulations. Non-residents of Ontario or non-residents of Canada may fish in Quetico waters with the appropriate license. Such a visitor may get a four-day tag ($10.00 Canadian), a twenty-one day tag ($20.00), a twenty-one day renewal tag ($10.00), or a seasonal tag ($30.00. A Spousal tag costs $40.00. If the fisherman is after muskellunge or lake trout, species tags are required at $5.00 *per species* in addition to the basic fishing license. Detailed fishing regulation information is available where licenses are issued. As with the Park reservations, personal checks are not accepted at Park Ranger Stations, though cash, travelers checks, money orders and bank drafts are acceptable.

MANITOBA

Manitoba has a network of over 150 provincial parks of the same sorts as Ontario. Just a short (relatively speaking) distance from northern Minnesota and running north along the Ontario-Manitoba border is a series of provincial parks in lake and river country. They are Atikaki Wilderness, Whiteshell, and Nopiming Provincial Parks. Atikaki Wilderness Provincial Park is the only *wilderness* park (as contrasted with *recreation* or other park designation) in the system. To the northwest of Lake Winnipeg, Grass River Provincial Park offers canoeing with history.

Manitoba boasts of 100,000 lakes and numberless rivers; a canoeist can find anything suitable to skill level and interest.

The Manitoba Recreational Canoeing Association is an information source on canoe routes in the province. Write MRCA Resource Committee, Box 2663, Winnipeg, MB R3C 4B3 or call 204/985-4103.

Open fires are prohibited from April 1 to November 15 unless the fire is in an approved fire pit. If approved fire pit is not available, meals must be cooked over a camp stove.

Manitoba fishing license regulations. A fishing license for a non-resident is $30, or $15 for a non-resident Conservation license. The difference is in the catch limit on some kinds of fish. Fishing regulations vary in the three sport fishing divisions of the province.

SASKATCHEWAN

Saskatchewan is a huge province, part of the historic fur trade country. The northern two-thirds of it are thoroughly peppered with lakes and streaked with streams, terrain that continues east into Manitoba. Highways are sparse in this whole region, but outfitters with base camps and outposts are fairly numerous (over 300 in the province). The province boasts numerous provincial parks, many of which are located on rivers and lakes.

Tourism Saskatchewan produces a beautiful, wonderfully comprehensive brochure overing fishing, hunting, canoeing, outfitting and package tours. It contains additional addresses for further information on any of the categories. The province has documented more than 50 canoe routes, listing length, time necessary to traverse, and number of portages. Of those, seven were identified as "suitable for novice canoeists." Tourism Saskatchewan also has several pertinent publications (available free of charge).

Saskatchewan Environment and Resource Management manages the provincial parks.

QUEBEC

Québec has several huge provincial parks: remote La Verndrye, Laurentides Park (both are much larger than Ontarios's Algonquin), Chibougamau Park, and Mont Tremblant Park. Smaller, but similarly remote (lightly-inhabited areas) parks are La Belle Papineau, Mastgouche (abuts St. Maurice *National* Park), St. Maurice, and Portneuf. All are north of the St. Laurence River.

CANADA'S NATIONAL PARKS

Among Canada's National Park system are several that are appropriate for canoeing and camping, though not necessarily full-fledged wilderness camping. The list (not comprehensive) would include Pukaskwa (Ontario), Prince Albert (central Saskatchewan), Nahanni National Park Reserve (the Northwest Territories), Wood Buffalo National Park (Alberta and Northwest Territories), and Riding Mountain National Park (Manitoba). Other parks, such as the Pacific Rim in British Columbia, may offer possibilities for sea-kayaking, but I have no experience with kayaks.

For general information (the sort that whets the appetite), write or call the Parks Service Regional Offices. (See Sources.)

Prince Albert National Park (Saskatchewan) features several canoe routes, three sizeable lakes and numerous smaller ones, plus numerous hiking trails. A full range of camping options is available, from trailer park to backcountry camping. It's a great park for wildlife, particularly white pelicans and bison.

Riding Mountain National Park (Manitoba) lists canoeing as an activity; however, the terrain would not sem to encourage canoe *travel*. The Park accommodates trailers and campers.

Wood Buffalo National Park (Alberta and Northwest Territories) is one of the biggest national parks in the world, and is truly a wildlife reserve, where the Peace and Athabasca Rivers flow. Even so, visitor center facilities are wheelchair accessible.

Nahanni National Park Reserve has very little in the way of development or visitor facilities. Neither is it easily accessible. The country is mountainous, with the consequent canyons and rapids. The Nahanni River is famed among expert canoeists; it and the Flat (also in the Reserve) are "beautiful and relentless." They are *not* for beginners.

Kouchibouguac (New Brunswick, in the Atlantic Region) would seem to be a northern cousin of the coastal waters of the Everglades, with salt marshes, sand dunes, offshore barrier islands, seals and terns.

Pukaskwa's White and Pukaskwa Rivers (Ontario) offer wilderness whitewater adventure. Pukaskwa's brochure notes that all visitors travelling in areas other than the Coastal Hiking Trail *must* contact a Park Warden to register their trip agenda and schedule and sign out on completion of trip. Registration by mail is not accepted.

USEFUL AND INTERESTING READING

These books are useful and interesting reading; some are superb resource books as well.

CAMPING AND CANOEING TECHNIQUES

American Red Cross, The. *Canoeing and Kayaking.* The American Red Cross. New York, NY: Doubleday, 1981. The classic, basic book for reference on the full scope of un-powered water craft and safety in using them.

—. *Standard First Aid and Personal Safety.* Prepared by the American National Red Cross, 1977. At least one member of the party, better yet, several, should be well-versed in first aid and cardio-pulmonary resuscitation (CPR).

Cary, Bob. *The Big Wilderness Canoe Manual.* New York, NY: Arco Publishing Inc., 1978, 1983. Cary has guided in the BWCA and in Canadian regions. This book includes camping expedition accounts with his wife, which I liked; there has seemed to be very little female presence in the canoeing books I have read. Cary is wilderness-oriented, and I mean the wilderness *beyond* the BWCA. A very practical book and fun to read.

Cassidy, John. *Klutz Book of Knots: How to tie the world's 25 most useful hitches, ties, wraps, and knots.* Palo Alto, CA: Klutz Press, 1985. This is a great little book! Well-illustrated with pictures of the finished knot and how-to drawings, it includes pieces of cordage and holes in the appropriate pages for practice tying. I highly recommend it.

Cheney, Theodore A. *Camping by Backpack and Canoe.* New York, NY: Funk & Wagnalls, 1970. One interesting part of this book discusses Indian canoe construction. Camping books published before 1980 are astonishing indicators of the extent to which equipment and philosophy have changed. One piece of equipment he does like to take is a pressure cooker. Cheney's style is lively and conversational; the book is delightful reading.

Drabik, Harry. *The Spirit of Canoe Camping. A Handbook for Wilderness Camping.* Minneapolis, MN: Nodin Press, 1981.

Forgey, M. D., William. *Wilderness Medicine.* ICS Books, Inc., Merrillville, IN. 1987. Dr. Forgey is serious about wilderness activities. This book covers all sorts of situations, injuries, ailments, etc., that could possibly occur. The book seems focussed more toward expeditions (longer than two week trips). He speaks of outfitting with quite a few medications that may or may not be readily available to the average paddler.

Furtman, Michael. *A Boundary Waters Fishing Guide.* Minocqua, WI: NorthWord Press, 1990. Really excellent for beginners. Includes key of species for every lake in BWCA. We took this with us for one trip and found it very helpful. Friend Spouse particularly likes Furtman's method of dressing northern pike.

—. *Canoe Country Camping: Wilderness Skills for the Boundary Waters and Quetico.* Duluth, MN: Pfeifer-Hamilton. 1992. Attractive book; his point of view is that of young, frequent trekker. Tends to overlook needs of less vigorous. Does at least focus on camping trips with small parties (i.e., him and his wife).

Hartley, Joel, M.D. *First Aid Without Panic.* New York, NY: Grosset & Dunlap, 1982. Full of sound, practical advice for outdoors people.

Jacobson, Cliff. *The NEW Wilderness Canoe & Camping.* Merrillville, IN: ICS Books. 1986. Lots of information from a prolific writer in the field.

Landy, Paul, and Mattay McNair. *The Outward Bound Canoeing Handbook.* New York, NY: Lyons & Burford, Publishers. 1992. I haven't read this, but considering the source, it should be useful.

Malo, John W. *Malo's Complete Guide to Canoeing and Canoe Camping.* New York, NY: Times Books, NY Times Publishing Company, Inc., 1967, revised 1974, 1983. This is a good overall book on canoe construction, types, and handling; on paddles and how to use them. He devotes about one-fourth of the book to canoe camping, and is somewhat general on it. Also included is a listing by state of other good canoeing areas in the United States and Canada.

Maughan, Jackie Johnson, and Ann Puddicombe. *Hiking the Backcountry.* Harrisburg, PA: Stackpole Books, 1981. Comprehensive. I like this book very much; not only are there many, many useful tips for the backpacker, and particularly the female backpacker, there are also extensive and illuminating discussions on women's physiology relating to outdoor activity. Backpackers do a different thing from canoeists, and consequently do many other matters differently, but there are many points of common ground. Notes on sources; many helpful hints for women hiking alone.

Meyer, Kathleen. *How to Shit in the Woods. An environmentally sound approach to a lost art.* Berkeley, CA: Ten Speed Press. 1989. This is an excellent, practical and thoughtful book. Meyer deals with questions every camper has but is embarrassed to ask. The disposal of human waste is a topic most people prefer to evade, but Meyer approaches it in a forthright and extremely practical manner.

Ormond, Clyde. *Complete Book of Outdoor Lore and Woodcraft.* New York, NY: Outdoor Life Books, 1964 (1970, 1981). Ormond approaches the topic with a hunter's eye. The chapters on animal tracking and tree identification can add greatly to enjoyment of wilderness. There is a major emphasis on survival lore and techniques, though nothing on mishaps that can occur in the wild.

Riviere, Bill. *Pole, Paddle & Portage.* New York, NY: Van Nostrand Reinhold Company, 1969. This is one of the classic books on canoeing. Chapter XVII Canoe country gives a state by state, as well as province by province in Canada, rundown on canoeing possibilities. An appendix lists information sources by state and organized groups in that state, some of which may be out of date.

— , with the staff of L.L. Bean. *The L. L. Bean Guide to the Outdoors.* New York, NY: Random House, NY, 1981. While some of the material (on fabrics, for instance) is out of date, nonetheless the book provides much useful information on what to look for in equipment and clothing. L.L. Bean, the founder of the renowned store, would have appreciated the term "elegance," as that was part of his style.

Rutstrum, Calvin. *The New Way of the Wilderness.* New York, NY: The MacMillan Company, 1958. (Also his *North American Canoe Country.* A grand old man of wilderness life, Rutstrum describes how to do it (canoeing, camping and living in the backcountry). His experience dates from early in this century, and at least in part addresses canoeing in Canada and the American High West. Much is sadly out of date because of changes in amount of traffic in wilderness, changes in technology (the equipment has improved greatly), and in attitudes toward the environment. Fine book for canoe handling technique and for a sense of the wilderness as it was. Rutstrum died in 1982.

Stensaas, Mark. *Canoe Country Wildlife: A Field Guide To The Boundary Waters And Quetico.* Duluth, MN: Pfeifer-Hamilton. 1993. This book is a delight. More than the usual field guide, this lively book identifies creatures common to its target area by scientific names and tells a bit of its biological data, but then goes on to add observations, and assorted tidbits of interest. The illustrations by Rick Kollath are particularly attractive.

Webre, Anne and Janet Zeller. *Canoeing and Kayaking for Persons with Physical Disabilities.* Newington, VA; American Canoe Association Book Service, 1990. I have not read this; however, it comes highly recommended for its collection of techniques and adaptations for the paddler with disabilities. The aim of the book is to open up this area of water sports previously thought closed to people with disabilities. Webre is a canoeing instructor; Zeller is a longtime paddler, now disabled.

CANOEING AREAS

Beymer, Robert. *Boundary Waters Canoe Area, Volume 1: The Western Region,* 1988, and *Volume 2: The Eastern Region.* Berkeley, CA: Wilderness Press, 1985, 1991. These two volumes are superb in their detailing of trip routes and lengths. Also have solid advice for equipment. Author clearly loves the country. We have carried Volume 2 and his *Guide to Quetico Provincial Park,* to the greater enjoyment of our trips.

— . *A Paddler's Guide to Quetico Provincial Park.* Virginia, MN: W.A. Fisher, 1984. Also an excellent piece of work, and rather more fun to read, as Beymer weaves into his descriptions of routes some of the historical background.

— . *Superior National Forest.* Seattle, WA: The Mountaineers, 1989. Beymer continues to do what he does so well: this time he widens the range of wilderness activities available in northern Minnesota's Superior National Forest to include backpacking and hiking as well as canoeing.

Carter, E.F., and J.L. Pearce. *A Canoeing and Kayaking Guide to the Streams of Florida, Volume 1: North Central Peninsula and Panhandle.* Birmingham, AL: Menasha Ridge Press. 1985.

DuFresne, Jim. *Voyageurs National Park: Water Routes, Foot Paths and Ski Trails.* Seattle, WA: The Mountaineers, 1986. DuFresne does for Voyageurs what Beymer did for the BWCA with an additional section on hiking and skiing.

Glaros, L. and D. Sphar. *A Canoeing and Kayaking Guide to the Streams of Florida, Volume 2: Central and South Peninsula.* Birmingham, AL: Menasha Ridge Press. 1987.

Jamieson, Paul, & Donald Morris. *Adirondack Canoe Waters — North Flow.* Glens Falls, NY: Adirondack Mountain Club, Inc. Third edition, 1988. This is the Adirondack equivalent to Robert Beymer's books, which is to say it is invaluable for the new visitor to the Adirondack region. There is a companion book, *Adirondack Canoe Waters — South and West Flow.*

Kalma, Dennis. *Boat and Canoe Camping in the Everglades Backcountry and Ten Thousand Islands Region.* Miami, FL: Florida Flair Books. 1988. This little (64 pages) book is a good one to get if you are considering an Everglades trip, and at $4.95, the price is certainly right. Kalma gives a good overview, with attention on pre-trip planning, route planning, campsites, emergencies, several suggested routes, and sections on the natural and human histories of the region.

Truesdell, William G. *A Guide to the Wilderness Waterway of the Everglades National Park,* revised 1985. Coral Gables, FL; University of Miami Press. This book is recommended by people who know the Park as the guide for planning routes in the Park.

Umhoefer, Jim. *Minnesota All-Seasons Guide to Minnesota Parks, Canoe Routes and Trails.* Minocqua, WI; NorthWord Press, 1984. One of severable books this knowledgeable guide writes about Minnesota and Wisconsin.

GENERAL INTEREST, BOUNDARY WATERS

Blacklock, Les, with Sigurd F. Olson. *The Hidden Forest.* New York, NY: Viking Press, 1969. Text by Olson, photographs by Blacklock. Blacklock produced numerous wildlife and nature books and calendars, many singly, some in collaboration with his photographer son Craig Blacklock.

—. *Our Minnesota.* Stillwater, MN: Voyageur Press, 1978. Text by wife Fran, photographs and captions by Les. The Blacklocks' work is wonderful for providing a real sense and feel of the wilderness.

Breining, Greg, and Stebbins, Jerry. *Boundary Waters.* Minneapolis, MN: Nodin Press, 1983. Coffee table book, with solid photography by Jerry Stebbins, text by Greg Breining.

Jaques, Florence Page. *Canoe Country.* Minneapolis, MN: University of Minnesota Press. 1937. (Reprint) A charming account of a honeymoon trip on the boundary lakes on Minnesota, when wilderness travel was definitely roughing it, by a young woman who saw it all with the eyes of an artist and newcomer.

Kerfoot, Justine. *Woman of the Boundary Waters.* Grand Marais, MN: Women's Times Publishing, 1986. Justine Kerfoot has lived on the Gunflint Trail for some fifty years, and is an archetypical voice of life in the wilderness. Highly recommended for the view of a bygone way of life.

Olson, Sigurd. *The Singing Wilderness* (1956), *Wilderness Days* (1972), *Listening Point* (1958), *Open Horizons* (1969), *Reflections from the North Country, of Time and Place.* New York: Alfred A. Knopf, Borzoi Books. The first two are especially recommended. Olson was deeply involved as a wilderness preservationist; we who enjoy the North Country are greatly indebted to him. He wrote lovingly and enchantingly of the region.

Searle, R. Newell. *Saving Quetico-Superior: A Land Set Apart.* St. Paul, MN: Minnesota Historical Society. 1977. Ernest Oberholtzer, a pioneer conservationist featured in this book, has been called "the original architect of the border wilderness."

Sevareid, Eric. *Canoeing with the Cree.* St. Paul, MN: Minnesota Historical Society, Historical Reprint Edition, 1968. Originally pub lished in 1935, based on a diary kept during the trip and on a series of newspaper articles filed *en route,* it is Sevareid's own account of the 1930 canoe journey he and his friend Walter Port made during the summer they graduated from high school. They were the first to canoe from Minneapolis, MN, up the Minnesota River and continue by canoe and portage all the way (some 2,250 miles) to York Factory on Hudson Bay. For comparison, the length of the Mississippi River is some 2,344 miles long. The book vividly reminds of difficulties that have been reduced in the intervening years.

CAMPING WITH CHILDREN

Brown, Jr., Tom with Judy Brown. *Tom Brown's Field Guide To Nature and Survival For Children.* New York, NY.: Berkeley Publishing Group, 1989. Reported to be useful for planning family trips, though I have not read it.

Caduto, Michael and Joseph Bruchac. *Keepers Of The Earth: Native American Stories And Environmental Activities For Children.* Golden, CO: Fulcrum, Inc., 1988. Aims at teaching environmental conscious-ness; I have not read it.

Euser, Barbara. *Take 'em Along: Sharing The Wilderness With Your Children.* Evergreen, CO: Cordillera Press, 1987. This could be useful; I have not read it.

Liston, Beverly. *Family Camping Made Simple: Tent and rv Camping with Children.* Chester, CT: Globe Pequot Press. 1989. She writes of camping with very young children (and up), with more attention to camping in areas such as National Forests. The chapter on recreation is very good on acquiring some basic woods skills, and excellent on getting children into nature study.

Shanberg, Karen, and Stan Tekiela. *Plantworks: A Wild Plant Cookbook, Field guide and Activity Book For the Novice & Naturalist.* Cambridge, MN: Adventure Publications, 1991. Identifies fifteen plants or trees commonly found in the eastern half of the United States, with their habitats, the seasons when the plants may be found, and recipes for safely harvesting and preparing. Excellent starter book for budding naturalists. Useful and extensive bibliography.

Silverman, Goldie. *Backpacking With Babies And Small Children*. Berkeley, CA: Wilderness Press, 1986. This little book is full of practical information on its title subject.

FOOD

Axcell, Claudia, Diana Cooke, and Vikki Kinmont. *Simple Foods For the Pack*. San Francisco, CA: Sierra Club Books. 1986. The authors have gathered 180 trail-tested recipes (these are backpacker's recipes, and those that call for canned items of course are not useful in areas where cans are banned.) Quite a few items look to be very interesting, providing considerable variety to menus. The emphasis is on "natural" foods, and some of the items may not be to everybody's taste. One good feature is a set of menus for trips of different lengths.

Barker, Harriet. *Supermarket Backpacker*. Chicago, IL: Contemporary Books. 1977. I wish I had found this book in the early years when we were just started camping. While written primarily for backpackers, there are many, many good ideas that are applicable to wilderness restrictions. She includes a section on home-drying of foods for trips, discusses nutrition.

—. *The One-Burner Gourmet*. Chicago, IL: Contemporary Books. 1981. One of the larger cookbooks for campers (nearly 300 pages), it is primarily useful for family camping in areas like National Forests, where it is feasible to carry a grub box and cans are no problem. Recipes rely heavily on the use of fresh food and canned items. One particularly helpful feature is a buying guide on campstoves. Her suggestion to dig a shallow trench for foil cooking is totally out of line for wilderness camping.

McHugh, Gretchen. *The Hungry Hiker's Book of Good Cooking*. New York, NY: Alfred A. Knopf, 1982. Basically a backpacker's book, it offers much useful information on cooking equipment as well as 135 recipes and menus. Also gives list of mail-order backpacking supply houses.

White, Joanna. *The Dehydrator Cookbook*. San Leandro, CA: Bristol Publishing Enterprises, Inc., Nitty Gritty Cookbooks. 1992. Bristol Publishing Enterprises publishes a nifty Nitty Gritty series. While many of the recipes using home-dehydrated foods are not particularly useful for wilderness camping, the directions for drying a wide range of foods are pertinent.

MISCELLANEOUS

Freier, Ph. D., George D. *Weather Proverbs: How 600 proverbs, sayings and poems accurately explain our weather.* Tucson, AZ: Fisher Books. 1989. Dr. Freier, a physicist by training, is recognized as an expert on lightning, and here he makes understanding weather phenomena quite accessible and points out how folklore, appearing in proverbs, makes it easy to make short term weather predictions.

Leopold, Aldo. *A Sand County Almanac, with Essays on Conservation from Round River.* New York, NY: Ballantine Books (originally published in 1949 by Tamarack Press). I particularly like the "Taste for Country" essays, which are very strong in their cry for the preservation of wilderness. Remember he wrote those before 1953, hence was a prophet calling for conservation, preservation of wilderness, and in general, greater respect for the land and all its creatures. He gave a wake-up call that reverberates (as well it should) down to the present time. The floods of 1993 serve to underscore his points.

Niemi, Judith, and Wieser, Barb, Editors. *Rivers Running Free: Stories of Adventurous Women.* Seattle, WA: Seal Press, 1992. A delightful and fascinating collection of stories, articles and journal excerpts from women canoeists. Some of the writings appeared in the early part of this century. A welcome voice among what is predominantly a masculine literature.

USEFUL BROCHURES AND BOOKLETS

"Canoe America." National Marine Manufacturers Association, 401 North Michigan Avenue, Chicago, IL 60611. This is an excellent information source, a 32-page booklet listing addresses, national and state by state, to which canoeists may write for a variety of free information, including maps, travel indexes, camping guides and canoe routes. Also lists tips about safety, state canoe regulations, attractions, activities and how to rent of buy a canoe.

TRAVELING IN CANADA WITH DISABILITIES

"Easy Wheeling Manitoba." Canadian Paraplegic Association, 825 Sherbrook Street, Winnipeg, MB R3 1M(204/786-4753) Booklet, available free of cost from CPA or from Travel Manitoba outlets (see Sources). Inquiry might produce more information on camping opportunities.

REFERENCES AND RESOURCES

I drew on the following helpful resources, in addition to many on the preceding list:

Chalmers, J. Alan. *Atmospheric Electricity,* 2nd edition. Long Island City, NY: Pergamon Press, Oxford, 1967.

Hartley, Joel, M.D. *First Aid Without Panic.* New York, NY: Grosset & Dunlap, 1982. This has a lot of sound, practical advice for outdoors people.

Henderson, John, MD. *Emergency Medical Guide,* 4th edition. New York, NY: McGraw-Hill Book Co. Information on burns, heat exhaustion, heat prostration.

Kavaler, Lucy. *Freezing Point: Cold As A Matter of Life and Death.* New York, NY: The John Day Company, 1970. Chapter 2.

Lappé, Frances Moore. *Diet for a Small Planet.* New York, NY: Ballantine Books. Particularly from Part III. C.

Pozos, Robert, and Born, David O. *Hypothermia: Causes, Effects, Prevention.* Piscataway, NJ: New Century Publishers, Inc., 1982. Dr. Pozos very kindly reviewed the section on hypothermia in this book.

Wood, Peter. *Running the Rivers of North America.* Barre, MA: Barre Publications, 1978. Chapter IV, on canoe camping, very good; Part II, on the Rivers of America, very helpful on where to get more information on rivers.

I adapted several recipes from some in the following cook books:

Clark, Morton Gill. *A World of Nut Recipes.* New York, NY: Funk & Wagnalls. 1967.

Blair, Eulalia C. *Quick -To-Fix Desserts.* Boston, MA: CBI Publishing Company, Inc. 1980.

Leibenstein, Margaret. *The Edible Mushroom.* New York, NY: Fawcett Columbine. 1986.

EQUIPMENT SOURCES

This is not intended to be a comprehensive list; I have included products and companies I know about. I would appreciate knowing about similar, well-worthwhile products. Write me in care of Cat's-paw Press.

Adventure Medical Kits, P O Box 2586, Berkeley, CA 94702.

Audubon Workshop. The "Audible Audubon" — mini-phonograph with some eighteen Sound Plates. $39.95 for mini-phono with one Sound Plate; other plates each $7.95. Phone (312/729-6660, or write Audubon Workshop, 1501 Paddock Drive, Northbrook, IL 60062, for catalogue. Several companies specializing in nifty outdoor interest items list this in their catalogues now.

Cabela's, 812 Thirteenth Avenue, Sidney, NE 69160. Order telephone: 800/237-4444. Specializes in clothing and accessories for the hunter or fisherman.

Campmor, P O Box 997, Paramus, NJ 07653. Phone 800/526-4784 to order, 201/445-5000 for product information. Specialists in camping equipment, they offer a tremendous assortment of tents, sleeping bags, backpacks and all manner of outdoor accoutrements.

Duluth Tent & Awning Company, Box 16024, 1610 Superior Street, Duluth, MN 55816-0024. Phone 800/777-4439 to order. They make the traditional Duluth packs (gave them the name, in fact), and other good stuff. Good basic equipment at reasonable cost.

EMS (Eastern Mountain Sports), Vose Farm Road, Peterborough, NH 03458. Has numerous stores across the country, particularly in the eastern half. Their primary interest, as the name indicates, is mountaineering, but they have tents, sleeping bags, cooking equipment and practical clothing. Their packs are more of interest to backpackers and hikers rather than canoeists.

Eddie Bauer's, Fifth and Union, P O Box 3700, Seattle, WA 98124. Order by telephone, 800/426-8020. Has stores around over the country, several in Canada. Similar to REI, but more fashion-conscious. Has tents, cooking gear, etc., for camping, fishing and hunting.

General Ecology, Inc., 151 Sheree Boulevard, Lionville, PA 19353 (215/363-7900; fax: 215/363-0412). Water purifier, mid-price range.

Grade VI, P O Box 8, Urbana, IL 61801 (800/533-5250). Well-regarded company for making high quality packs and sacks.

Granite Gear, Inc., P O Box 278, Industrial Park, Two Harbors, MN 55618 (218/834-6157). These are the makers of "Big Blue" and "Lady Blue." They are not the only makers of internal frame packs, but they certainly do know canoeing, and their products are high quality. They have a

Granite Gear, Inc., P O Box 278, Industrial Park, Two Harbors, MN 55618 (218/834-6157). These are the makers of "Big Blue" and "Lady Blue." They are not the only makers of internal frame packs, but they certainly do know canoeing, and their products are high quality. They have a growing line of other useful packs and bags (and our collection is growing, too). I am very partial to their packs.

James Alexander Corporation, RD. 3, Box 192, Blairstown, NJ 07825 (800/Tick-Kit or 800/842-5548). Their Tick Kit™ is aimed at preventing Lyme disease by means of easy spotting and disposal of ticks; contains magnifying glass, mounted on curved tweezers, five antiseptic swabs.

L. L. Bean, Inc., Freeport, ME 04033. Order telephone, 800/221-4221. Clothing. This has long been a classic purveyor of good sturdy outdoor wear. Ask for specialized catalogue for equipment.

Medic-Alert Foundation International, P O Box 1009, Turlock, CA 95381-1009. A lifetime Membership cost is $15, which includes cost of stainless steel emblem, with your special medical condition engrave on back, with special "call collect" number that provides instant access to your emergency medical records and the names of physicians or relatives to be contacted. Special medical conditions can include such particulars as organ donation or contact lens wearing, specific allergies that are potentially lethal, heart condition, etc.

Northwest River Supplies, Inc., P O Box 9186, Moscow, ID 83843-9186. As name implies, they specialize in river travel; lots of stuff on sea kayaking, too. They have waterproof bags, and they have portage packs, with their own house brand. Internal suspension similar to climbing, backpacking systems. NRS also has a summer version of boater's gloves, with suede palms and mesh back.

Piragis Northwoods Company, 105 North Central Avenue, Ely, MN 55731 (800/223-6565). These people have an excellent catalog with high quality merchandise. Ely is known as the gateway to Canoe Country, near the heart of the Boundary Waters Canoe Area. Consequently, Piragis knows and carries "the right stuff" for comfortable, safe traveling. They also can help outfit for a trip.

Quetico Superior Canoe Country Packs, CLG Enterprises, P O Box 6687, Minneapolis, MN 55406 (612/721-5785.) Good source for relatively inexpensive packs.

PUR, 2229 Edgewood Avenue South, Minneapolis, MN 55426. For catalog, call 800/845-PURE. Water purifier, mid-price range.

REI (Recreational Equipment Inc.), P O Box C-88125, Seattle, WA 98188. To order, phone 800/426-4840. Wide range of equipment for numerous outdoor activities (began as specialist for mountain climbing), clothing, trail foods. This is a cooperative; the membership fee is $10, though membership is not required for purchasing items. Their prices are competitive with comparable stores. Also has an "expertise" line (206/575-1009) for information.

Rich Craft, Box 125, Kershaw, SC 29067. They advertise a stainless steel indentification tag for $3.5; two tags with a neck chain, $4.95. Tag hold six lines or sixteen spaces.

Sawbill Canoe Outfitters, Tofte, MN 55615. Voyageur packs.

Stormy Bay, P O Box 345, Grand Rapids, MN 55744. The Wanigan™ Pantry Pack. Floatable, waterproof; fits well in canoe; for a well-organized kitchen in the woods.

FOOD SUPPLIERS

If a food supplier also offers equipment, look to the earlier listing for address. Many of them sell through camping supply or outdoor recreation stores, including some of the equipment sellers mentioned above.

Alpine Aire, P O Box 926, Nevada City, CA 95959.

Backpackers' Pantry, 1540 Charles Drive, Redding, CA 96003.

Campmor.

EMS (Eastern Mountain Sports).

Eddie Bauer's.

Harvest FoodWorks, 40 Hillcrest Drive, Toronto, Ontario M6G 2E3. Trail foods. Good products, reasonable price.

Myers Meats, Box 132, Parshall, ND 58770. Beef jerky ($12, 12 oz.)

Northwest River Supplies, Inc.

REI (Recreational Equipment Inc.).

Richmoor Corporation, Van Nuys, CA 91406. Natural High is their brand.

Taste Adventure. Distributed by Will-Pak Foods, San Pedro, CA 90731. Offers several interesting items through better supermarkets. I liked their Black Bean chili.

The Camper's Pantry, P O Box 293, Farmington, MN 55024-0293. (1-800-726-8796). Wide assortment of the good brands. Catalog includes useful products as well. They well understand the canoeist's needs.

Woodland Pantry, Forest Foods, Inc. P O Box 375, River Forest, IL 60305. Mushrooms (dried).

World Variety Produce, Inc., P O Box 21127, Los Angeles, CA 90021. Melissa's Brand dried fruits; some items are expensive but close to the fresh thing for taste. The blueberries worked beautifully in pancakes. Send a self-addressed, stamped envelope with a request for free recipe brochures.

UNITED STATES MAP SOURCES

DeLorme Mapping Company, Main Street, P O Box 298Q, Freeport, ME 04032. DeLorme produces the *Maine Atlas* and the *Gazeteer*, a geographical encyclopedia locating and describing parks, canoe trips, historic sites, etc. Like the McKenzie, Fisher or USGS maps, detailed topographical maps are available on specific sections.

McKenzie Products, 315 West Michigan Street, Dept 15, Duluth, MN 55802 . (218) 727-2113). Excellent maps for Boundary Waters region of northern Minnesota and Quetico Provincial Park. Ask for 53 Map Index (free) for overview.

National Oceanic and Atmospheric Administration (NOAA), Distribution Division N) CG33, National Ocean Service, 6501 Lafayette Avenue, Riverdale, MD 20737. Charts on coastal and interior waterways in Florida. For traveling in the backcountry of Everglades National Park and the Ten Thousand Islands Region, the NOAA Nautical Charts of the area are essential. Appropriate charts are Numbers 11430, 11432 and 11433. Order from International Sailing Supply, 320 Cross Street, Punta Gorda, FL 33950. (813/639-7626.)

The National Cartographic Information Center, Reston, VA 22092. They produce topographic maps.

United States Geological Survey, Distribution Section, 1200 South Eads Street, Arlington, VA 22202. Topographical maps of the entire U.S. Write for an index sheet (available free) for the state or area that you are interested in visiting and a price list.

W.A. Fisher, Virginia, MN 55792. Source of excellent maps for Boundary Waters region of northern Minnesota and Quetico Provincial Park.

Geological Survey maps do not show campsites. The Superior-Quetico maps from the W. A. Fisher Company and McKenzie Products of Duluth are excellent showing the locations of campsites and lengths of portages as well as the lakes and rivers. Printed on a water-resistant paper , these maps hold up quite well in face of the occasional shower and frequent folding and refolding.

CANADIAN MAPS AND INFORMATION SOURCES

TOPOGRAPHICAL MAPS

Publications Services Centre, Ministry of Natural Resources, Parliament Building, Whitney Block, Toronto, ON N7A 1W3. National Series Topographic Maps.

Department of Energy, Mines, and Resources, Surveys and Mapping Branch, 615 Booth Street, Ottawa, ON K1A 0E9 (613/952-7000). Topographical maps, such as for Wood Buffalo National Park.

The Hydrographic Chart Distribution Office, Department of Fisheries and Oceans, 1675 Russell Road, P O Box 8080, Ottawa, ON K1G 3H6. Hydrographical charts.

Department of Natural Resources, Survey and Mapping Branch, 1007 Century Street, Winnipeg, MB R3H 0W4 (204/945-6666). Canoe route maps.

Outfitters generally sell topographical maps.

PARKS INFORMATION SOURCES

ONTARIO

General information on provincial parks, write

Ontario Ministry of Natural Resources, Provincial Park & Wildlife, Whitney Block — Queen's Park, 99 Wellesley Street West, Toronto, M7A 1W3, for information on Provincial Parks, or MNR, Natural Resources Information Centre, Room M1-73 Macdonald Block, 900 Bay Street, Toronto, ON M7A 2C1 or phone 416/314-1717 (Telecommunications Device for the Deaf (TDD), 416/314-6557). For Ontario Travel, from the Toronto calling area, call 416/965-4008 (English), or 416/965-3448 (French). Excepting from Yukon and the Northwest Territory and Alaska, call 800/ ONTARIO; for TDD, 416/965-6027. Their Public Information Centre, Room 1640, carries current publications by the Province Ministry on Ontario parks and price lists. Call 416/965-3081 for personal shopping and mail orders.

The Ministry of Tourism and Recreation, Province of Ontario, Queen's Park, Toronto, M7A 2R9.

All prices quoted in this section are in Canadian funds.

ADDITIONAL SOURCES FOR PARTICULAR PLACES

For information on non-operating parks, call 416/314-1717. Contacts for the parks mentioned in Canoeing in Canada:

Algonquin, P O Box 219, Whitney, K0J 2M0 (705/633-5572). Call 705/633-5538 for reservation application forms. Friends of Algonquin Park (Box 248, Whitney, K0J 2M0) sell books and provide other information.

Bon Echo, R R I, Cloyne, K0H 1K0 (613/336-2228)

Charleston Lake, R. R. 4, Lansdowne, K0E 1L0 (613/659-2065)

Chapleau-Nemegosenda, 190 Cherry St., Chapleau, P0M 1K0 (705/864-1710)

Esker Lakes, P O Box 129, Swastika, P0K 1T0 (705/567 4849)

French River, P O Box 3500 Station A, Sudbury, P3A 4S2 (705/522-7823)

Frontenac, P O Box 11, Sydenham, K0H 2T0 (613/376-3489)

Halfway Lake, P O Box 3500, Station A, Sudbury, P3A 4S2, (705/567-4849)

Kesagami, P O Box 730, Cochrane, P0L 1C0 (705/272-4365)

Lady Evelyn-Smoothwater,P O Box 38, Temagami, P0H 2H0 (705/569-3622)

Lower Madawaska River, P O Box 220, Pembroke, K8A 6X4 (613/732-3661)

Killarney, Killarney, P0M 2A0, (705/287-2900)

Friends of Killarney, Killarney, P0M 2A0. Killarney Park Interior Users Map ($2.50, 1992). Identifies campsites, portages, hiking trails. Killarney Outfitters, HW 637, Killarney, P0M 2A0. (705/287-2828).

Mattawa River, (address not given), North Bay, (705/474-5550)

Mississagi River (based with Chapleau-Nemegosenda, and The Shoals and Wakami Lake), 190 Cherry Street, Chapleau, P0M 1K0 (705/864-1710)

Murphy's Point, RR 2, Perth, K7H 3C7 (613/267-5060)

Opasquia, P O Box 5003, Red Lake, P0V 2M0 (807/727-2253)

Quetico Provincial Park, Ministry of Natural Resources, Atikokan, P0T 1C0, or phone 807/597-2735 for reservations and Park Rules.

General information on canoeing or kayaking in Ontario : Ontario Recreational Canoeing Association, 1220 Sheppard Avenue East, Willowdale, M2K 2X1. Also the Canadian Recreational Canoeing Association, Box 500 1029 Hyde Park Road, Hyde Park, N0M 1Z0. Silent Lake, P O Box 500, Bancroft, K0L 1C0 (416/722-8061)

Sleeping Giant (formerly known as Sibley) General Delivery, Pass Lake, P0T
    2M0 (807/933-4332)
Wabamimi, P O Box 970, Nipigon P0T 2J0 (807/857-2120)
White Lake, P O Box 1160, Wawa, P05 1K0 (807/822-2447)
Winisk River, P O Box 640, Geraldton, P0T 1M0 (807/854-1030).
Woodland Caribou, P O Box 5003, Red Lake, P0V 2M0 (807/727-2253)

MANITOBA
Department of Natural Resources, Room 800, 1495 St. James Street, Winnipeg,
    MB R3H 0W9, for general information.
Department of Natural Resources, Room 500, 191 Broadway, Winnipeg, R3C
    4B2. Obtain fishing license by mail to this address.
Travel Manitoba, Department 8036, 7th Floor, 155 Carlton Street, Winnipeg,
    R3C 3H8 (800/665-0040, ext. 36), for literature and information, includ-
    ing fishing regulations. Ask for "Canoeing in Manitoba" for description of
    an enticing assortment of canoe trips.

SASKATCHEWAN
Saskatchewan Environment and Resource Management, 3211 Albert Street,
    Regina, SK S4S 5W6, manages the provincial parks.
Saskatchewan Trade & Convention Centre, 1919 Saskatchewan Drive,
    Regina, S4P 3V7 (800/667-7191 toll-free).
Tourism Saskatchewan, 2103 Eleventh Avenue, Regina, S0C 0K0 (800/
    667-5822 toll-free).

NATIONAL PARKS

FOR GENERAL INFORMATION

PARKS SERVICE REGIONAL OFFICES:
Western Region, Room 520, 220 Fourth Avenue South East, Calgary,
    Alberta T2P 3H8 (403/292-4440)
Prairie and Northern Region, 457 Main Street, 4th Floor, Winnipeg,
    Manitoba, R3B 3E8 (204/983-2110)
Ontario Region, 111 Water Street East, Cornwall, Ontario K6H 6S3 (613/
    938-5866)
Quebec Region, 3 Buade Street, Haute Ville, Québec, Québec G1R 4V7
    (418/648-4177)
Atlantic Region, Historic Properties, Upper Water Street, Halifax, Nova
    Scotia B3J 1S9 (902/426-3457)

FOR INFORMATION ON SPECIFIC PARKS:
Prince Albert National Park, P O Box 100, Waskesiu Lake, SK S0J 2Y0
    (306/663-5322)
Wood Buffalo National Park, Box 750, Fort Smith, North West Territories,
    X0E 0P0 (403/872-2349)
Nahanni National Park Reserve, Postal Bag 300, Fort Simpson, NWT X0E
    0N0 (403/695-3151, phone; 403/695-2446, fax)
Pukaskwa National Park (Highway 627, Hattie Cove, Heron Bay, ON P0T 1R0
    (807/229-0801)
    Friends of Pukaskwa, General Delivery, Heron Bay, ON P0T 1R0 (807/
229-0801). They can also sell fishing licenses as well as maps.

DISTANCES AND AREAS

Americans and Canadians do not use the same ways of counting distances and areas. The canoeist using BWCA maps is accustomed to portage distances given in rods. The Canadian is accustomed to meters for the standard unit. The average American is more apt to think of feet and yards. So here are the typical units and their equivalents.

DISTANCE

1	meter	equals 1.09 yards
1	meter	equals 3.28 feet
1	yard	equals .91 meter
1	rod	equals 16.5 feet
1	rod	equals 5.03 meters
320	rods	equals 1 mile
1	mile	equals 5280 feet
1	mile	equals 1.61 kilometer
1	kilometer	equals 1,000 meters
1	kilometer	equals 3281 feet
1	kilometer	equals .62 mile
1	kilometer	equals 198.85 rods

AREA

1	acre	equals 43,560 square feet
1	sq. mile	equals 640 acres
1	sq. mile	equals 2.59 square kilometers
1	sq. kilometer	equals .3861 square mile
1	hectare (ha)	equals 2.47 acres
1	hectometer	equals 100 meters
1	dekameter	equals 10 meters

MASTER CHECKLISTS

THE BASICS
Canoe
Paddles
Personal Flotation Devices
Maps
Map envelope
Permit or reservation
Tent
Loft for tent
Small whiskbroom
Ground cloth
Tarp or large (about 9' x 12') plastic sheet with grommets,
20' rope for ridgepole, 100' ¼ inch nylon cord for corners
Packs
Sleeping bag
Mattress
Flashlight
Bear rope, two 35' -50' pieces
Additional rope (¼ inch), 10'
Clothes pins
Saw (folding)
Backpacker's trowel (optional in the BWCA)
Compass
Notebook and pen
Plastic bags
Optional Items
Space Blanket
Pillow
Small back pack or day pack
Notebook and pen
Camp seat
Hiking Staff
Binoculars
Fishing gear
Dip net
Lantern (candle or gas)
Hatchet with sheath
String Hammock
Sun Shower

Books or other "playthings"
Photographic equipment

FOOD PREPARATION GEAR
Cook kit (e.g., nested kettles)
Eating utensils (forks, spoons)
Plates or bowls
Knife
Cups
Pancake turner or spatula
Canteen or water bottle
Collapsible water jug
Pot scrubber
Dish towels
Matches and butane lighter
Pot holders or oven mitts
Camp stove
Wind screen for stove
Fuel container for stove
Filter funnel, if stove requires
<u>Optional Items</u>
Aluminum foil
Long-handled wooden spoon

HEALTH AND SAFETY KIT
Aspirin or aspirin substitute (acetaminophen)
Antihistamine
Antacid (e.g., Pepto-Bismol, Di-Gel)
Antiseptic or antibiotic cream (e.g., Betadyne)
Cortisone ointment (0.5% hydrocortisone)
Eye drops
Topical analgesic
Lip protection
Personal prescribed medications
Insect repellant
Sunscreen
Water purification means (mechanical or chemical)
Adhesive bandages, assorted sizes
Telfa™ pads, assorted sizes
Gauze and tape
Moleskin
Safety pins, assorted sizes
Triangle bandage
Ace (elastic) bandage
Splint, rigid or inflatable (for joint injuries)
Reusable splint (e.g., Sam Splint)
Thermometer (fever)
Whistle
Small mirror
<u>Optional</u>
Baking soda (4 ounces)

Pre-moistened towelettes
Tincture of benzoine, (Tough Skin™) to prevent blisters

CLOTHING AND PERSONAL GEAR
Sturdy pants; shorts optional
Suspenders (optional, according to body build)
Tee shirts or tank tops
Long-sleeved shirt
Nylon wind-breaker or shell jacket
Woolen or chamois unlined jacket/shirt
Underwear
Sleepwear
Socks
Shoes: trail shoes and camp shoes
Rain gear
Hat
Sunglasses
Gloves (optional, according to season)
Toothbrush and dentifrice
Soap
Towels (can substitute moistened towelettes)
Toilet paper
Pocket knife and sharpening stone
Personal identification tags
Optional
Head net

REPAIRS KIT
Duct tape
Emery board or nail file
Nail clippers
Needle and thread (heavy and light)
Safety pins (or in Health and Safety Kit)
Small scissors (not nail or cuticle)
Tweezers
Spare parts for functions that would lead to disaster if broken and
    unreplaced

FOOD SUGGESTIONS
(From the Supermarket)
Breadstuffs
Bagels or bagel sticks
Cinnamon (toast) rusks or other breakfast toasts
Zweiback
Graham crackers or vanilla wafers
Pilot biscuit
Ry-Krisp or Vasa Brod
English muffins
Italian bread sticks
Salad crackers of various sorts

Rye crackers
Pita (Near Eastern pocket bread)
Whole wheat or stoned wheat crackers
Hard rolls such as French rolls or Kaiser buns
White, whole-wheat or rye bread
Ordinary loaf bread
Croissants
Pop-tarts or similar breakfast bars
Pumpkin or zucchini bread
Steamed date bread
Biscotti (Italian cookies or biscuits)

Baking Mix

Commercial baking mixes (such as Bisquick) or homemade
Corn bread mix

Cereals

Cereal, cold — individual packets
Cereal, quick-cooking — oatmeal, farina, mixed grains, couscous, grits, Roman Meal
Granolas

Pastas

Pasta, "bare" (from rice-like to broad ribbons and shapes)
Macaroni and cheese
Pasta and sauce dishes
Raviolini or tortellini (dehydrated)
Ramen noodles

Main Dishes and The Makings

Potato dishes (au gratin, hash-browned, scalloped)
Casserole-type meals (shelf-stable, microwaveable, boil in the bag, etc.)
Falafel
Mashed potatoes, instant
Pilaf (packaged rice and vegetable combinations)
Quick-cooking rice, singly or combined with other ingredients
Bacon Bits or Bac-Os
Edam or similar hard cheese
Mozzarella (string) cheese
Country ham or prosciutto (any heavily cured and aged ham)
Vegetables (peas, mushrooms, carrots, green beans, black Chinese mushrooms)

Lunch Items

Beef jerky or beef sticks
Dry salami
Summer sausage
Cheese spreads (tube cheese or small tubs)
Cheese and crackers snack packs
Peanut butter and crackers snack packs

Sweets

Instant puddings
Gelatin desserts (Jello is one)
Packaged cookies
Biscotti

Snacking cake mixes
Fruit bars or packaged brownies
Dried fruits (apples, apricots, banana slices, cherries, cranberries, dates,
    figs, pears, pineapple, golden and black raisins, combinations)
Jelly, marmalade, preserves or honey (use for pancakes)

Soups
Instant soups

Drinks
Instant flavored coffee drinks
Bouillon cubes
Fruit drink mix, powdered
Kool-aid
Tea (tea bags, plain or specialty; instants; flavored instants)
Coffee (fresh-ground or instant)
Coffee drink mixes, instant
Cocoa mix (combine cocoa mix and powdered milk)

Nibblings
Aplets (also Grapelets or Cotlets)
Chocolate bars
Fruit leather, fruits dried or fresh
Granola bars
Halvah
Hard candies
Milk bars
Nuts (cashews, peanuts, pecans, walnuts, pistachios) for snacks or
    cooking
Seeds (pumpkin seeds, sunflower seeds, corn nuts, soy nuts)
Stuffed dates
Trail Mix variations
Yogurt bar
Yogurt-covered raisins or peanuts
Marshmallows

Staples
Oil or ghee
Salt and pepper
Margarine
Butter Buds or similar product
Baking mix
Jelly, marmalade, or honey
Coffee or tea
Cocoa mix
Fruit-flavored drink powder
Dry milk
Bouillon, cubes or instant
Cornmeal
Lemon juice
Tabasco sauce or cayenne pepper
Cinnamon sugar, 2-ounce jar

INDEX

ORDER FORM

9561 Woodridge Circle
Eden Prairie, Minnesota 55347
612/941-5053

Please send me:

_____ copy (copies) of *Roughing It Elegantly: A Practical Guide To Canoe Camping, Second edition,* by Patricia J. Bell (ISBN 0-9618227--0-8). $14.95 (plus $0.91 sales tax, if in Minnesota)

_____ copy (copies) of *The Prepublishing Handbook: What you should know before you publish your first book,* by Patricia J. Bell (ISBN 0-9618227-2-4). $12 (plus $0.78 sales tax, if in Minnesota)

_____ copy (copies) of *The Paddler's Planner* (ISBN 0-9618227-3-2)
            $7.95 (plus $0.52 sales tax, if in Minnesota)

Include $3.50 for shipping for each copy.

Name _____

Address_____

_____

Yes, I would like the above book(s) autographed to:

_____

Another *award-winner from Cat's-paw Press*

THE *Prepublishing Handbook* —*What you should know* BEFORE *you publish your first book,* by Patricia J. Bell, with Foreword by Dan Poynter, author of *The Self-publishing Manual.* 1993 winner of the prestigious Benjamin Franklin award in Language/Writing.

What are
- the risks and rewards of publishing independently?
- the roles and tasks of a one-person publishing house?
- the expenses and what are they for?
- the processes of producing and promoting a book?
- the places to find more information?

THE *Prepublishing Handbook* guides to the right decision for you.

Excellent basic information on beginning the process—lots of resources and dips included. Essential material for anyone considering publishing as a business or as a "labor of love."

"This is the one to start with if you've considered putting your time and hard-earned money into a book venture, but are not sure what's involved. Introduction by Day Poynter of *Self-Publishing Manual* fame."
Cliff Martin, publishing consultant,
in *The Millenium Whole Earth Catalog*

A *must* read for all writers and potential publishers. THE *Prepublishing Handbook* is one of those books that I refer to again and again. Pat uses simple, straightforward language to lead you through the steps needed to become a successful independent publisher. Don't publish your book without first reading THE *Prepublishing Handbook* by Patricia Bell
Marcella Chester, Walking Bridge Press

Enthused with a dream and powered by ambition [a great many people] launch into publishing only to be rewarded for their efforts and financial investment by a garage full of unsold copies and a feeling of "where did I go wrong?" Basically the answer is: "You didn't do your homework. " You wouldn't expect to be able to fly a plane without first learning how to operate the controls. Don't expect to successfully publish without first learning the basics of what to do — and what not to do! Here's where Pat Bell's THE *Prepublishing Handbook* —*What you should know* BEFORE *you publish your first book* is invaluable...THE *Prepublishing Handbook* is vital reading for anyone contemplating becoming an independent publisher — and a useful reference for established publishers as well! **Midwest Book Review**— Reviewer's Bookwatch, July 1996

Your book would have saved us money if it had existed when we entered the fray. Publisher, Beebe Books.